CHRIST

AND HIS

SALVATION:

IN SERMONS VARIOUSLY RELATED THERETO.

BY

HORACE BUSHNELL.

NEW YORK:
CHARLES SCRIBNER, 124 GRAND ST.
1864.

STEREOTYPED BY R. H. HOBBS,
Hartford, Conn.

TO

JOSEPH SAMPSON, Esq.,

OF NEW YORK.

MY DEAR FRIEND:

When resigning my pastorship, five years ago, you will remember that you put it before me to consider myself engaged now in a "Ministry at Large;" serving in it, by the pen, or by whatever method, according to the ability left me, the cause we both have made our own. In this modified ministry, I have had the sense of a worthy and sacred charge upon me still as before, and in it, as I have occupied, I seem also to have prolonged, my life. This, with another volume, on The Vicarious Sacrifice, which is ready in due time to follow, are the principal fruit of my broken industry. Without consent obtained, I venture to connect them with your name, as the spontaneous tribute of my true respect and strong personal friendship.

HORACE BUSHNELL.

Hartford, June 10, 1864.

CONTENTS.

I.

CHRIST WAITING TO FIND ROOM.

II.

THE GENTLENESS OF GOD.

III.

THE INSIGHT OF LOVE.

IV.

SALVATION FOR THE LOST CONDITION.

V.

THE FASTING AND TEMPTATION OF JESUS.

VI.

CONVICTION OF SIN BY THE CROSS.

VII.

CHRIST ASLEEP.

VIII.

CHRISTIAN ABILITY.

IX.

INTEGRITY AND GRACE.

X.

LIBERTY AND DISCIPLINE.

XI.

CHRIST'S AGONY, OR MORAL SUFFERING.

CONTENTS.

XII.

THE PHYSICAL SUFFERING, OR CROSS OF CHRIST.

XIII.

SALVATION BY MAN.

XIV.

THE BAD CONSCIOUSNESS TAKEN AWAY.

XV.

THE BAD MIND MAKES A BAD ELEMENT.

XVI.

PRESENT RELATIONS OF CHRIST WITH HIS FOLLOWERS.

XVII.

THE WRATH OF THE LAMB.

XVIII.

CHRISTIAN FORGIVENESS.

XIX.

CHRIST BEARING THE SINS OF TRANSGRESSORS.

XX.

THE PUTTING ON OF CHRIST.

XXI.

HEAVEN OPENED.

I.

CHRIST WAITING TO FIND ROOM.

"*And she brought forth her first-born son, and wrapped him in swaddling clothes, and laid him in a manger, because there was no room for them in the inn.*"—LUKE ii. 7.

In the birth and birthplace of Jesus, there is something beautifully correspondent with his personal fortunes afterward, and also of the fortunes of his gospel, even down to our own age and time. He comes into the world, as it were to the taxing, and there is scant room for him even at that.

A Roman decree having been issued, requiring the people to repair to their native place to be registered for taxation, Joseph and Mary set off for Bethlehem. The khan or inn of the village is full, when they arrive, and, being humble persons, they are obliged to find a place in the stall or stable, where the holy child is born. It so happens, not by any slight of the guests, in which they mock the advent of the child, for he makes his advent only as the child of two very common people. But there is a great concourse and crowd—senators, it may be, landowners, merchants, money-changers, tradesmen, publicans, peddlers, men of all sorts—and the most forward, showiest, best attended, boldest in airs of consequence, take up all the places, till in fact no place is left. What they have secured too it is their conceded right to keep. If the carpenter and his wife are in a plight, people as humble as they can well enough take the stable, when there is nothing better to be had.

So it was, and perhaps it was more fitting to be so; for the great Messiah's errand allows no expectation of patronage, even for his infancy. He comes into the world and finds it preöccupied. A marvelous great world it is, and there is room in it for many things; room for wealth, ambition, pride, show, pleasure; room for trade, society, dissipation; room for powers, kingdoms, armies and their wars; but for him there is the smallest room possible; room in the stable but not in the inn. There he begins to breathe, and at that point introduces himself into his human life as a resident of our world—the greatest and most blessed event, humble as the guise of it may be, that has ever transpired among mortals. If it be a wonder to men's eyes and ears, a wonder even to science itself, when the flaming air-stone pitches into our world, as a stranger newly arrived out of parts unknown in the sky, what shall we think of the more transcendent fact, that the Eternal Son of God is born into the world; that proceeding forth from the Father, not being of our system or sphere, not of the world, he has come as a Holy Thing into it—God manifest in the flesh, the Word made flesh, a new divine man, closeted in humanity, there to abide and work until he has restored the race itself to God! Nor is this wonderful annunciation any the less welcome, or any the less worthy to be celebrated by the hallelujahs of angels and men, that the glorious visitant begins to breathe in a stall. Was there not a certain propriety in such a beginning, considered as the first chapter and symbol of his whole history, as the Saviour and Redeemer of mankind?

But I am anticipating my subject, viz., *the very impressive fact that Jesus could not find room in the world, and has never yet been able to find it.*

I do not understand, you will observe, that this particular subject is formally stated or asserted in my text. I only conceive that the birth of Jesus most aptly introduces the whole subsequent history of his life, and that both his birth and life as aptly represent the spiritual fortunes of his gospel as a great salvation for the world. And the reason why Jesus can not find room for his gospel is closely analogous to that which he encountered in his birth; viz., that men's hearts are preoccupied. They do not care, in general, to put any indignity on Christ; they would prefer not to do it; but they are filled to the full with their own objects already. It is now as then and then as now; the selfishness and self-accommodation, the coarseness, the want of right sensibility, the crowding, eager state of men, in a world too small for their ambition—all these preoccupy the inn of their affections, leaving only the stable, or some by-place, in their hearts, as little worthy of his occupancy and the glorious errand on which he comes.

See how it was with him in his life. Herod heard

the rumor that the Messiah, that is, the king, was born, and it being specially clear that there was no room for two kings in Galilee, raised a slaughter general among the children, that he might be sure of getting this particular one out of the way. Twelve years later when Joseph and his mother turned back to seek the child at Jerusalem, where they had left him, and found him sitting with the doctors of the temple, asking them questions and astonishing their comprehension by his answers; when also his mother, remonstrating with him for remaining behind, hears him say that he "must be about his Father's business," and goes home pondering his strange answer in her heart; how clear is it that they, none of them, have room, even if they would, to take in the conception of his divine childhood, or the history preparing in it. John the Baptist, again, even after he has testified in the Spirit on seeing him approach—"Behold the Lamb of God that taketh away the sins of the world!" and has all but refused to baptize him because of his superior dignity, grows doubtful afterward, yields to misgivings, gets perplexed, like any poor half-seeing sinner, with his mystery, and finally sends to inquire whether he is really the Christ, or whether some other is still to be looked for! His great ministry, wonderful in its dignity and power, wins but the scantiest hospitality; he journeys on foot through many populous towns and by the gates of many palaces, sleeping in desert places of the mountains, as he slept his first night in a manger, not having where to lay his head. Nicodemus, and many others probably in the higher conditions of life, felt the sense of some mysterious dignity in him, and went, even by night, to receive lessons of spiritual instruction from him, yet never took him to his house, and too little conceived him to so much as break silence at his trial by a word of vindication. The learned rabbis could have bid him welcome, if he had come teaching "corban," or the precise mode or merit of baptizing cups, or tithing anise, but when he spoke to them of judgment and mercy and the right of doing good on Sundays, they had no room, in their little theologies, for such a kind of doctrine. His own disciples got but the slenderest conception of his person and mission from his very explicit teachings. They still wanted even the explanations of his parables explained. It was as if the sun had broken out upon a field of moles—there was a wonderful incapacity and weakness in all their apprehensions; he shone too brightly and they could see only the less. The priests, and rabbis, and magistrates, saw enough in him to be afraid of him, or rather of his power over the people. They charged him, before Pilate, with a design to make himself king instead of Cæsar, and when he answered, in effect, that he came only to be king of the truth, Pilate, greatly mystified by his answer, and the more that he had the sense of some strange power in his person, wanted still, like a child, to know what he could mean by the truth? On the whole it can not be said that Christ ever once found room, and a clear receptivity for his person, any where, during his mortal life. Mary and Martha did their best to entertain him and give him a complete hospitality, and yet their hospitality so little conceived him as to assume that being nicely lodged, and complimented with a delicate housewifery, was a matter of much more consequence than it was; even more, a great deal, than to fitly receive the heaven-full of honor and beauty brought into their house in his person. And so it may be truly said of him that he came unto his own, and his own received him not. He was never accepted as a guest of the world any more than on that first night in the inn. There was not room enough in the world's thought and feeling to hold him, or even to suffer so great a presence, and he was finally expelled by an ecclesiastical murder.

At the descent of the Spirit there was certainly a great opening in the minds of his disciples concerning him, and there has been a slow, irregular, and difficult progress in the faith and perception of mankind since that day, but we shall greatly mistake, if we suppose that Christ has ever found room to spread himself at all in the world, as he had it in his heart to do, when he came into it, and will not fail to do, before his work is done.

Were a man to enter some great cathedral of the old continent, of which there are many hundreds, survey the vaulted arches and the golden tracery above, wander among the forests of pillars on which they rest, listen to the music of choirs and catch the softened light that streams through sainted forms and histories on the windows, observe the company of priests, gorgeously arrayed, chanting, kneeling, crossing themselves, and wheeling in long processions before the great altar loaded with gold and gems; were he to look into the long tiers of side chapels, each a gorgeous temple, with an altar of its own for its princely family, adorned with costliest mosaics, and surrounded, in the niches of the walls, with statues and monumental groups of dead ancestors in the highest forms of art, noting also the living princes at their worship there among their patriarchs and brothers in stone—spectator of a scene so imposing, what but this will his thought be: "surely the infant of the manger has at last found room, and come to be entertained among men with a magnificence worthy of his dignity." But if he looks again, and looks a little farther in—far enough in to see the miserable pride of self and power that lurks under this gorgeous show, the mean ideas of Christ, the superstitions held instead of him, the bigotry, the hatred of the poor, the dismal corruption of life—with how deep a sigh of disappointment will he confess: "alas, the manger was better and a more royal honor!"

So if we speak of what is called Christendom, comprising, as it does, all the most civilized and powerful nations of mankind, those most forward in learning, and science, and art, and commerce, it may well enough seem to us, when we fix the name Christendom—Christ-dominion—on these great powers of the earth, that Christ has certainly gotten room, so far, to enter and be glorified in human society. And it is a very great thing, doubtless, for Christ to be so far admitted to his kingly honors—more, however, as a token of what will sometime appear, than as a measure of power already exerted. Still what multitudes of out-lying populations are there that have never heard of him. And the states and populations that acknowledge him,—how unjust are their laws, how intriguing and dishonest their diplomacies, how cruel their wars, what oppressions do they put upon the weak, what persecutions raise against the good, what abuses and distortions of God's truth do they perpetrate, what idolatries and mummeries of superstition do they practice, and, to include all in one general summation, how little of Christ, take them all together, appears to be really in them. Now and then a saint appears, a real Christly man, but the general mass are sharp for money and dull to Christ, and whether sharp or dull, are for the most part extremely ignorant as regards all spiritual knowledge, even if they happen, as men, to be specially intelligent, or practiced much in philosophy. The savor of Christ, in short, is so weak that we can scarcely get the sense of it once in a day. A wind blowing off from his cross might almost be expected to carry as much grace with it—so slight, evanescent, scarcely perceptible, doubtfully real is the evidence shown of a genuine Christly power, even in just those upper tiers of humanity, which are called the Christendom, or Christ-dominion itself.

But we must take a closer inspection, if we are to see how very little room Christ has yet been able to obtain, and how many things conspire to cramp the efficacy and narrow down the sway of his gospel. Great multitudes, it is well understood, utterly reject him, and stay fast in their sins. They have no time to be religious, or the sacrifices are too great. Some are too poor to have any heart left, and some are too rich—so rich, so filled up with goods, that a camel can as well get through a needle's eye, as Christ get into their love. Some are too much honored to receive him, and some too much want to be. Some are in their passions, some in their pleasures, some in their expectations. Some are too young and wait to give him only the dry remains of life, after the natural freshness is gone. Some are too old and are too much occupied with old recollections and stories of the past forever telling, to have any room longer for his reception. Some are too ignorant, and think they must learn a great deal before they can receive him. Others know too much, having stifled their capacity already in the dry-rot of books and opinions. The great world thus, under sin, even that part of it which is called Christian, is very much like the inn at Bethlehem, preoccupied, crowded full in every part, so that, as the mother of Jesus looked up wistfully to the guest-chambers that cold night, drawing her Holy Thing to her bosom, in like manner Jesus himself stands at the door of these multitudes, knocking vainly, till his head is filled with dew, and his locks are wet with the drops of the night.

So it should be, as you will easily perceive beforehand; for Christianity comes into the world by supposition, just because the world is not ready to receive it.

The very problem it proposes is to get room where there is none, to open a heart where there is no heart, to regenerate opposing dispositions, to sweeten soured affections, to beget love where there is selfishness, to institute peace in the elemental war of the soul's disorders. This being true, we can see beforehand that the grand main difficulty of the gospel in restoring the world, is to get room enough opened for its mighty renovations to work. It will come to be received where there is no receptivity. Mankind will even seem to be shutting it away by a conspiracy of littleness and preoccupied feeling, when formally preparing to receive it.

What shall Constantine, the first convert king do, for example, when he enters the fold, but bring in with him all his regal powers and prerogatives, and wield them for the furtherance of the new religion; never once imagining the fact that, in doing it, he was bringing church and gospel and every thing belonging to Christ, directly into the human keeping and the very nearly insulting patronage of the state. And so the gospel is to be kept in state pupilage, in all the old-world kingdoms, down to the present day—officered, endowed, regulated, by the state supremacy. Spiritual gifts have no place under the political regimen of course. Lay ministries are a disorder. No man comes to minister because he is called of God, or goes because he is sent of God, but he buys a living, or he has it given him, as he might in the army or the post-office. And so the grand, heaven-wide, gospel goes into quarantine, from age to age, getting no room to speak, or smite, or win, or save, beyond what worldly state-craft gives it. Call we this making room for the gospel?

Church-craft meantime has been quite as narrow, quite as sore a limitation as state-craft. Thus instead of that grand, massive, practically educated, character, that Christ proposes to create in the open fields of duty, by sturdy encounter with wrong, by sacrifices of beneficence and the bloodier sacrifices of heroic testimony for the truth, it contrives a finer, saintlier, more superlative, virtue, to be trained in cells and nightly vigils!—poor, unchristly, mean imposture, it turns out to be of course. To give the church the prestige of a monarchy, under one universal head, a primacy is finally created in the bishop of Rome, and now, behold the august father, occupied, as in Christ's name, in blessing rosaries, preparing holy water, receiving the sacred puffs of censers, and submitting his feet to the devout kisses of his people! O how wretched and barren a thing, how very like to a poor mummery of imposture, have these ecclesiastics, contriving thus to add new ornaments and powers, reduced the gospel of heaven's love to men!

And the attempted work of science, calling itself theology, is scarcely more equal to its theme. The subject matter outreaches, how visibly, and dwarfs all the little pomps of the supposed scientific endeavor. What can it do, when trying, in fact, to measure the sea with a spoon! A great question it soon becomes, whether Christian forgiveness covers any but sins committed before baptism; as if the flow of God's great mercies in his Son could be stopped by the date of a baptism, and the sins of his children, afterward, left to be atoned by purgatorial fires! The death of Christ is conceived and taught, for whole centuries, as being a ransom paid to the devil; then, after so many centuries have worn the superstition fairly out, as an offering, or suffering, to appease the wrath of God. Meantime it is carefully held, to save God's dignity in him, that he does not suffer at all as divine, but is even impassible; so that what he certainly suffers in his moral sensibilities, even because they are perfect—all to make the cross an expression of divine feeling powerful on the heart of sin—subsides into a stifled, unmoved, immovable mercy that, in fact, belongs to the stones. It becomes a great article of opinion also, that God only wants to save a particular number, and that exactly is the number He predestinates. Next, to coincide with this, Christ is shown to have died only for this particular part of mankind. Next to coincide with this, a limited or special grace is affirmed under the same restrictions. Regeneration, again, is wrought by baptism. Repentance subsides into doing penance. And the forgiveness of sins becomes a priestly dispensation.

But the most remarkable thing of all is that, when the old, niggard dogmas of a bigot age and habit give way, and emancipated souls begin to look for a new Christianity and a broader, worthier faith, just there every thing great in the gospel vanishes even more strangely than before. Faith becomes mere opinion, love a natural sentiment, piety itself a blossom on the wild stock of nature. Jesus, the Everlasting Word, dwindles to a mere man. The Holy Spirit is made to be very nearly identical with the laws of the soul. God himself too is, in fact, put under nature, shut in back of nature and required to stay there; the incarnation, the miracles, the Gethsemane, the Calvary, all the flaming glories of the gospel are stifled as extravagances, and the new Christianity, the more liberal, more advanced, belief, turns out to be a discovery that we are living in nature, just as nature makes us live. Salvation there is none, nothing is left for a gospel but development, with a little human help from the very excellent person, Jesus.

Now the blessed Lord wants room, we all agree; we even profess that we ourselves want mightily to be enlarged. Why then is it always turning out, hitherto, that when we try to go deepest, we drag every thing down with us? What, in fact, do we prove but that, when we undertake to shape theologically the glorious mystery of salvation by Christ, we just as much reduce it, or whittle it down, as human thought is narrower and tinier than the grand subject matter attempted.

But saddest of all is the practical depreciation of Christ, or of what he will do as a Saviour, experimentally, from sin. The possibilities of liberty, assurance, a good conscience, a mind entered into rest, are, by one means or another, let down, obscured, or quite taken away. To believe much is enthusiasm, to attempt much, fanaticism. The assumption is, that Christ will, in fact, do only a little for us, just as there is only a little done; when the very sufficient reason is, that there is only a little allowed to be done. As to any common footing with the ancient saints in their inspirations, guidances, and gifts—it is even a kind of presumption to think of it. They had their religion at first hand, we are now a degree farther off. They had the inbirth of God, and knew him by the immediate knowledge of the heart. We only read of him and know about him and operate our minds, alas! how feebly, toward him, under the notions, or notional truths, gotten hold of by our understanding. O it is a very sad picture! Dear Lord Jesus can it never be that better room shall be given thee?

True there is no grace of Christ that will suddenly make us perfect; but there is a grace that will take away all conscious sinning, as long as we sufficiently believe, raising us above the dominating power of sin into a state of divine consciousness, where we are new-charactered, as it were, continually, by the righteousness of God, spreading itself into and over and through the faith, by which we are trusted to his mercy. All this Christ will do. In this state of power and holy endowment, superior to sin, he can, he will establish every soul that makes room wide enough for him to enter and bestow his fullness. He will be a Saviour, in short, just as mighty and complete as we want him to be, just as meager and partial and doubtfully real as we require him to be. O what meaning is there, in this view, in the apostle's invocation—"That he would grant you, according to the riches of his glory, to be strengthened with might by his Spirit in the inner man; that Christ may dwell in your hearts by faith; that ye, being rooted and grounded in love, may be able to comprehend, with all saints, what is the length, and breadth, and depth, and height; and to know the love of Christ that passeth knowledge, that ye might be filled with all the fullness of God." This heavy, long-drawn sigh, whose wording carries such a weight of promise still—what does it invoke but that Christ may somehow, any how, get fit room, as he never yet has done, in these stunted human hearts.

And this same sigh has been how fit a prayer for all ages. Probably nothing comparatively of the power of Christ, as a gift to the world, has ever yet been seen or realized in it. And a main part of the difficulty is, that Christ is a grace too big for men's thoughts, and of course too big for their faith,—the Eternal Word of God robed in flesh, the humanly manifested love and feeling of God, a free justification for the greatest of sinners and for all sin, a power of victory in the soul that raises it above temptation, supports it in peace, and makes obedience itself its liberty. Such a Christ of salvation fully received, embraced in the plenitude of his gifts—what fires would he kindle, what tongues of eloquence loosen, what heroic witnessings inspire! But, as yet, the disciples are commonly men of only a little faith, and it is with them according to their faith. They too often almost make a merit of having no merit, and think it even a part of Christian modesty to believe that Christ will do for them, only according to what they miss, or really do not undertake for themselves.

And so it comes to pass, my brethren, that our gospel fails, hitherto, of all its due honors, because we so poorly represent the worth and largeness of it. What multitudes are there, under the name of disciples, who maintain a Christian figure scarcely up to the line of common respect—penurious, little, mean, sordid, foul in their imaginations, low-minded, coarse-minded every way. Until Christ gets room in the higher spaces of their feeling, and their consciousness gets ennobled by a worthier and fuller reception, it must be so. Others are inconstant, falling away so feebly as to put a weak look on the gospel itself; as if it were only able to kindle a flare in the passions, not to establish a durable character. This too must be so, till Christ is fully enough received to be the head of their new capacity and growth. Multitudes, again, are not made happy as they should be, wear a long-faced, weary, dissatisfied, legally constrained look, any thing but a look of courage and joy and blessed contentation. Yes, and for the simple reason that there is nothing so wretched, so very close to starvation, as a little, doubtfully received grace. True joy comes by hearts'-full and when there is room enough given for Christ to flood the feeling, the peace becomes a river—never till then.

Discordant opinions and strifes of doctrines endlessly propagated are another scandal. And since heads are little and many, full of fractious and gaunt notions, all horning or hoofing each other, as hungry beasts in their stall, what wonder is it if they raise a clatter of much discord? No, the true hospitality is that of the heart, and if only the grand heart-world of the race were set open to the full entertainment of Jesus, there would be what a chiming of peace and unity in the common love.

Why, again, since Christianity undertakes to convert the world, does it seem to almost or quite fail in the slow progress it makes? Because, I answer, Christ gets no room, as yet, to work, and be the fire in men's hearts he is able to be. We undertake for him as by statecraft and churchcraft and priestcraft. We raise monasteries for him in one age, military crusades in another. Raymond Lull, representing a large class of teachers, undertook to make the gospel so logical that he could bring down all men of all nations, without a peradventure, before it. Some in our day are going to carry every thing by steam-ships and commerce; some by science and the schooling of heathen children; some by preaching agents adequately backed by missionary boards; some by tracts and books. But the work, however fitly ordered as respects the machinery, lingers, and will and must linger, till Christ gets room to be a more complete inspiration in his followers. They give him the stable when they ought to be giving him the inn, put him in the lot of weakness, keep him back from his victories, shut him down under the world, making his gospel, thus, such a secondary, doubtfully real, affair, that it has to be always debating in the evidences, instead of being its own evidence, and marching forward in its own mighty power.

But what most of all grieves me, in such a review, is, that Christ himself has so great wrong to endure, in the slowness and low faith of so many ages. Why, if I had a friend, who was always making me to appear weaker and meaner than I am, putting the flattest construction possible on my words and sayings, professing still, in his own low conduct, to represent my ideas and principles, protesting the great advantage he gets, from being much with me, in just those things where he is most utterly unlike me—I could not bear him even for one week, I should denounce him utterly, blowing all terms of connection with him. And yet Christ has a patience large enough to bear us still; for he came to bear even our sin, and he will not start from his burden, even if he should not be soon through with it.

All the sooner, brethren, ought we to come to the heart so long and patiently grieving for us. Is it not time, dear friends, that Christ our Master should begin to be fitly represented by his people—received in his true grandeur and fullness as the Lord of Life and Saviour of all mankind; able to save to the uttermost; a grace all victorious; light, peace, liberty, and power; wisdom, righteousness, sanctification, and redemption. Be it yours then so to make room for him, even according to the greatness of his power—length, breadth, depth, height. Be no more straitened in your own bowels, stretch yourselves to the measure of the stature of the fullness of Christ. Expect to be all that he will make you, and that you may be, open your whole heart to him broad as the sea. Give him all the widest spaces of your feeling—guest-chambers opened by your loving hospitality. Challenge for him his right to be now received by his disciples, as he never yet has been. Tell what changes and wondrous new creations will appear, when he finally breaks full-orbed on human experience—his true second coming in power and great glory. For this great consummation it is that every thing is preparing, and if there be voices and calls chiming through the spaces round us, which, for deafness, we have all these ages failed to hear, what is their burden but this—Lift up your heads, O ye gates, and be ye lifted up, ye everlasting doors, and the King of Glory shall come in.

II.

THE GENTLENESS OF GOD.

"*Thy gentleness hath made me great.*"—Ps. xviii. 35.

Gentleness in a deity—what other religion ever took up such a thought? When the coarse mind of sin makes up gods and a religion by its own natural light, the gods, it will be seen, reveal both the coarseness and the sin together, as they properly should. They are made great as being great in force, and terrible in their resentments. They are mounted on tigers, hung about with snakes, cleave the sea with tridents, pound the sky with thunders, blow tempests out of their cheeks, send murrain upon the cattle, and pestilence on the cities and kingdoms of other gods—always raging in some lust or jealousy, or scaring the world by some vengeful portent.

Just opposite to all these, the great God and creator of the world, the God of revelation, the God and Father of our Lord Jesus Christ, contrives to be a gentle being; even hiding his power, and withholding the stress of his will, that he may put confidence and courage in the feeling of his children. Let us not shrink then from this epithet of scripture, as if it must imply some derogation from God's real greatness and majesty; for we are much more likely to reach the impression, before we have done, that precisely here do his greatness and majesty culminate.

What then, first of all, do we mean by gentleness? To call it sweetness of temper, kindness, patience, flexibility, indecisiveness, does not really distinguish it. We shall best come at the true idea, if we ask what it means when applied to a course of treatment? When you speak, for example, of dealing gently with an enemy, you mean that, instead of trying to force a point straight through with him, you will give him time, and ply him indirectly with such measures and modes of forbearance as will put him on different thoughts, and finally turn him to a better mind. Here then is the true conception of God's gentleness. It lies in his consenting to the use of indirection, as a way of gaining his adversaries. It means that he does not set himself, as a ruler, to drive his purpose straight through, but that, consciously wise and right, abiding in his purposes with majestic confidence, and expecting to reign with a finally established supremacy, he is only too great to fly at his adversary, and force him to the wall, if he does not instantly surrender; that, instead of coming down upon him thus, in a manner of direct onset, to carry his immediate submission by storm, he lays gentle seige to him, waiting for his willing assent and choice. He allows dissent for the present, defers to prejudice, watches for the cooling of passion, gives room and space for the weaknesses of our unreasonable and perverse habit to play themselves out, and so by leading us round, through long courses of kind but faithful exercise, he counts on bringing us out into the ways of obedience and duty freely chosen. Force and crude absolutism are thus put by; the irritations of a jealous littleness have no place; and the great God and Father, intent on making his children great, follows them and plies them with the gracious indirections of a faithful and patient love.

It is scarcely necessary to add that there are many kinds of indirection, which are wide, as possible, of any character of gentleness. All policy, in the bad sense of the term, is indirection. A simply wise expedient has often this character. But the indirections of God are those of a ruler, perfectly secure and sovereign, and their object is, not to turn a point of interest for himself, but simply to advance and make great the unworthy and disobedient subjects of his goodness.

This character of gentleness in God's treatment, you will thus perceive, is one of the greatest spiritual beauty and majesty, and one that ought to affect us most tenderly in all our sentiments and choices. And that we may have it in its true estimation, observe, first of all, how far off it is from the practice and even capacity generally of mankind. We can do almost any thing more easily than consent to use any sort of indirection, when we are resisted in the exercise of authority, or encounter another at some point of violated right.

There is a more frequent approach to gentleness, in the parental relation, than any where else among men.

And yet even here, how common is the weak display of a violent, autocratic, manner, in the name of authority and government. Seeing the child daring to resist his will, the parent is, how often, foolishly exasperated. With a flush of anger and a stern, hard voice, he raises the issue of peremptory obedience; and when, either by force or without, he has carried his way, he probably congratulates himself that he has been faithful enough to break his child's will. Whereas, raising an issue between his own passions and his child's mere fears, he is quite as likely to have broken down his conscience as his will, unnerving all the forces of character and capacities of great manhood in him for life. Alas how many parents, misnamed fathers and mothers, fancy, in this manner, that when self-respect is completely demolished in their poor defenseless child, the family government is established. They fall into this barbarity, just because they have too little firmness to hold their ground in any way of indirection or gentleness. They are violent because they are weak, and then the conscious wrong of their violence weakens them still farther, turning them, after the occasion is past, to such a misgiving, half apologizing manner, as just completes their weakness.

It will also be observed, almost universally, among men, that where one comes to an issue of any kind with another, matters are pressed to a direct point-blank Yes or No. If it is a case of personal wrong, or a quarrel of any kind, the parties face each other, pride against pride, passion against passion, and the hot endeavor is to storm a way through to victory. There is no indirection used to soften the adversary, no waiting for time, nothing meets the feeling of the moment but to bring him down upon the issue, and floor him by a direct assault. To redress the injury by gentleness, to humble an adversary by his own reflections, and tame his will by the circuitous approach of forbearance and a siege of true suggestion—that is not the manner of men, but only of God.

True gentleness, we thus perceive, is a character too great for any but the greatest and most divinely tempered souls. And yet how ready are many to infer that, since God is omnipotent, he must needs have it as a way of majesty, to carry all his points through to their issue by force, just as they would do themselves. What, in their view, is it for God to be omnipotent, but to drive his chariot where he will. Even Christian theologians, knowing that he has force enough to carry his points at will, make out pictures of his sovereignty, not seldom, that stamp it as a remorseless absolutism. They do not remember that it is man, he that has no force, who wants to carry every thing by force, and that God is a being too great for this kind of infirmity; that, having all power, he glories in the hiding of his power; that holding the worlds in the hollow of his hand, and causing heaven's pillars to shake at his reproof, He still counts it the only true gentleness for Him to bend, and wait, and reason with his adversary, and turn him round by His strong Providence, till he is gained to repentance and a volunteer obedience.

But God maintains a government of law, it will be remembered, and enforces his law by just penalties, and what room is there for gentleness in a government of law? All room, I answer; for how shall he gain us to his law as good and right, if he does not give us time to make the discovery of what it is? To receive law because we are crammed with it, is not to receive it as law, but only to receive it as force, and God would spurn that kind of obedience, even from the meanest of his subjects. He wants our intelligent, free choice, of duty—that we should have it in love, nay have it even in liberty. Doubtless it is true that he will finally punish the incorrigible; but He need not therefore, like some weak, mortal despot, hurry up his force, and drive straight in upon his mark. If he were consciously a little faint-hearted he would, but he is great enough in his firmness to be gentle and wait.

But some evidence will be demanded that God pursues any such method of indirection, or of rectoral gentleness with us. See then, first of all, how openly he takes this altitude in the scriptures.

When our first father breaks through law, by his act of sin, he does not strike him down by his thunders, but he holds them back, comes to him even with a word of promise, and sends him forth into the rough trials of a world unparadised by guilt, to work, and suffer, and learn, and, when he will, to turn and live. The ten brothers of Joseph are managed in the same way. When they could not speak peaceably to him, or even endure his presence in the family, God lets them sell him to the Egyptians, then sends them down to Egypt, by the instigations of famine, and passes them back and forth with supplies to their father, allowing them to feed even the life of their bodies out of Joseph's bounty, till finally, when he is revealed as their brother and their father's son, they are seen doing exactly what they had sworn in their wrath should never be done—bowing their sheaf to the sheaf of Joseph. Here too is the solution of that very strange chapter of history, the forty years' march in the wilderness. The people were a slave-born people, having all the vices, superstitions, and unmanly weaknesses, that belong to slavery. God will not settle his land with such, and no thunders or earthquakes of discipline can drive the inbred weakness suddenly out of them. So he takes the indirect method, puts them on a milling of time and trial, marches them round and round to ventilate their low passions, lets some die and others be born, till finally they become quite another people, and are fitted to inaugurate a new history.

But I need not multiply these minor examples, when it is the very genius of Christianity itself to prevail with man, or bring him back to obedience and life by a course of loving indirection. What we call the gospel is only a translation, so to speak, of the gentleness of God—a matter in the world of fact, answering to a higher matter, antecedent, in the magnanimity of God. I do not say that this gospel is a mere effusion of divine sentiment apart from all counsel and government. It comes by counsel older than the world's foundations. The salvation it brings is a governmental salvation. It is, at once, the crown of God's purposes and of his governmental order. And the gentleness of God must institute this second chapter of gracious indirection, because no scheme of rule could issue more directly in good without it. For it was impossible in the nature of things that mere law—precept driven home by the forces of penalty—should ever establish a really principled obedience in us. How shall we gladly obey and serve in love, which is the only obedience having any true character, till we have had time to make some experiments, try some deviations, sting ourselves in some bitter pains of trials, and so come round into the law freely chosen, because we have found how good it is; and, what is more than all, have seen how good God thinks it himself to be, from what is revealed in that wondrous indirection of grace, the incarnate life and cross of Jesus. Here the very plan is to carry the precept of law by motives higher than force; by feeling, and character, and sacrifice. We could not be driven out of sin by the direct thrust of omnipotence; for to be thus driven out is to be in it still. But we could be overcome by the argument of the cross, and by voices that derive a quality from suffering and sorrow. And thus it is that we forsake our sins, at the call of Jesus and his cross, freely, embracing thus in trust, what in willfulness and ignorance we rejected.

Nor does it vary at all our account of this gospel, that the Holy Spirit works concurrently in it, with

Christ and his cross. For it is not true, as some Christian teachers imagine, that the Holy Spirit works conversion by a direct, soul-renewing fiat or silent thunderstroke of omnipotence. He too works by indirection, not by any short method of absolute will. Working efficiently and, in a certain sense, immediately in the man, or subject, he still circles round the will, doing it respect by laying no force upon it, and only raising appeals to it from what he puts in the mind, the conscience, the memory, the sense of want, the fears excited, the aspirations kindled. He moves upon it thus by a siege, and not by a fiat, carries it finally by a process of circumvallation, commonly much longer even than the ministry of Jesus. He begins with the child, opening his little nature to gleams of religious truth and feeling —at the family prayers, in his solitary hours and dreams, in the songs of praise that warble on the strings of his soul, and among the heavenly affinities of his religious nature. And thenceforward he goes with him, in all the future changes and unfoldings of his life, turning his thoughts, raising tender questions in him, working private bosom scenes in his feeling, forcing nothing, but pleading and insinuating every thing good; a better presence keeping him company, and preparing, by all modes of skill and holy inducement, to make him great. So that, if we could follow a soul onward in its life-history, we should see a Spirit-history running parallel with it. And when it is really born of God, it will be the result of what the Spirit has wrought, by a long, and various, and subtle, and beautiful process, too delicate for human thought to trace.

Holding this view of God's gentleness in the treatment of souls, and finding even the Christian gospel in it, we ought also to find that his whole management of us and the world corresponds. Is it so—is there such a correspondence?

See, some will say, what terrible forces we have ravening and pouring inevitably on about us day and night—roaring seas, wild hurricanes, thunder-shocks that split the heavens, earthquakes splitting the very world's body itself, heat and cold, drought and deluge, pestilences and deaths in all forms. What is there to be seen but a terrible, inexorable going on, still on, everywhere. The fixed laws everywhere refuse to bend, hearing no prayers, the great worlds fly through heaven as if slung by the Almighty like the smooth stone of David, and the atoms rush together in their indivertible affinities, like the simples of gunpowder touched by fire, refusing to consider any body. Where then is the gentleness of such a God as we have signaled to us, in these unpitying, inexorable, fated, powers of the world? Is it such a God that moves by indirection? Yes, and that all the more properly, just because these signs of earth and heaven, these undiverted, undivertible, all-demolishing and terrible forces permit him to do it. He now can hide his omnipotence, for a time, just at the point where it touches us; he can set his will behind his love. for to-day and possibly to-morrow; simply because he has these majestic inexorabilities for the rear-guard of his mercies. For we can not despise him now, when he bends to us in favor, because it is the bending, we may see, of firmness. Able to use force, he can now use character, and time, and kindness. Real gentleness in Him, as in every other being, supposes counsel, order, end, and a determinate will. A weak man can be weak and that is all. Not even a weak woman can be properly called gentle. No woman will so much impress others by her gentleness, when she is gentle, as one that has great firmness and decision. And so it is the firm, great God, he that goes on so inflexibly in the laws, and the inexorable forces and causes of the creation—He it is that can, with so much better dignity, gentle himself to a child or a sinner.

See then how it goes with us in God's management of our experience. Doing every thing to work on our feeling, temperament, thought, will, and so on our eternal character, He still does nothing by direct impulsion. It is with us here, in every thing, as it was with Jonah when the Lord sent him to Nineveh. It was a good long journey inland, but Jonah steers for Joppa, straight the other way, and there puts to sea, sailing off upon it, and then under it, and through the belly of hell, and comes to land nobody knows where. After much perambulation, he gets to Nineveh and gives his message doggedly, finally to be tamed by a turn of hot weather and the wilting of a gourd. Just so goes the course of a soul whom God is training for obedience and life. It may be the case of a young man, setting off willfully, with his face turned away from God. Whereupon God lets him please himself a little in his folly, and finally pitch himself into vice, there to learn, by the bitter woes of his thraldom, how much better God is to him than he is to himself, how much worthier of trust than he ever can be to himself. Or he takes, it may be, a longer course with him—gives him a turn of sickness, then of bankruptcy, then of desertion by friends, then of slander by enemies, taming thus his pride, sobering his feeling, making the world change color, but not yet gaining him to the better life. Then he fetches him out of his disasters by unexpected vindications and gifts of mercy, such as soften unwontedly the pitch of his sensibilities. A faithful Christian wife, gilding his lot of adversity before, by her gentle cares, and quite as much, his recovery now, by the beautiful spirit she has formed in his and her children, by her faithful training—making them an honor to him as to herself—wins upon his willful habit, melts into his feeling, and operates a change in his temperament itself. Meantime his years will have been setting him on, by a silent drift, where his will would never carry him, and changing, in fact, the current of his inclination itself. Till at length, dissatisfied with himself, as he is more softened to God, and more softened to God, as he is more diverted from the satisfaction he once had in himself, he turns, with deliberate consent, to the call of Jesus, and finds what seemed to be a yoke, to be easy as liberty itself.

The change is great, nay almost total in his life, and yet it has been carried by a process of indirection so delicate, that he is scarcely sensible by what steps and curiously turned methods of skill it has been brought to pass. And so God is managing every man, by a process and history of his own; for he handles him as he does no other, adapting every turn to his want and to the points already gained, till finally he is caught by the gentle guile of God's mercies and drawn to the rock of salvation; even as some heavy and strong fish, that has been played by the skillful angler, is drawn, at last, to land, by a delicate line, that would not even hold his weight.

In a similar way God manages, not seldom, to gain back infidels and doubters. First he commonly makes them doubt their doubts. Their conceit he moderates, meantime, by the sobering effect of years and sorrow. By and by he sharpens their spiritual hunger, by the consciously felt emptiness of their life, and the large blank spaces of their creed. Then he opens some new vista into the bright field of truth, down which they never looked before, and the mole eyes of their skepticism are even dazed by the new discovered glory of God's light.

Disciples who are lapsed into sin, and even into looseness of life, are recovered in the same way of indirection. God does not pelt them with storms, nor jerk them back into their place by any violent seizure. He only leads them round by his strong-handed yet gentle tractions, till he has got them by, or out of, their fascinations, and winnowed the nonsense out of their fancy or feeling, by which they have been captivated. And so at length he gets their feet upon the rock again never to be moved.

Indeed I may go farther. Even if you desire it, God will not thrust you on to higher attainments in religion, by any forcible and direct method. He will only bring you out into the rest you seek, just as soon as you are sufficiently untwisted, and cleared, and rectified, under his indirect methods, to be there. Commonly your light will spring up in quarters where you look not for it, and even the very hidings and obscurations you suffer, will give you out some spark of light, as they leave you. The obstacles you conquer will turn out to be, in some sense, aids, the discouragements that tried you will open, when they part, as windows of hope.

Having traced the manner and fact of God's condescension to these gentle methods, let us now pass on to another point where the subject properly culminates; viz., to the end he has in view; which is, to make us great. He may have a different opinion of greatness from that which is commonly held by men—he certainly has. And what is more, he has it because he has a much higher respect for the capabilities of our human nature, and much higher designs concerning it, than we have ourselves. We fall into a mistake here also, under what we suppose to be the Christian gospel itself; as if it were a plan to bring down, not the loftiness of our pride, and the willfulness of our rebellion, but the stature and majesty of our nature itself. Thus we speak of submitting, or losing our will, being made weak and poor, becoming little children, ceasing to have any mind of our own, falling into nothingness and self-contempt before God. All which are well enough as Christian modes of expression; but we take them too literally. They are good as relating to our wrong will and wrong feeling, not as relating to our capacity of will and feeling itself. On the contrary, while God is ever engaged to bring down our loftiness in evil and perversity, he is just as constantly engaged to make us loftier and stronger in every thing desirable—in capacity, and power, and all personal majesty. We do not understand him, in fact, till we conceive it as a truth profoundly real and glorious, that he wants to make us great—great in will, great in the breadth and honest freedom of our intellect, great in courage, enthusiasm, self-respect, firmness, superiority to things and matters of condition; great in sacrifice and beneficence; great in sonship with Himself; great in being raised to such common counsel, and such intimate unity with him in his ends, that we do, in fact, reign with him.

Take, for example, the first point named, the will; for this, it will be agreed, is the spinal column even of our personality. Here it is that we assert ourselves with such frightful audacity in our sin. Here is the tap-root of our obstinacy. Hence come all the woes and disorders of our fallen state. Is it then His point to crush our will, or reduce it in quantity? If that were all, he could do it by a thought. No, that is not his way. His object is, on the contrary, to gain our will—gain it, that is, in such a manner as to save it, and make it finally a thousand fold stouter in good and sacrifice, than it has been, or could be, in wrong and evil. He will make it the chariot, as it were, of a great and mighty personality, inflexible, unsubduable, tremendous in good forever.

So of the intellect. Blinded by sin, wedded to all misbelief and false seeing, he never requires us to put violence upon it, never to force an opinion or a faith, lest we break its integrity; he only bids us set it for seeing, by a wholly right intent and a willingness even to die for the truth; assured that, in this manner, Time, and Providence, and Cross, and Spirit, will bring it into the light, clearing, as in a glorious sun-rising, all the clouds that obscure it, and opening a full, broad heaven of day on its vision. Recovered thus without being forced or violated, it feels itself to be a complete integer in power, as never before; and having conquered such obstacles under God, by the simple honesty of its search, it has a mighty appetite sharpened for the truth, and a glorious confidence raised, that time and a patient beholding will pierce all other clouds, and open a way for the light.

And so it is that God manages to save all the attributes of force and magnanimity in us, while reducing us to love and obedience. Take such an example as Paul. Do we speak of will? why he has the will-force of an empire in him. Of intelligence? let it be enough that he goes down into Arabia, and that in three years' time his mind has gone over all the course of Christian truth and doctrine, helped by no mortal, but only by God's converse with him, and his own free thought. Of courage, firmness, self-respect? what perils has he met, what stripes endured, and what offscouring of the world has he been taken for, unhumbled still, and erect in the consciousness of his glorious manhood in Christ —sorrowful yet always rejoicing, poor yet making many rich, having nothing yet possessing all things; confounding Athens and Ephesus and the mob at Jerusalem, out-pleading Tertullus the lawyer, convincing Felix and Agrippa, commanding in the shipwreck, winning disciples to the faith in the household of Cæsar, and planting, in fact, all over Cæsar's world-wide empire, the seeds of a loftier and stronger empire by which it is finally to be mastered.

Such now are God's mighty ones—humble it may be and poor, or if not such by social position, most effectually humbled, some will think, by their faith, yet how gloriously exalted. God renounces all the point-blank methods of dealing, that he may give scope and verge to our liberty, and win us to some good and great feeling, in glorious affinity with his own. He wants us to be great enough in the stature of our opinions, principles, courage and character, that he may enjoy us and be Himself enjoyable by us. Hence also it is that, when we are born of God, and the divine affinities of our great nature come into play unbroken, unimpaired, and even wondrously raised in volume, we, for the first time, make discovery of ourselves. Our heads touch heaven, as it were, in the sense of our regenerated dignity, and joys like the ocean roll through our nature, that before could only catch some rill or trickling drop of good. And with it comes what strength, a mighty will, a sense of equilibrium recovered, an all appropriating faith, superiority to things, immovable repose.

And now at the crowning of this great subject, what shall more impress us than the sublime and captivating figure God maintains for Himself and his government in it. Easy enough were it for him to lay his force upon us, and dash our obstinacy to the ground. He might not thrust us into love, he could not into courage and confidence, but he might instantly crush out all willfulness in us forever. But he could not willingly reduce us, in this manner, to a weak and cringing submission. He wants no slaves about his throne. If he could not raise us into liberty and make us great in duty, he would less respect both duty and Himself. He refuses therefore to subdue us unless by some such method that we may seem, in a certain other sense, to subdue ourselves. Most true it is that he carries a strong hand with us. He covers up no principle, tempers the exactness of no law. There is no connivance in his methods, no concealment of truths disagreeble and piercing, no proposition of compromise or halving, in a way of settlement. His Providence moves strong. His terrors flame out on the background of a wrathful sky. He thunders marvelously with his voice. And so his very gentleness stands glorious and strong and sovereignly majestic round us. Were he only soft or kind, bending like a willow to our wicked state, there were little to move and affect us even in his goodness itself. But when we look on Him as the Almighty Rock, the immovable Governor and Keeper of the worlds, girding himself in all terrible majesty, when he must, to let us know that impunity in wrong is impossible, then it is that we behold Him in the true meaning of his gentleness—how good! how firm! how adorably great! Come nigh O thou sinning, weary prodigal, and acknowledge and receive, in blissful welcome, the true greatness of thy God! Be not jealous any more that religion is going to depress your manly parts, or weaken the strength of your high aspirations. In your lowest humiliations and deepest repentances, you will be consciously raised and exalted. Every throb of heaven's life in your bosom will be only a throb of greatness. Every good affection, every holy action, into which your God may lead you, all your bosom struggles, your hungers and tears and prostrations, will be the travailing only of a princely birth, and a glorious sonship with God.

Holding such a view too of God's ends and the careful indirections by which he pursues them, we can not fail to note the softened aspect given to what are often called the unaccountable severities of human experience. The woes of broken health and grim depression; the pains, the unspeakable agonies by which human bodies are wrenched for whole years; the wrongs of orphanage; pestilence, fire, flood, tempest and famine—how can a good God launch his bolts on men, we ask, in severities like these? And the sufferers themselves sometimes wonder, even in their faith, how it is that if God is a Father, he can let fall on his children such hail-storms of inevitable, unmitigated disaster. No, suffering mortal! a truce to all such complainings. These are only God's merciful indirections, fomentations of trouble and sorrow that he is applying, to soften the rugged and hard will in you. These pains are only switches to turn you off from the track of his coming retributions. If your great, proud nature could be won to the real greatness of character, by a tenderer treatment, do you not see, from all God's gentle methods of dealing with mankind, that he would gladly soften your troubles? And if diamonds are not polished by soap, or oil, or even by any other stone, but only by their own fine dust, why should you complain that God is tempering you to your good, only by such throes and lacerations and wastings of life, as are necessary?

Again, to vary the strain of our thought, how strangely weak and low, is the perversity of many, when they require it of God to convert them by force, or drive them heavenward by storm. You demand, it may be, that God shall raise the dead before you, or that He shall speak to you in an audible voice from the sky, or that he shall regenerate your life by some stroke of omnipotence in your sleep—something you demand that shall astound your senses, or supersede your freedom. You require it of God, in fact, that He shall manage you as he did Sennacherib, that He shall put his hook into your nose, and his bridle into your lips, and lead you back, in that manner, out of sins you will not consentingly forsake. How preposterous and base to ask it thus of your Father, that He will storm you with his power and thrust you into goodness by his thunder-bolts! Instead of being jealous, with a much finer class of souls, that God and religion are going to reduce your level, you even require to be made little by Him, nay, to be unmade, and even thrust out of your personal manhood. How much better to give a ready welcome to what God is doing for you and in you, without force, doing in a way to save and even to complete your personal manhood.

Last of all let us not omit, in such a subject as this, the due adjustment of our conceptions to that which is the true pitch and scale of our magnanimity and worth as Christian men. It is easy, at this point, to flaunt our notions of dignity, and go off, as it were, in a gas of naturalism, prating of manliness, or manly character. And yet there is such a thing to be thought of, revelation being judge, as being even great—great in some true scale of Christian greatness. A little, mean-minded, shuffling, cringing, timorous, selfish soul—would that many of our time could see how base the figure it makes under any Christian name. I will not undertake to say how little a man may be and be a Christian; for there are some natures that are constitutionally mean, and it may be too much to expect that grace will ennoble them all through in a day. Judging them in all charity, it must none the less be our conception for ourselves, that God is calling us even to be great, great in courage and candor, steadfast in honor and truth, immovable in our promises, heroic in our sacrifices, right, and bold, and holy—men whom He is training, by His own great spirit, for a world of great sentiment, and will, and might, and majesty. For when we conceive the meeting in that world, and being there compeers with such majestic souls as Moses, and Paul, and Luther, and Cromwell, nay with thrones and dominions otherwise nameless, we do not seem, I confess, to be so much raised in the sense of our possible stature in good, as when we simply meditate God's gentle methods with us here, to raise our fallen manhood to its place; his careful respect for our liberty, the hidings of His power, the detentions of his violated feeling, the sending of his Son, and his Son's great cross, the silent intercessions of his Spirit—all the changes through which he is leading us, all the careful trainings of care and culture by which he is bringing us back at last, stage by stage, to the final erectness and glory of a perfect life. Even as when the mother eagle lifts her young upon the edge of her nest, holding them back that they may not topple off, and puts them fluttering there and waving their pinions that they may get strength to lift their bodies, and finally to scale the empyreal heights. And when we shall be able, ascending thus our state of glory, to look back and trace all this, in a clear and orderly review, what a wonderful and thrilling retrospect will it be.

Conscious there of powers not broken down or crushed into servility, but of wills invigorated rather by submission, with what sense of inborn dignity and strength shall we sing—Thy gentleness hath made us great. All the littleness of our sin is now quite gone. We are now complete men, such as God meant us to be; —great in the stature of our opinions, great in our feelings, principles, energies of will and joy; greatest of all in our conscious affinity with God and the Lamb. Be it ours to live, then, with a sense of our high calling upon us, abiding in all the holy magnanimities of love, honor, sacrifice and truth; sincere, exact, faithful, bountiful and free; showing thus to others and knowing always in ourselves, that we do steadily aspire to just that height of good, into which our God himself has undertaken to exalt us.

III.

THE INSIGHT OF LOVE.

"*She hath done what she could; she is come aforehand to anoint my body to the burying.*"—MARK, xiv. 8.

It takes a woman disciple after all to do any most beautiful thing; in certain respects too, or as far as love is wisdom, any wisest thing. Thus we have before us, here, a simple-hearted loving woman, who has had no subtle questions of criticism about matters of duty and right, but only loves her Lord's person with a love that is probably a kind of mystery to herself, which love she wants somehow to express. She comes therefore with her box of ointment, having sold we know not what article, or portion of her property, to buy it, for it was very costly, and pours it on the Saviour's head—just here to encounter, for the first time, scruples, questions, and rebuffs of argument. For though she is no casuist herself, no debater of cases of conscience, there are abundance of such among the Lord's male disciples present, Judas among them, and they have more reasons, a great many, to offer than she, poor child of love, has ever thought of. "Hold woman," they say, and particularly Judas in the representation of John, "Why this extravagance and foolish waste? Is not the Lord always teaching us to consider the poor, and do good in every thing, and what immense good might you have done, had you sold this ointment and put it to the uses of beneficence; why, the trains of benefit you might have set agoing by the money are even endless, and now it is thrown away for just nothing." She makes no answer, has nothing at all to say, and does not see, most likely, why she has not been as foolish as they think.

But Christ answers for her. "No, children, no," he says, "do not trouble the woman, she has an oracle in her love wiser than yours that you have in your heads; she has done a good work on me, fitting, altogether, to be done by her, if not by you. Nay, she has even prophesied here, taken hold practically of my future—just that which I have never been able to make you conceive, or guess. The poor you have always with you, be it yours to bless them, but me ye have not always. She is come aforehand—dear prophetic tribute!—to anoint my body for the burying. Is it nothing that I die in the fragrant odors of this dear woman's love? Verily I say unto you, wheresoever this gospel shall be preached throughout the whole world, this also that this woman hath done, shall be told for a memorial of her."

No such commendation was ever before or after conferred by the Saviour on any mortal of the race. He testified for the Gentile centurion, that he had found no such faith as his even in Israel. He tacitly commended his three favorite disciples, Peter, James and John, by the peculiar confidence into which he took them. But the little gospel, so to speak, of this loving woman's devotion, he declares shall go forth with his, to be spoken of, and felt in its beauty, and breathed in its fragrance, in all remotest regions of the world, and latest ages of time.

And what is the lesson or true import of this so much commended example? What but this?—do for Christ just what is closest at hand, and be sure that you will so meet all his remotest, or most unknown times and occasions. Or, better still, follow without question the impulse of love to Christ's own person; for this when really full and sovereign, will put you along easily in a kind of infallible way, and make your conduct chime, as it were, naturally with all God's future, even when that future is unknown; untying the most difficult questions of casuistry without so much as a question raised.

And precisely here, not elsewhere, is the great contribution Christ has made to morality, or the department of duty. He inaugurates, in fact, a new Christian morality, quite superior to the natural ethics of the world. Not a new morality as respects the body of rules, or code of preceptive obligations, though even here he instituted laws of conduct so important as to create a new era of advancement, but new in the sense that he raised his followers to a new point of insight, where the solutions of duty are easy, and the otherwise perplexed questions of casuistry are forever suspended; even as this woman friend of Jesus saw more through her love, and struck into a finer coincidence with his sublime future, than all the male disciples around her had been able to do by the computations of reflective reason. Nay, if Judas who, according to John, was the more forward critic, had been writing just then a treatise on the economies of duty, her little treatise of unction was better.

But we shall not understand either her, or the subject we are proposing to illustrate, if we do not—

I. Bring into view the inherent difficulty that besets all questions of casuistry that rise under the laws, or precepts of natural morality. By casuistry we mean, as the word is commonly used by ethical writers, the settlement of *cases*, sometimes called *cases of conscience*. The rules or precepts of morality are easy for the most part, it is only their applications to particular cases that are difficult. And they are often so difficult as to cause the greatest perplexity in the most conscientious and thoroughly Christian minds; as many of you will know perhaps from the struggles of your own moral experience. Ready to do any thing which duty requires, ready to fulfill any precept, or law, which is obligatory, you have yet been tormented often with doubts, it may be, regarding what this or that rule of duty required of you, in the particular case which had then arrived. For the rules, or precepts of obligation, are all general or generic in their nature, while the cases are particular, and appear to even run into each other, by subtle gradations of color, so as to be separable by no distinct lines. Every case is peculiar, it is more, it is less, it is different—does the rule of duty apply?

Take for example, the statute "thou shalt not kill," either as a statute of the decalogue, or of natural morality. Under this, as an accepted law, there will come up, in the application, questions like these—Whether one can rightly be a soldier for the defense of his country? Whether he can rightly execute a criminal under the sentence of death? Whether it is murder to shoot a robber at one's bed-side in the night? Whether one can rightly defend a poor fugitive, hunted by his master, by assailing the master's life? Whether as a christian he may rightly pursue the murderer of his child, and bring him to trial, under a charge that subjects him to capital punishment? Whether he may order a surgical operation done upon a child, which there is much reason to fear will only shorten life? Whether he can run this or that considerable risk of his own life for purposes of gain, without incurring the guilt of suicide?

The same is true of any other main precept of morality or statute of the decalogue. Accepting the law general, endless questions arise regarding its particular applications, which it seems impossible to solve.

Or we may take the great principle which requires doing good, the utmost good possible. And then the question will arise continually, in new forms endlessly varied, what is best to be done? And here we find ourselves thrown at every turn, upon a search that requires an immense fore-reaching, or impossible, knowledge of the future. What are God's plans in regard to the future? shall we meet them and chime with them, by this course or by that? Or, if we only try to find what will be most useful, we can see but an inch forward, and how can we decide. Thus if the woman had been asking how she could use her box of ointment so as to do most good with it, she would either have fallen into utter doubt and perplexity, or else she would have taken up the same conclusion with Judas, and given it to the benefit of the poor. And so if you have on hand the question, whether, in the way of being useful in the highest possible degree, you will educate your son as a Christian minister? there come up immediately questions like these—Whether he will live to be of any service to the world? Whether he has talents to be useful? Whether he will maintain a character to be useful? Whether even God will make him eloquent, or keep him grounded thoroughly in the truth? A thousand unknown matters regarding his future, baffle you in coming to any intelligent solution of your duty. Any sort of business you propose to undertake as a way of usefulness, depends in the same way on a thousand unknown contingencies—the probable characters of partners and customers, the winds, wars, fires, seasons, markets of the years to come. In this measure you are brought up shortly, under the questions of duty, by the discovery that you can see but a little way, what ever you propose, and that all your computations of usefulness or means of usefulness to be obtained, are too short in the run to allow the satisfactory settlement of any thing.

These difficulties, it is true may be exaggerated. Some men never have a trouble about duty in their lives, just because they have practically no conscience about it. Really conscientious persons, too, settle most of their questions as they rise, without debate. It is here exactly as it is in the law; for what is called the common law is a product of pure moral casuistry from beginning to end—ten thousand obligations are discharged without litigation to one that is settled by it, and yet the few to be thus settled are how many and troublesome. The reported volumes multiply till no one can read them, and yet the new cases come; the work is never done—never in fact to be done. Just so it is with our troubles of casuistry. The really conscientious man will be continually graveled by some question he can not solve by his reason, and one such question is enough to break his peace. However perfect and simple the code of preceptive duty, the applications of it will often be difficult, and sometimes well nigh impossible, without some better help than casuistry, which better help I now proceed,

II. To show is contributed by Christ and his gospel. By him is added to the code of duty, what could, by no possibility be located in it, a power to settle right applications to all particular cases, without casuistry, or any such debate of reasons, as allows even a chance of perplexity.

Thus, begetting in the soul a new personal love to himself, practically supreme, Christ establishes in it all law, and makes it gravitate, by its own sacred motion, toward all that is right and good in all particular cases. This love will find all good by its own pure affinity, apart from any mere debate of reasons; even as a magnet finds all specks of iron hidden in the common dust. Thus if the race were standing fast in love, perfect love, that love would be the fulfilling of the law without the law, determining itself rightly by its own blessed motions, without any statutory control whatever. It is only under sin, where the love is gone out as a principle, that we get up rules, work out adjudications, creep along toilsomely into moral customs and codes, contriving in that manner to fence about life and make society endurable. These are laws that God enacts for the lawless and disobedient; or which they, under God, elaborate for their own protection. But who will go to love and say, thou shalt not steal, or kill, or lie—does not love know that beforehand? These decalogue statutes—love wants none of them, she fulfills them before they are given. She can shape a life more beautifully by her own divine impulse, than it could be done by any and all ethical statutes, or refinements under them. And accordingly when Christ restores this love in a soul, it will be a new inspiration of duty, just according to its degree of power. In so far as the love is weak, or incomplete, the fences of precept and rule will be wanted. But the new affinity it creates, ought to be so clear as to make all questions of duty more and more easy, till finally the sense of all such rules is nearly or quite gone by, leaving only the love to be its own interpreter and light of guidance.

Again it is a further consideration, drawing toward

the same conclusion, that Christ incarnates a perfect and complete morality in his own person, so that when the soul in its new love embraces his person, it embraces, or takes into its own affinities, a complete morality. Consider who Christ is; the eternal Word of God for whom, and by whom, all the worlds were made; in whom as being in the form of God, all God's ends, creations, principles, counsels, providences, and future ongoings, are in a sense contained and totalized. Whoever loves him, therefore, loves in fact, all that he is in his perfection, and all that he means in the world, all that he is doing and going to do in it; and so loving him, all the currents of his soul run out with his, to meet as by a true inspiration, all his deepest purposes and most future and remotest appointments. He is in a state of mind that cleaves instinctively, and by hidden sympathies, to all that is in the Lord's person. Where the reasons of the understanding are short of reach, and ethical solutions of all kinds doubtful, he is drawn by the indivertible affinities of his heart, into easy coincidence with all that Christ means for him, and so into a certain divine morality. He is not a philosopher, not wise, as we commonly speak, and yet Christ, who is being formed in him, is made unto him wisdom. As the worlds are fashioned to serve His plans, and work out, in the sublime progression of ages, all His counsels of good, he falls into that same progression to roll on with it, not knowing whither, and how, and why, by any wisdom of the head, yet chiming faithfully with all that Christ is doing, or wants to be done.

At the risk now of a little repetition, let us recur a moment to the singularly beautiful example of the woman, whose conduct gives us our subject, and see how completely these suggestions are verified. The wise male brethren who stood critics round her, had all the casuistic, humanly assignable, reasons plainly enough with them. And yet the wisdom is hers without any reasons. She reaches further, touches the proprieties more fitly, chimes with God's future more exactly, than they do, reasoning the question as they best can. It is as if she were somehow polarized in her love by a new divine force, and she settles into coincidence with Christ and his future, just as the needle settles to its point without knowing why. She does not love him on debate, or serve him by contrived reasons, but she is so drunk up in his person, so totally captivated by the wondrous something felt in him, that she has and can have no thought other than to love him, and do every thing out of her love. To bathe his blessed head with what most precious ointment she can get, and bending low to put her fragrant homage on his feet, and wind them about in the honors of her hair, is all that she thinks of, and be it wise or unwise, it is done. Whereupon it turns out that she has met her Lord's future, as no other one of his disciples had been able; anointed his brow for the thorns, his feet for the nails, that both thorns and nails may draw blood in the perfume of at least one human creature's love. And this she has done, you perceive, because her life is wholly in Christ's element; tempered to him more fitly and totally than it could be by her understanding. By a certain delicate affinity of feeling that was equal to insight, and almost to prophecy, she touches exactly her Lord's strange, unknown future, and anoints him for the kingdom and the death she does not even think of, or know. Plainly enough no debate of consequences could ever have prepared her for these deep and beautifully wise proprieties.

Now in just this manner it is, that Christianity comes to our help, in all the most difficult, most insoluble questions of duty, those I mean which turn upon a computation of consequences. To compute such consequences, we need to know, in fact, a thousand things that belong to the future, and we know scarcely one of them—on what particular ends God is moving, by what means he will reach them, what effects will follow, or not follow, a supposed act of usefulness, what trains of causes will be put agoing, what trains checked and baffled. Here it is that our casuistry breaks down continually. At this point, all merely preceptive codes are inherently weak and well nigh impracticable. They command us to good, or beneficence, and leave us to utter perplexity in all computations of consequences that reach far enough to settle the real import or effect of any thing. Nothing plainly but some inspiration, or some new impulsion of love, such as puts the soul at one with all God's character and future, as when it embraces Christ and a completely incarnated morality in his person, can possibly settle our applications of duty and give us confidence in them. Just what helped the woman to come aforehand in the anointing of the Lord's body, is wanted by us all, at every turn of life.

And this I will now add, as a last consideration, is what every Christian has found many times, if not always, in his own experience. Thus, in some trying condition, where he has not been able, by the understanding, to settle any wise course of proceeding, how very clear has everything been made to him, step by step, by the simple and consciously single-eyed impulse of love to his Master. And when all is over, when his crisis is past, his course fought out, his adversaries confounded, his cause completely justified, his sacrifice crowned, how plain is it to him that he has been guided by a wisdom in his loving affinities, which he had not in the reasons of his understanding; all in a way so easy as even to be an astonishment to himself. Not to say this, my brethren, out of my own experience would be to withhold a good confession that is due. And I can not persuade myself that any thoroughly Christian person is ignorant of the experience I describe. All our best determinations of duty are those which come upon us in the immediate light of our immediate union to Christ.

I ought, perhaps, to add that the doctrine I am wishing to unfold, does not exclude the use of the understanding. It is one thing to use the understanding *under* love, as being liquified and molded by it, and quite another to make it the oracle or sole arbiter of duty. Christ himself gives precepts to the understanding, just because we are not perfected in love, and require, meantime, to have the school-master's keeping, under a preceptive and statutory control. Nothing was further off from God's design than to add so many preceptive regulations by Christ and the apostles, to help out the natural code of morality, and be applied as that code is, and with it, by natural reason. He gives them only because we are not ripe enough in the good impulse of love to be kept right by that alone. We might take our passions for love, and become fanatics and fire-brands of duty. The false heats of our indignations against wrong, too little qualified by love, might fill us with personal animosities. Our lusts might steal the name of love and fool us by the counterfeit. Therefore he puts dry precepts in the understanding for a time, where, if they are legal and precisional in their way, the fogs of distemper and passion will be just as much less able to reach them.

Let me add now, a few distinct suggestions that crowd upon us, naturally in the closing of such a subject. And—

1. The great debate which has been going on for some time past, with our modern infidelity, is seen to be joined upon a superficial and false issue. The superior preceptive morality of the Gospel of Christ, which used to be conceded, is now denied, and the learned champions of denial undertake to refute our claim, by citing from the explored literature of the ancient Pagan writers, every particular maxim, or pre-

cept that we most value, or suppose to be most original, in the teachings of Christ. Which if they can do, as they certainly can not, their argument is only a very transparent sophistry. For, when they have hunted all treasures of learning through, picking up here one thing and here another, to match the teachings of Christ, and claim as the result, that they have matched every thing, their conclusions amounts to simply this, not that Christ is the equal of some man, but that he is just as competently wise as all men taken together. Besides they make him none the less original; for no one can pretend that Christ obtained, or raked together so many precepts, by any such hunt of learned exploration as is here resorted to; he must have given them out of his own creative intelligence. And then again, what signifies a great deal more, it is not here after all, that he made his grand contribution to the life of duty. The issue tried is wholly one side of his chief merit; viz., that he brings relief and clearness where all the natural codes of duty break down. These codes are grounded in natural reason, by that also to be applied. The chief maxims may be right, but the applications are still to be settled as no mortal man can settle them—by analogies, by subtle distinctions, drawn where there are no definite lines of distinction; by computations of usefulness depending on a knowledge of the future that is impossible. Every maxim wants a volume of casuistry to settle its application to this or that case in practice; and then new cases, equally difficult, will be rising still—even as they do at common law, which covers only a very small corner of the general field of duty. Baxter wrote an immense folio on cases of conscience, thinking, I suppose, that he had made every thing clear to the end of the world; when in fact he had started more questions in doing it than twenty folios could settle. Handled in this way, the law of duty runs to endless refinements; and as men are corrupt, to endless sophistries and abortions; yielding codes in fact, that are codes of immorality, framing mischief by a law; codes of Jesuitry, codes of hideous and disgusting practice, such as heathen peoples propagate with endless perversity. How much then does it mean that Christ has a perfect morality incarnated in his person—all beauty, truth, mercy, greatness, wise counsel of life; so that when he is embraced, all casuistries are well nigh superseded, and the humblest, most unreasoning disciple, is able by a course of applications, wiser than he knows himself, to fill up a beautiful life, meet, with a glorious consent of practice, all the grandest meanings, and remotest future workings of God. The life of duty passes in a clear element, tossed by no perplexities, happy and sweet and strong, because the soul in Christ's love has a light of immediate guidance. In presence of this manifestly divine fact, how weak and sorry is the attempt to break down Christ's sublime superhuman evidences, by showing that his contributions to the mere preceptive code of duty, have been more or less nearly anticipated.

2. All conscientious Christian persons who get confused and fall into painful debates of duty in particular

cases, may here discover the secret of their trouble and the way to have it relieved. Their difficulty is that they fall back on the modes of casuistry, and attempt to settle their question of duty, as Jesuits or heathens do, by computations of reason. Shall I do this? shall I do that? shall I give myself, or my son, or my husband to the army of my country? keeping one day in seven, how shall I keep it? training up my child for God, what indulgences shall I give, what pleasures shall I allow? having adversaries, shall I be silent? willing to make every thing a sacrifice for God, shall I give or not give all my time and talent to the immediate duties of religion?—ten thousand such questions are rising every hour, this with one person, this with another. The debate is begun and kept up day and night, till the soul is weary. The darkness increases, the confusion grows painful, the longer and more critical the debate is, till finally the soul, thrown back upon itself, sinks into a kind of nervous dread, close akin to horror. How many such cases have I met, in past years, and they are among the saddest to which I have been called to minister. The question of duty was turned round and round, till the multitude of reasons made distraction. It was even as if duty were the only thing impossible to be found. Have I any such afflicted soul before me now? O, my friend, that I could show you the root of your difficulty. You carry your case to the wrong tribunal, to the casuistries of ethics and not to Christ. You get tangled in questions, when you should be clear in love. Go where Mary went, or rather where

Mary's heart went. Cease from your refinements, refuse to be caught any more in the mouse-trap questions and scruples of duty, and let it be enough to lay your soul on Christ's bosom. Resting quietly thus, in the sacred bliss of love to Christ's person, wanting nothing but to be with him and for him, your torment will soon be over. The question of duty will be ended even beforehand, just because the soul of all duty is in you. The current of your feeling will run to it and settle it, even before you ask where it is.

3. It is no good sign for a Christian person, that he is always trying to settle his duty by calculations, and wise presagings of the future; and it is all the worse, if he pleases himself in the confidence that he succeeds. Doing nothing by faith, making no room for impulse or the inspiration of christian love, he takes the easy method of sagacity—easy to the fool as to the wise man—determining his questions of course mostly in the negative; for, if there is any doubt, it is always a brave thing, and always looks sagacious to say, No; and then, since he undertakes no duty which he can not see to the end of, even by his eyes, which is about the same as to undertake no duty at all, he conceives that he has a more solid way of judging than others. He will do nothing out of a great sentiment of course, he will break no box of ointment on the head of anybody; he will educate no son for the ministry, for example, lest possibly he should be only a martyr for the truth, and all that has been spent upon him, should only be anointing him for his burial. Meantime, what is the

love of Christ doing in him? what great impulse of love does he trust enough to follow it? He makes a winter in the name of piety, and because nothing is melted in the heat of it, blesses himself in the solidity of his practice! Possibly there may be a little of the christian love in such a person, but the signs are bad. To be politic is no certain way of being good, and the man who tries it, perils every thing.

4. We have a striking, and at the same time, most inviting conception here given us, of the perfect state of society and character in the future life. Calculation, criticism, moral codes and precepts, none of these are wanted longer to regulate the conduct, all the legalities are gone by. There is no debate of reasons, no casuistry. The reign of simple love has come. The impulse that moves has its law in itself, and every man does what is good, just because only good is in him. There is no scruple, no friction, no subtlety of evil to be restrained. The conduct of all is pure water flowing from a pure spring. And as springs are unconscious of their sweetness, thunders of their sublimity, flowers of their beauty, so the perfection of character and conduct is consummated in a spontaneous movement that excludes all self-regulation, and requires no dressing of the life by rules and statutes. All best and noblest things are done, as it were naturally; for Christ, who is formed within, must needs appear without in acts that represent himself. All acts of beauty and good are like that of the woman, coming to anoint her Lord—inspirations of the beauty she loved, wise without

study or contrivance, unconscious, spontaneous, and free. This now is society, this is character, to this heighth of perfection, this blessedness in good, our God is raising all that love him.

After having sunned ourselves, my friends, in this bright picture above, some of you, it may be, will now return to the earth with a feeling more wearied and worn by duty than ever. This everlasting and compunctious study of duty, duty to children, husband or wife, duty to poor neighbors, and bad neighbors, and impenitent neighbors, duty to Sunday Schools, duty to home missions and missionaries, duty to heathens and savages, duty to contrabands and wounded soldiers, and wooden legs in the streets, and limping beggers at the door, duty to every body, everywhere, every day; it keeps you questioning all the while, rasping in a torment of debates and compunctions, till you almost groan aloud for weariness. It is as if your life itself were slavery. And then you say, with a sigh, "O, if I had nothing to do but just to be with Christ personally, and have my duty solely as with him, how sweet and blessed and secret and free would it be." Well, you may have it so; exactly this you may do and nothing more! Sad mistake that you should ever have thought otherwise! what a loss of privilege has it been! come back then to Christ, retire into the secret place of his love, and have your whole duty personally as with him. Only then you will make this very welcome discovery, that as you are personally given up to Christ's person, you are going where he goes, helping what he does, keeping ever dear, bright company with him, in all his motions of good and sympathy, refusing even to let him suffer without suffering with him. And so you will do a great many more duties than you even think of now; only they will all be sweet and easy and free, even as your love is. You will stoop low, and bear the load of many, and be the servant of all, but it will be a secret joy that you have with your Master personally. You will not be digging out points of conscience, and debating what your duty is to this or that, or him or her, or here or yonder; indeed you will not think that you are doing much for Christ any way—not half enough—and yet he will be saying to you every hour in sweetest approbation—"Ye did it unto me."

IV.

SALVATION FOR THE LOST CONDITION.

"*For the Son of Man is come to save that which was lost.*"—MATH. xviii. 11.

Every kind of work supposes something to be done, some ground or condition of fact to be affected by it; education the fact of ignorance, punishment the fact of crime, charity the fact of want. The work of Christ, commonly called a work of salvation, supposes in like manner the fact of a lost condition, such as makes salvation necessary. So it is that Christ himself conceives it, "For the Son of Man is come to save that which was lost." He does not say, you observe, "that which is about to be, or in danger of being, lost," but he uses the past tense, "*was lost*," as if it were a fact already consummated, or, at least, practically determined. This work, therefore, is to be a salvation, not as being a preventive, but as being a remedy after the fact; a supernatural provision by which seeds of life are to be ingenerated in a lapsed condition where there are none. At this point then Christianity begins, this is the grand substructural truth on which it rests, that man who is to be saved by it, is a lost being—already lost.

And yet there will be many who recoil from this

assumption of Christ, and, without any willing disrespect to his person, take up a suspicion that he somehow over-states the fact of our condition. They could admit, without difficulty, that they are imperfect, that they sometimes do wrong, and that there is often great perversity in men, or it may be in themselves. It would not shock them, if it were declared that every human being wants forgiveness; but to say that we are lost beings, appears to be an extravagance. They do not see it in the tolerably comfortable state of the world, and they are not conscious of it in themselves; they think they have even a kind of instinctive conviction against it, and feel obliged to repel it as injurious and without evidence.

Probably some of you before me are in just this position of mind regarding the great point stated. You feel obliged to make issue with the Lord Jesus in respect to it—doing it, as you believe, not from any disposition to have a conflict with him, but simply because you can not assent to his words, and seem even to know that the fact he assumes can not be true. The disagreement you will admit is very unequal, but how can you assent to a position that so far violates your honest convictions.

What I propose then at the present time, not in the way of controversy, but for your sake and Christ's sake, is to go over this matter in a careful revision, offering, if I can, such a statement of it that, going out as it were from your own center and sentiment, you will meet the mind of Christ approvingly. Perhaps you will so take his meaning as to meet him with a felt tenderness in it, such as he most certainly reveals to you; concluding this friendly negotiation, so to speak, in a reverent, believing acceptance of him as your own great, necessary Saviour. To this end let us,

I. Clear away some obstructions, or points of misconception, that may put your feeling at unnecessary variance with Christ's doctrine, or give you a sense of revulsion from it that is not really occasioned by any thing in it.

Thus, when he says "was lost," using the past tense, as if the lost condition were a fact accomplished, you do not see that either you, or the world is in a state of undoing so completely reprobate. But he does not mean, when he says "was lost," that the lost condition is literally accomplished in the full significance of it, but only that it is begun, with a fixed certainty of being fully accomplished; that, as being begun, the causes that are loosed in it contain the certainty of the fact, as truly as if the fact were fully executed. Thus if you see a man topple off the brink of a precipice a thousand feet high, you say inwardly, the moment he passes his center of gravity, "he is gone;" you know it as well as when you see him dashed in pieces on the rocks below; for the causes that have gotten hold of him, contain the fact of his destruction, and he is just as truly lost before the fact accomplished as after. So if a man has taken some deadly poison and the stupor has begun to settle upon him already, you say that he is a lost man; for the death-power is in him, and you know as well that he is gone, as if he lay dead at your feet. So a soul under evil once begun, has taken the poison, and the bad causation at work is fatal; it contains the fact of a ruined immortality, in such a sense that we never adequately conceive it, save as we give it past tense, and say, "was lost."

Again, you have heard of such a thing as "total depravity," and the declaration of Christ may be somehow associated with such a conception; a conception which you instinctively repel as unjust and extravagant, and contrary plainly to what you know of the many graces and virtues that adorn our human life. But this notion of total depravity is no declaration of Christ, and he is not responsible for it. It is only a speculated dogma of man, which can be so stated as to be true, and very often is so stated as to be false. You have nothing to do with it here.

It has much to do, again with your impressions on this subject, that you are so completely wide of all sensibility to, or consciousness of, the lost condition Christ assumes. Have you considered the possibility that you may be rather proving the truth of it in that manner? "If our gospel be hid," says an apostle, "it is hid to them that are lost." If you have no sense of being in the lost condition Christ speaks of, if the salvation he proposes seems, in that view, to be an exaggeration, a fiction, it may be true and is very likely to be, that the want of proportion is in you and not in it. I say not that it is, I only suggest that it may be. If it is, then it will appear by the positive evidence hereafter to be given.

Again, your mind is an active principle, and it keeps suggesting, or putting in your way, thoughts that run, as it were, to a contrary conviction; as that God is good, and will not put a race in being, to be lost regarding all good ends of being, or that he is a great being, competent every way to keep his foster children safe. The argument is short and easy, it seems even to invent itself. But there is another counter suggestion that is quite as likely to be true, and has weight enough cer tainly to balance it; viz., that God wanted possibly, in the creation of men, free beings like himself, and capable of common virtues with himself—not stones, or trees, or animals—and that, being free and therefore not to be controlled by force, they must of necessity be free to evil; consequently never to be set fast in common virtues with himself, except as he goes down after them into evil and a lost condition, to restore them by a salvation. This being true, creatures may be made, that perish, or fall into lost conditions. Besides the world is full of analogies. The blossoms of the spring cover the trees and the fields, all alike beautiful and fragrant; but they shortly strew the ground as dead failures, even the greater part of them, having set no beginning of fruit. And then of the fruits that are set how many die as abortive growths, strewing the ground again. How many harvests also are blasted, yielding only straw. In the immense propagations of the sea, what myriads die in the first week of life.

Thus we find nature everywhere struggling in abortive growths, fainting, as it were, in the perfecting of what her prolific intentions initiate. And all these abortions are so many tokens in the lower forms of life, of the possibility that there also may be blasted growths in the higher.

Once more the amiable virtues, high aspirations, and other shining qualities, you see in mankind, make the assumed fact of our lost condition seem harsh and extravagant—you could not believe it if you would. But considering how high and beautiful a nature the soul is, it should not surprise you that it shows many traces of dignity even after it has fallen prostrate, and lies a broken statue on the ground. Besides, Christ himself had even a more appreciative feeling, in respect to what may be called our natural character than you. When a certain young man, rich, but conscientiously upright and nobly ingenuous, came to him asking what he should do "to inherit eternal life?" though he was obliged in faithfulness to answer, "one thing thou lackest,"—requiring him to suffer a total change of life, in the sacrifice of all he had, and the assumption of his cross—his manner and look were so visibly and affectingly tender, nevertheless, as to attract the special attention of his disciples, and from them it passed into the narrative, as a distinctly noted element of description—"Then Jesus beholding him, loved him." You might not yourself have put any such terms of requirement upon him; I fear that you would not, but would you, with all you sensibilities to natural excellence, have loved him as much, or shown it by signs as beautifully impressive?

Having noted, in this manner, so many points of unnecessary revulsion from the fact of a lost condition, assumed by Christ in his work of salvation, I think I may take it for granted that you are ready—

II. To look at the evidence of the fact and accept the conclusion it brings you.

And the first thing here to be considered is, that our blessed Master, in assuming your lost condition, is not doing it harshly, or in any manner of severity. He is no dogmatist, making out his article of depravity. He is not a teacher of that light quality that permits him to be pleased with appalling severities of rhetoric, and over-drawn allegations of fact, without any due sense of their meaning. His feeling is tender, never censorious. Sometimes, by a kind of divine politeness so to speak, he puts a face on human character and relations that avoids a look of impeachment where impeachment would be true; as when he speaks of "laying down his life for his friends." He could have said "enemies" quite as truly, or even more so, but did not like to put that now upon his disciples. In the same kind way of consideration, but with a deeper feeling, he apologizes to God for his murderers, even in the article of death, and apparently comforts himself in the allowance—"Father forgive them, for they know not what they do." Is it such a being that will thresh you in random charges, the severity of which is apparent to you and not to him? You can not say it, or even be willing to think it.

Furthermore, it must be evident to you, as it has been to all most unrestrained critics and deniers, that his moral sentiments and standards are high and sharp beyond comparison—higher and sharper certainly than yours. He has also a most piercing insight of all that is deepest in character and its wants; as, by force of his most singular purity alone, he must of necessity have; what then will you sooner think of, when he calls you a lost man, than that, possibly, he knows you more adequately than you know yourself? Having then some better right than you to know, what does he in fact say?

I might go to the other scriptures, citing declarations from them; and especially from the writings of Paul, who discusses this very point many times over, showing by the most cogently close and formal arguments, the fallen state of disability and subjection to evil, out of which Christ has undertaken to raise you; but I prefer to keep the question still and altogether between you and him, and therefore I shall not cite any words but his. Notice then his parables of the lost sheep, and the lost piece of money, not omitting to observe that he is here sharpening no point of allegation against men, but only setting forth the joy that will accrue to the angels of God, and all good beings, when they are restored. Is it in this attitude of feeling that he is launching hard or unjust judgments upon them? He also speaks of a state of "condemnation," declaring in a manifestly gentle feeling, that he has not come to condemn but to save the world, yet still obliged to add—"he that believeth not is condemned already." What is this state condemned of God but a lost condition under another figure? He uses also the figure of death, spiritual death, in the same manner, saying—"I am the life." "My Son was dead and is alive again, was lost and is found." "Is passed from death unto life." "For God so loved the world, that he gave his only begotten Son, that whosoever believeth on him should not perish, but have everlasting life." Death is the condition of disorder and spiritual dissolution, which is a lost condition. Life is salvation, because it is the condition of harmony restored; where part answers again to part, function to function, in a complete living order. The lost condition he also calls a state of "darkness" and "blindness," and to it he comes as "the light" and "the way." Who is more profoundly lost than he that walks groping for the wall? He conceives the lost condition as a state of moral disability, in which men "have eyes" which "can not see," and "ears which can not hear," and are able no longer to convert, or heal themselves. It even requires a divine power in us, he conceives, if we are to make any real approach to good—"No man can come to me, except the Father which hath sent me draw him." Not to multiply citations further, take the one practical exhibition of his discourse on regeneration. The doctrine is that man, as he conceives him, is in such a condition that nothing short of a divine movement upon him, can bring him back, into that character and felicity for which he was made. "Verily, verily I say unto you, except a man be born again"—"born of the Spirit,"—"he can not see the kingdom of God."

These now are Christ's convictions, most tenderly, faithfully, and variously expressed, concerning man, or the lost condition of man—your lost condition. He does not come to some very bad men, saying these things, but he speaks comprehensively to the race, and grounds his work of salvation fixedly upon the lost condition affirmed.

You will not hear them disrespectfully. Still it will not be strange if your feeling is unsatisfied. "If it be so with me," you will ask, "why may it not somehow be made to appear?" Let me take you then a step further, into another field, where I think it will appear.

As the matter lies between you and Christ, and he has spoken already, I will take you now to yourself. Think it not strange, if your heart answers, after all, to the heart of Jesus, and re-affirms exactly what he has testified.

You live in a world where there is certainly some wrong—you have seen it, suffered from it, and consciously done it. But all wrong, it will be agreed, is something done against the perfect and right will of God, and a shock must of necessity follow it. Suppose a machinist to produce a machine, some one wheel of which will somehow run directly the other way from what was intended—does run the other way for some space, longer or shorter, every few hours. It will go into confusion of course and become a total wreck. So a soul going against the will of God, in acts of wrong, breaks God's order in it. Taken as a functional structure, all the parts of which are to play harmoniously into each other, disorder and ruin begins just when wrong begins, and all its goings on afterward accelerate and aggravate the disorder. As the junctures and functions are no more in heaven's order, it is practically undone. Then, as the body is the soul's organ, the damage is propagated as disease in that. And then, as society is made up of souls and bodies, that also becomes an element of discord, infested with lies, grudges, enmities, jealousies, breaches of trust and of contract, deeds of injustice and robbery; history itself a volume, the main chapters of which report the conflicts of war, the oppressions of slavery, the wrongs of woman, the hard fortunes of industry, the corruptions of courts and governments, the intrigues of diplomacy, the persecutions of the good.

But I refer you to society thus only in a way of transition, and return immediately to the main question as it stands in the revelations of your own personal consciousness. It has always seemed to me that whoever will accurately note his own inward working, for but one half hour, must even be appalled by the discoveries he will make. You distinguish first of all a certain shyness, or feeling of recoil from God—why should you withdraw instinctively thus from a being wholly good and pure? It was just this feeling that

Adam had, after the sin, when he withdrew and hid himself in the garden. Guilt is at the bottom of this shyness. And what is a more certainly lost feeling than the feeling of guilt? Who can stop it, or smooth it away, by any thing done upon himself? It testifies to a fact—can you ever annihilate that fact? No more can you stop the guilt which is only a fit remembrance of it.

You discover also a certain look of disproportion, that is painfully significant. Your ambition is too high for your possibilities and your place. Your passions are too strong for your prudence. Your prudence too close for your affections. Your irritabilities too fiery at times for both. Your resentments are too impetuous for your occasions. Your appetites too large for your possibilities of safe indulgence. Your will over-rules your conscience. Your inclinations master the dictates of your reason. And what is more sadly humiliating than any thing else, your great aspirations have some weight upon them which they can not lift, falling back baffled and spent, with no power left but to notify you of their constant failure. Your great ideals too, revealing, as it were, the summits of a magnificent nature, and lifting their flags of inspiration there, are yet draggled somehow and drugged by low impulses, that make you a mockery to yourself in your attainments. A kind of inversion appears in every thing—sure indication of disorder.

There is disagreement also, as well as disproportion. Your practical judgments of things disagree with your real wants, magnifying toys of sense, to leave you aching for God and the unseen good of the mind. Your eyes discover good in shows and outward preferments, your convictions place it in truth and character. Your generous and high sentiments look down with scorn upon the sordid and cowardly impulses of your selfishness, to be, in turn, alas! how often, mastered in the conflict with them. Your feeling of independence knuckles to conventionalities, and what begun as a war, is ended as a truce, in which you agree, as a kind of independent abject, to hold every thing in scorn that is not under the fashion. Your eternal convictions quarrel with your passions, and your will quarrels feebly with both, misgiving under one, succumbing to the other. The whole internal man is a troubled element. You hardly know, many times, what to think, on the plainest subjects of duty and religion, and are most facile to what you least approve. You ask where you are? and think you do not know; what to believe? and say you can not find; what to do? and do what you would not; what to avoid? and do it. Your mind is full of distraction—in endless mazes lost.

Take another and simpler view of your disorder do just what so few men ever did, sit down for an hour, and watch the run of your thoughts. Nothing flows in regular causation, no law of suggestion can be more than faintly traced. As a man who is lost in a deep forest, turns confusedly one way and the other, unable to set his mind in a train of deliberative order, so it is with you. Your thoughts huddle on, crossing all lines, breaking through all trains, refusing all terms of order, uncontrolled, uncontrollable; even as droves in the jostle of panic before a prairie fire. The law of right proceeding appears to be somehow broken, the suggestions are, how often, base, impure, and low, and withal defy any look of system. What jumps of transition! how incongruous, unaccountable, and wild! Could the internal picture be mapped to the eye, what eye could trace it! It is as if the soul were an instrument played by demons. How unlike to the sweet flow of order and health in the mind of an angel. The metaphysicians do indeed make up their solutions, showing how every thing goes on by a law of suggestion or association in a strictly normal process. Their farthing candle gives a very little faint light, wholly insufficient, however, as regards the main question. The single word *disease* tells more than all their speculations. Watching these wild ways of thought, we distinguish a ferment of death, and not the flow of life. The look is abnormal; as if the soul were in a kind of dissolution. No man, duly observing thus himself, will easily doubt that he is somehow lost. The appalling doubt, whether he can ever be saved will be more natural. What a work indeed to save him, restore him, that is, to the state of inward health, raise him up into the orderly movement of angelic life, and make the currents flow melodious and clear.

Glance now a moment, at the disabilities that have somehow come upon you, in what the Saviour calls your lost condition. You never encountered any trouble, it may be, on this point, never thought of being under any such disability as he speaks of. Have you not your will, your strong will left? Yes, but the difficulty is to execute, or carry through what you will to be done. When you resolve to govern yourself, thus or thus, or to be this or that, according to some ideal conceived, does your soul mind you? do you become forthwith such as you undertook to be? Are there no currents of habit encountered, no floods of contrary impulse, no volcanic fires of irritation, that prove quite too strong for you? Suppose you determine with all seriousness, now, or at some future time, to begin a religious life. Is it begun? You find base motives creeping into your mind, which you disrespect and determine to shut them away. Do you succeed? You grow sick of the world in one form or another, and rise up to cast it out. Does it go? You conceive a true notion of spiritual dignity and beauty of character, and set yourself to the attainment. Do you reach it? Try a thing more brave and certainly not less necessary; take stiff hold of your thoughts, set your will down upon them and still their tumult, and tame their wild way, into the sweet order of health and rational proceeding. Can you do it? Could any thing be more preposterous even than to try? And yet there is no true perfection of soul that does not include even this; including also, in the same way, all that belongs to internal order, proportion, agreement, and a full consent of all functions and powers. Have you courage to undertake such perfection? This now is the very profound disability in which Christ finds you yourself. Perhaps you never saw it before, but he looks upon you tenderly in it, and counts you to be lost—is any thing more certainly, manifestly true? This brings me to speak—

III. Of the salvation—what it is, and by what means or methods it is wrought. Too short a space is left me, you will see, to allow any thing but a very condensed statement. Excluding then all that may be held, or contended for, as regards the matter of expiation for sin, or the final satisfaction of God's justice, in the death of Christ—which can, at the most, be no proper salvation from the inward disorder and disability we have discovered—we come directly to the question, how the death is quickened, how the lost condition of the old man is, or is to be, renewed by Christ, in his work considered as a salvation?

Manifestly this can be done only by some means, or operation, that respects the soul's free nature, working in, upon, or through consent in us, and so new ordering the soul.

Not then, by some divine act in the force principle of omnipotence, some new creating stroke from behind, that restores our disorder; the change thus accomplished is a mending by repair, and not a recovery; omnipotence, not Christ, is the Saviour.

As little is it by some help given to your development, or self-culture, or even self-reformation. When Lord Chesterfield gives disquisitions on the elegant properties of good manners and polite conduct, he speaks to men as having a power to fashion themselves by his rules. Christ is no professor of goodness in that way. He calls you never to go about being better. He does not so much as call upon you to stifle your deep hunger, by satisfying your own wants. He does not even put you climbing after the glorious ideals you have, and the still more glorious he gives you from his own life and person; as if you could get inspiration from these to raise yourself. The Chesterfieldian method, and the merely moral of Socrates, are not his. These were instructors, not Saviours, speaking both to men, not to lost men—what you want, and what Christ undertakes to be, is a Saviour for lost men. No scheme of Christianity, so called, includes a gospel, which does not include this. Any Christ, who does not come to save lost men, is antichrist, or at best no Christ at all; for who can be the Lord's true Christ, not coming, as life to death, peace within to discord within, order to disorder, liberty to bondage.

We must look, in fact, for some such being as can be a World's Regenerator; making good the fact that God has not created us for a lost condition, but for salvation. Doubtless it may be true that God could not bring us on as free, by any straight line progress of development, into the character he meant for us, and the relation to Himself, that was to be our joy and his. As the ancient poets tell us of this or that hero of their's, who went down to hell, fought away the three-headed dog at the gate, and passed the Stygian river, and when the grim reconnoisance was over, forced his way back, even by the judgment bar of Radamanthus, out into the light; so there was to be, we may believe, an epic descent of souls into the hell-state of disorder and judicial condemnation, and a bursting up again, out of their penal imprisonment, into life and free dominion. But if the soul-history could not be a simply quiet educing of good, if it must be inherently terrible, plunging down through gulfs of disaster and loss, in the mad experiment of wrong, even as it is itself inherently free; then a Saviour is required who can sound the bottom of such gulfs, and bring up the lost ones, into that good and glory eternal for which they were made. This is Christ the Lord, coming, as in everlasting counsel, to execute a salvation prepared before the foundation of the world.

He works by no fiat of absolute will, as when God said "let there be light." He respects your moral nature, doing it no violence. He moves on your consent, by moving on your convictions, wants, sensibilities, and sympathies. He is the love of God, the beauty of God, the mercy of God—God's whole character, brought nigh through a proper and true Son of Man, a nature fellow to your own, thus to renovate and raise your own. Meeting you at the point of your fall and disorder, as being himself incarnated into the corporate evil of your state, he brings you God's great feeling to work on yours. He is deeply enough entered into your case, to let the retributive causes loosened by your sin roll over him in his innocence, doing honor thus to God's judicial order, that you may see it sufficiently hallowed without your punishment. And that he may get the greater and more constraining power over you, he reveals to you by his suffering death, the suffering state of God's perfection—stung by the wrongs, and moved in holy grief for the sad and shameful lot of his fallen children. His suffering is in fact the tragic hour of divine goodness; for what to our slow feeling, is even eternal goodness, till we see it tragically moved? Nay, it was even necessary, if transgressors were to have their dull heart opened to this goodness, that they should see it persecuted and gibbeted by themselves. Thus, and therefore, he dies, raising by his death at our hands, those terrible convictions that will rend our bosom open to his love—dies for love's sake into love in us. So he will become the power of God unto salvation, gathering you in, as it were, with all your disorders, into the infolding, new-creating sympathy of his own character in good; so that being thus infolded in him, all your disproportion, discord, disability, and all wild tumult of the mind will be new crystalized in his divine order. Thus ends the ferment of death, succeeded by the harmony and health of new born life. In this view it was that Christ said, "I am the life." And the same thing was differently put, when he said "and I, if I be lifted up, will draw all men unto me." He would draw by his death, moving on consent and choice, so to gather in all our disorder, into the molds of his own perfect life.

And this is salvation, the entering of the soul into God's divine order; for nothing is in order that is not in God, having God flow through it by his perfect will, even as he sways to unsinning obedience the tides of the sea, and the rounds of the stars. As we are lost men when lost to God, so we find ourselves when we find God. And then, how consciously do the soul's broken members coalesce and meet in Christ's order, when Christ liveth in them. In this new relationship, the spirit of love and of a sound mind, all strength, free beauty, solid vigor, get their spring—we are no more lost. All that is in God or Christ his Son, flows in upon us—wisdom, righteousness, sanctification, redemption. We are new men created in righteousness after God. Even so, "in righteousness;" for we are new-charactered in God, closeted so to speak in God's perfections—in that manner justified, as if we had never sinned, justified by faith. We have put on righteousness, and in it we are clothed; even the righteousness of God, which is by faith of Jesus Christ, unto all and upon all them that believe.

This is the salvation that our God is working in his Son, but as the great apostle here intimates, it is, and is to be, by faith; for the result can never be issued save as we, on our part believe. The very plan, or mode of his working supposes a necessity of faith in us. For as God comes nigh us in his son, he can be a salvation, only as we come nigh responsively to Him, yielding our feeling to the cogent working of his. And this we do in faith. Faith is the act by which one being confides in another, trusting up himself to that other, in what he is and undertakes. And there is nothing that puts a man so close to another's feeling, principle, and character, as this act of trust. When you put such faith in a man, his opinions, ways, and even accents of voice have a wonderfully assimilative power in you. It is as if your life were overspread by his, included in his. To be nigh a great good mind, accepted in trust and friendship, is, in this manner, one of the greatest possible advantages, and especially so for a young person. In this fact you have the reason of that faith in Christ which is made the condition of salvation. For it is even your chance of salvation, as a lost man, that a being has come into the world, so great in character and feeling, that turning to be with him, he shall be in you. And therefore, it is that his apostle says—"Christ the power of God to every one that believeth;" and he himself—"he that believeth shall be saved." He can be no sufficient power, work no principle of life, save as he is welcomed to the heart by faith. In the same way, he calls you to "come," for coming is faith. And when he says, "come unto me all ye that are weary and heavy laden, learn of me and ye shall find rest to your souls," he does not speak, as many think, to such as are only afflicted, world-sick, tired, pining in weak self-sympathy, but to them who are weary of their own evils, tossed and rent by their own disorders, thrown out of rest by the tumult of their thoughts and bosom troubles, starving in their own deep wants, crushed by their felt disabilities to good—in a word, lost men.

Thus he speaks to you. And you come when you truly believe in him. Then you rest, rest in God's harmony, rest in peace—knowing in the blissful revelation of fact, how much it means that the Son of Man is come to save that which was lost.

V.

THE FASTING AND TEMPTATION OF JESUS.

"*Then was Jesus led up of the Spirit into the wilderness to be tempted of the devil. And when he had fasted forty days and forty nights, he was afterward an hungered.*"—MATH. iv. 1–2.

I think I do not mistake, when I assume that this particular chapter of the gospel history, commonly called *the temptation*, is just the one that a good many theologians, and a much larger number of Christian disciples, do really, if not consciously, wish had not been written; that which most stumbles their speculation, and least fructifies their spiritual impressions; that which wears the most suspiciously mythic look, that which they skip most frequently in the reading, or, if they read, only gather up their minds to go on with due attention, after they are through with it.

Jesus Immanuel, the eternal Word incarnate, innocence itself and purity, the only perfect being that ever trod the earth, fasting! opening his great ministry of life in a fast of forty days, and a conflict with the devil for so long a time! Coming down, as he himself declares from heaven, to set up the kingdom of God among men, he goes to his work as if it were a deed of repentance—out of a desert, out of a fast—inaugurating his sublime kingship by austerities and fierce mental conflicts, such as guilty souls might undergo for their chastening. The picture is incongruous, many think, and revolting to faith. Besides they have a settled disrespect to fasting itself.

What I propose then at the present time, is a careful inquiry into the matter.—*The fasting of Jesus in the wilderness.* My hope is, that I shall be able to clear this remarkable scene of what many regard as its forbidding, or unwelcome aspect. I even hope to open up a conception of it that will place it along side of the agony and the cross, and will make it correspondently dear to all most thoughtful, practically earnest souls.

In the descent of the Spirit upon him at his baptism, he passes his great inward crisis of call and endowment, the effect of which the gospels report, in terms that require to be distinctly noted; saying, one that he is "led up," [transported,] another, that he is "led," [taken away,] another, that he is "driven" by the Spirit into the wilderness. Under all these rather violent forms of expression, the fact is signified, that the Spirit, coming here upon him in the full revelation of his call, raises such a ferment, in his bosom, of great thoughts and strangely contesting emotions, that he is hurried away to the wilderness, and the state of privacy before God, for relief and settlement. He was not wholly unapprised of his Messiahship before, but had come to no adequate impression of what, as Messiah, he was to do and to be. He began at twelve years of age, to talk, in words profoundly enigmatical to his friends, of being "about his Father's business." He was reading also, from that time onward, the prophets, so often quoted by him afterward, and his soul was making answer more and more consciously to their words, even as a bell that chimes responsively to some quivering harmony of sound that is felt upon the air. Still he was so far from expecting a public inaugural in John's baptism, that when John objects, saying "comest thou to me?" he only pleads the common reason of the multitude, a desire "to fulfill all righteousness," in the accepting of John's righteous ministry.

As he was human, so there was to be a humanly progressive opening of his mind, and a growing presentiment of his great future. All which makes the revelation, when it comes, only the greater and more astounding, because he is just so much more capable of taking the fit impression of it. Nor does it make any difference what particular account we frame of his person. If there is a divine-nature soul, and a human-nature soul, existing together in him as one person, that one person must be in the human type, unfolding by a human process, toward the consciously great Messiahship he is going to fulfill. If he is pure divinity incarnate, he is not simply housed or templed in the flesh, but inhumanized, categorized in humanity, there to grow, to learn, to be unfolded under human conditions of progress.

And then it is only a part of the same general view, that when his endowment settles upon him, as it does in the scene of his baptism, it raises in his feeling just the same kind of commotion that is raised in any very great and really upright human soul; as for example, in that of a prophet when his call arrives. There has been a mighty apprehension waking gradually in him before, and now there is a mighty breaking in, as it were at once, of the tremendous call; all the great movings attendant—sentiments, misgivings, joys of hope, agonies of concern—coming in with it, like the coming in of the sea. The surges break all round him, and the little skiff of humanity that he has taken for his voyage quivers painfully—quivers even the worse that it feels the heavy armament aboard of so great purpose and power.

An amazing transformation is suddenly wrought in his consciousness. As heaven opens above to let forth the voice, and let down the power, and the gate is set open before him to let him forward into his great future as a world's Redeemer; as every thing opens every way to prepare his mighty kingship, and he feels the Messianic forces heaving in his breast, he reels so to speak, under the new sense he has of himself and his charge, moved all through in a movement so tremendous that every faculty groans in the pressure, like a forest swaying in a storm. And the result is that he does what he must—tears himself utterly away from the incontinent folly of human voices, and the sorry conceit of human faces, and plunges into the deep silence and solitude of the wilderness; there to settle his great inward commotions and compose himself to his call. He is "driven of the Spirit," only in the sense that the crisis brought upon him by his call and felt endowment drives him. And he goes "to be tempted of the devil," only in the sense that, being so mightily heaved by his inward commotion, he both is and will be tempted thus, till he finds his point of rest, and settles into his plan of sacrifice.

As to the fast itself, it is not likely that he had any thought of fasting, when he betook himself to the retirement of the wilderness; he only found, when there, that a fast was upon him, and since it might help him to subdue his partly intractable humanity more completely to his uses, he took it for his opportunity, refusing to come out into the sight of the world's works and faces, to obtain his customary food. The great inward tumult he was in held him thus to his fasting for a whole forty days, and so deep was the stress of his feeling, that he does not appear to have been particularly conscious of hunger, till the very last of it; when as we are told "he began to be an hungered"—all which, as many are forward to say, is a myth, or, if not, a perfectly incredible story; no mortal organization being able to subsist for so long a time without food. And yet we hear every few months, of cases well attested that correspond. There appears in fact, to be a possible state of mental and nervous tension, that allows the subject to maintain life without food, for a much longer time than he could in the quiet equilibrium of a more natural state,

But what is Christ doing in this long solitude and

silence of the wilderness? To say that he is fasting does not satisfy our inquiry. The fast we can see, is total; not a fasting from food only, but from the comforts of human habitations, from conversation, from society, and even from public worship in the synagogue, where "his custom" was, even from his childhood, to be always present. Isolated thus from the great world, and closeted with God in that grim wilderness, there is of course, no one to report him and he has not chosen to report himself; save that, in the very closing scene of his exhaustion, which is often called "the temptation," he allows the veil to be lifted.

Who has not wished many times, that he could have the record of these forty days? And yet they may be worth even the more to us, that the record is not given—left with a veil hung over it, left to the imagination; by that only, as the purveyor to faith and sympathy, to be explored and pictured as it may be in its scenes, for there is nothing so fructifying as the supplying fondly of what is not given us in our Master's history, but is left, in this manner, to our creative liberty. In this view, certain blank spaces were even necessary, it may be to our complete benefit in the record of his life. Had he kept a complete diary for us of the forty days experience, it might have been a far less fruitful chapter, than the almost total blank he has left us to range in, loosing our love in tender explorations and reconnoisances, and constructing a history for our faith, out of the scantiest helps given to our understanding.

Among the few things given, or which we sufficiently know, are such as these; that he is not bewailing his sins; that he is not afflicting himself purposely in penances of hunger and starvation; that he is not wrestling with the question whether he will undertake the work to which he is called. The first he can not be doing, because he has no sins to bewail; nor the second, because he is no believer in the doctrine of penance; nor the third, because his choices are concluded always, by the simple fact that any thing right or good is given him to do. If by reason of his human weakness he suffers, for a time, great revulsions of body and mind, that do not pertain to his voluntary nature, that is quite another matter. We shall find reason to think it may be true.

But these are negations only, and I think we shall be able to fix on several very important points, where we know sufficient in the positive, to justify a large deduction, concerning the probable nature of the struggle through which Jesus is here passing.

1. He has a nature, that in part, is humanly derived, so far an infected, broken nature. He has never sinned, he has lived in purity, under this humanly impure investment; growing more and more distinctly conscious of those higher affinities by which he thus dominates over the human, unable to be soiled by its contact. But now it is opened to him in his call, that he is here not as here belonging, that he is sent, let down into the world, incarnated into human evil, into the curse. There must have been some time at which the sense of

this fact became fully developed in him; doubtless it was partly developed before, but it could not be completely till now, because his Messiahship, or mission of salvation to sinners, requiring him to be incarnated into the very fall and broken state of sin, was not before opened to him. Now it is opened, and the whole relation he is in flashes upon him. Before he had the contact of evil in a simply quiet mastery, now he has it in the grim discovery, that he is membered into it! Feeling himself incorporated thus into the corporate evil of the world, to bear its woe and shame, and hate and wrong, as being of the common humanity, he shudders in horrid recoil and revulsion—takes himself away into the desert, there to wrestle with his feeling, till he gets ready to bear the sin of the world with a mind leveled to the burden of its ignominy. For a time, he is just as much more disturbed and revolted, probably, as he is more consciously divine. In those forty days of trial, instinctively withdrawn from men, how often looking out upon them, did his divine chastity recoil from the fearful and even shocking relationship into which he was come. This in great part is the cross—not the wood, nor the nails, nor the vinegar, but the men, and the breath of hell, their malignity is breathing upon him.

2. It is not to be doubted that he had internal struggles of a different nature, growing out of his hereditary connection with our humanly disordered and retributively broken state. I refer, more especially, to what must have come upon him under the law of bad sug-

gestion. How it was with him in the closing scene, after he began to be an hungered—the bad thoughts that came to him, as by satanic suggestion—we are expressly told. And it is not to be doubted that his very call and spiritual endowment, raising, as they did, the sense of his kingly dignity and power, would also call out from his infected humanity, whole troops of bad thoughts or treacherous suggestions, even as the history declares. Raised in order and power, it is only human to be tempted by suggestions of the figure he can make, and the prodigious things he may do. It is not probably true that Jesus was contending, for the whole forty days, with such kind of temptations as came upon him at the close. But as certainly as his mind had a man-wise way of thinking, he must have had many thoughts coming upon him that required him to repeat his "get thee behind me," and turn his great nature home upon God and his work closely enough to pre-occupy it, and take away the annoyance. Neither let us shrink from such a mode of conceiving him, as if it were a derogation from his perfect character. Mental suggestion is not voluntary, but takes place under mental laws, going where it will, and running more or less wildly, where there is any contact of the nature with disorder. No crime is incurred by evil suggestion, when there is no encouragement of it, or yielding of the soul to it. As then Jesus was to be tempted in all points like as we are only without sin, it is even a fact included, that, when his tremendous call took him, an immense irruption of evil suggestions, bursting up from his low born humanity, must have taken him also. And this, I conceive, is what is meant, when he is declared to have been driven of the Spirit into the wilderness to be tempted of the devil. The very call of the Spirit brought this contest upon him. I do not exclude the possibility of some access of bad spirits concurrently working with the bad thoughts; for he was tempted just as men are, and as being a man. And he gained his victory, doubtless by a struggle often renewed and variously protracted.

3. It is not to be doubted that his human weakness made a fearful recoil from the lot of suffering, and the horrible death now before him. Human nature is keenly sensitive to suffering; but we manage often to bear a great deal of it, because we do not know of it beforehand, but have it coming upon us by surprises, or turns of Providence not expected. Hence there is nothing so common as the remark, from one or another, that he could not have borne such trials as have come successively upon him, if he had been advised, of them and had them in full view beforehand.

But the call of Christ, as it now opened, was a call to suffering; a call to be fulfilled by sorrow and pain, and consummated by the ignominy of a cross. The great Messiahship in which he was inaugurated, was to be a power of salvation for the world, as being a sublime tragedy of goodness. In this respect, his career of suffering was different, widely, from that of any mortal of the race, in the fact that he came into it with a full knowledge flashed upon him, of all that he was to bear from the sin he was to conquer. As we hear him speak in one of his earliest discourses of being "lifted up," recurring more than once to the same thing afterward, and using the same expression, calling his disciples also, many times over, to "take up the cross" and follow him, we can see for ourselves how the sorrow, and buffeting, and shame, and cross, all met him and stood in their appalling certainty always before him, from the first hour of his call onward. The recoil of his human nature from such a prospect must have been dreadful—mortally regarded, insupportable.

Let us not be misled, at this point, by the fact that he is a superior nature incarnate, imagining that he must also be superior, in that manner, to suffering. He has taken the human nature, and taken it as it is, by inheritance, and though it is good for symbol, as being the express image of God—better than all nature up to the stars beside—still it is weak for the matter of suffering, and is, in fact, only the more perfect for his uses on that account. Good, therefore, as symbol, it has to be conquered as organ. It wants staunching, for so dreadful a service, by some strong mastery, be it that of a fast, or of any other kind of discipline. Otherwise, being all weakness, it would even be treason if it could. Nothing could be farther off from the heroic in sacrifice, more susceptible to fear, more instinctively averse to the hatred of men, more unwilling to to die, and die hard, and die low. And what shall he do more naturally, in the confused struggles of his feel ing, than withdraw till the terrible revulsion is quelled or, what is the same, till he gets the poor, unsteady, low bred organ of his life brought up, into the scale of his sacrifice.

4. There comes upon him also, at the point of his call or endowment, still another and vaster kind of commotion, that belongs even to his divine nature, holding fit proportion with the greatness and perfection of it. The love he had before to mankind, was probably more like that of a simply perfect man. Having now the fallen world itself put upon his love, and the endowment of a Saviour entered consciously into his heart, his whole divinity is heaved into such commotion as is fitly called an agony; answering, in all respects, to the agony of the garden. How differently do we feel for any subject of benevolence the moment we have undertaken for him. He lies upon our heart-strings night and day, as a burden. We watch for him with a painful concern, we agonize for him. So when Jesus takes the world upon his love, it plunges him at once, into what may be called the suffering state of God; for it belongs to the goodness of God, just because it is good, to suffer, as being burdened in feeling for all wrong-doers and enemies. Every sort of love, the maternal, the patriotic, the christian, has for its inseparable incident, a moral suffering in behalf of its subjects. God has the same, in a degree of intensity equal to the intensity and compass of his love. And it is this moral suffering that now comes upon Christ, and is to be revealed by his incarnate ministry. The stress upon his feeling is too heavy to be supported by the frail

and tender vehicle of his humanity. It rolls in like a sea, and his human nature can not breast the heavy surge of it. He goes apart in the terrible recoil, both of his divine feeling and his human nature, sinks away into the recesses of the wilderness, crushed by the burden that has come upon his agonizing heart. As was just now intimated, his experience corresponds with that of his agony; for it was the same burden returning upon him, at that crisis, that threw him on the ground, and wrenched his feeling, in such throes of concern for his enemies, that his too feeble body gave way, and the gates of the skin flew open before the terrible pressure on his heart. I do not say that any such scene is transacted here in these forty days. I only know that Christ has the same weak body, and the same great feeling, burdened now for men, and, what is much to be considered, it has come upon him just as suddenly as the investiture and official endowment of his call. I do not see his prostrations. I do not catch the wail of his prayer, "let this cup pass from me," I only see that a great and dreadful commotion must be upon him—leaving him to cope with it as he best may, in that mysterious silence and solitude into which he has retreated from our human inspection.

Once more, the mind of Jesus, in his forty days retirement and fasting, must have been profoundly engaged and powerfully tasked in the unfolding of the necessary plan. He can not bolt into such a work, embracing such an immense reach of territory, and time, and kingly rule, without considering, beforehand,

and distinctly conceiving the what, and how, and when, and why, of his work. Doubtless there is a divine plan ready for him, and has been even from before the world's creation, but he, as being man, must think it consecutively out, step by step, in a certain human way of reception, or development, else he is not in it. No matter if the plan lay perfect in him as the Ancient of Days before he came into the world, still the counsel of it lay, not in words, or specific judgments, but in the infinite abyss of his boundless intuition. Now, in consenting to be man, he consents to be unfolded gradually in body and mind, to grow as he feeds, and know as he thinks. Nor does it make any difference if his thinking draws on the infinite; for to think the infinite into the finite, deific light into form and particularity, is a very considerable work that will not soon be done. His plan, therefore, must be thought, in order to be humanly had. Yesterday he had it not, to day the call has come that requires it, and a great soul-labor begins. Doubtless he has thought much, coasting round the subject before; he has read the Messianic prophets, and had their visions opened to his understanding, probably, as no other ever had before; his every faculty is clear, and broad, and deep, and rapid, in a degree surpassing all genius. Still, making all such allowance, how far off is he, at the coming of his call, from having any complete fact-form plan ready for it. The matter of it includes even the reasons of the creation, also the last ends of the creation, what between has been already done and what remains to be, in the great new future; all that affects God's relations to men, and men's to God, and the eternal kingdom as connecting both. In this great salvation-problem, therefore, touching always the infinite and finite together, what he shall do and teach; what, and when, and how, he shall suffer; by whom he shall organize, and for a time how long—in this problem, to be wrought out in a train of finite human thinking, his forty days will have enough to do, pour in fast and free as the stupendous revelation will. Full of all heaviest commotion therefore, on the side of his feeling, the great deep of intelligence also in Jesus must be mightily heaved, that his counsel may be adequately settled. O thou grim solitude of wilderness, what work is going on, these days, in thy silence!

How great and rapid the movement of his counsel has been, we may see, when coming out, after the forty days, into his ministry, he opens his mouth in his beatitudes and goes on with his wonderful first sermon, speaking, how decisively and calmly and with what evident repose; then beginning straightway his miracles, calling his apostles, and organizing his cause; evidently master of his plan even as a practiced general of his campaign—ready in all ripe counsel, to spread himself out on the great world-future of his kingdom.

Beginning thus at the call of Jesus, and making this large induction from what we know concerning him, I think you will agree, my friends, that these forty days of his in the wilderness must have been the most eventful days of his Messiahship, including beyond question, a vast, unknown, scarcely imaginable, but necessary and sublime, preparation for his work. No other chapter, I may safely say, in the whole history of Jesus, has a more fascinating and mysterious interest to our feeling, covered though it be in dimness and silence.

I have alluded once or twice to the agony of Jesus. I might also refer you to hours when the same deep conflict more than once, rolls back on him for a space, and his mighty "soul is troubled," venting itself in words. I can not resist the impression that the real agony of Jesus took him at the very first. How he bore himself in it for so many days in those desert wilds, his attitudes, his sleep or want of sleep, his prostrations and prayers, his groanings in spirit, his spaces of brightness and victorious courage and peace, his deep ponderings by day or night, sitting under the grim rocks—none of these are given us, but our heart will indulge itself in them and rightly may.

Some few incidents are given us which, taken together, signify much. Thus, he is not hungry, he is too powerfully wrought in by his thoughts and emotions to have the sense of hunger.

He is also alone. In the agony of the garden he has his friends with him, and looks to their sympathy for support. Here he has no friend with him, because he has not yet any friend enlisted, who can at all understand him, or yield him even a word of comfort.

I said he was alone—no he is not alone, but as Mark very casually intimates, "he is with the wild beasts." And this word *with* indicates a strange concomitancy, by which they are somehow drawn to come about him and be with him, in a way of harmless attention. For the term "*wild beasts*" does not mean simply wild animals, but the savage beasts of prey, such as lions, panthers, wolves, and the like. These are with Jesus, coming about him in his prostrations, drawing near in the moanings of his sleep, fawning about him tenderly when he sits in silence; going back, as it were, to the habit of paradise, and symbolizing, by their harmless companionship, that future paradise which he is to restore. Glad sign most surely, they, to his struggling heart.

Still another and very different class of beings come to him—I mean the angels. These we are told ministered unto him. Great joy was that to the angels! and it must have been as great to him! In such a state of long, long conflict and trial, how blessed were these visitors from the great world of peace above, their communications how sweet, how rich in assurance! So between the beasts and the angels, men being wholly away, Jesus gets tokens of sympathy that minister comfort, and help him to compose himself to the opening tragedy of his life.

We come, at last, to the final crisis of the trial, which many, by what appears to me a very great mistake, call the temptation; as if it covered the whole ground of the forty days. Exactly contrary to this the history says expressly—"And when he had fasted forty days and forty nights he was *afterward* an hungered." Or according to another gospel,—"when they were ended, he began to be an hungered." The three temptations follow. So powerfully had his mighty soul been wrought in, that he had not, till this time, been conscious of hunger. But now, at last, he is spent, and nature breaks under exhaustion. The representation appears to be that the fevered, half delirious state of hunger is upon him; and the phantoms of lying suggestion rush into his weakened brain, to bear down, if possible, his integrity. But it is not possible; even his broken, reeling, faculty is too strong in its purity for the utmost art of his enemy. And his triumph is thus finally completed, in the fact that any shred of his sinless majesty is seen to be enough to hold him fast, when the shattered vehicle of his humanity has quite given way.

That this, or something like it, is the true account to be taken of the story, is hardly to be questioned. It must have been derived from his own report; for no one else was privy to the matter of it. And he simply meant, I have no doubt, in the three temptations recited, to report what appeared to him, visionally speaking; or how they stood before his fevered brain. To believe that he was actually taken up by the devil, and set on the pinnacle of the temple, when fifty miles away; or that he was taken up into a mountain so exceedingly high, that he could see all the kingdoms of the round world from the top, is fairly impossible. He only re-reported the seemings of his hunger-fevered state. All temptations are but seemings. The devils bait their hook, never with truths, always with illusions. Nor were the temptations any the less real, or satanic, as being phantoms of exhaustion. This, in fact, was to be his victory, that not even his unsettled, weakened, faculty could be seduced by such phantoms, whether of internal or external suggestion. In this victory the trial of Jesus was finished—"And when the devil had ended all the temptations, he departed from him for a season." Now therefore he is ready, and the great Messianic ministry begins.

Scarcely necessary is it, my brethren, to say that it will be such a ministry as the great first chapter of the fast prepares—such and no other. I know not any point beside, in the history of his life, where you may take your stand and see the whole course of it open, with such intelligible unity and clearness. As the dawn prepares the day, so the forty days prepare the three wonderful years. Taking the fast for your initial point, and carefully distinguishing what goes on there, and is done or made ready, every thing appears to come out naturally, in a sense, from it. Here, in fact, as you may figure, Christ officially young, levels himself to his aim; and then, as age is not the count of years but of works, puts himself into his great ministry with such momentum and constancy, giving so much counsel, expending so much sympathy, suffering so great waste of sorrow, that he dies, at the end of three years, like one ripened by full age. The unsteadiness, the overdoing, the romance, of unpracticed energies, nowhere appears, but the regular gait of sagacity, patience, sound equilibrium, as of one who has his counsel ready, brings him on to his close. Whether this maturity is unfolded by the very rapid development of his crowded, heavy-pressing, all-doing ministry, or was really prepared, for the most part, in the fiery forty days of his trial, it may be difficult to say. Only this is abundantly clear, that he came out of that trial, to make his beginning, both strong and ready. If he did not seem to be as old when he gave the sermon on the mount as when he answered before Pilate, he was as thoroughly assured, and as completely master of the situation. From that time onward his equipoise is perfect, and his movement restful and smooth—never hurrying after counsel not yet arrived, but visibly set on by counsel, such as leaves no room for surprise, or a moment's faltering. The sweetness, and repose, and readiness he is in, are such as indicate a mental graduation into counsel, and victory already accomplished—as he had, in fact, conquered, beforehand, the world, and the devil, and his own humanity, and had come to such kind of settlement as a victor only gets. Many martyrs have borne themselves heroically when the doom was on them, and the pressure of the hour riveted their firmness. But Christ was a martyr at large and beforehand, who had taken the sentence of death in the wilderness, and bowed himself in consecration upon it, coming out to live martyr-wise; but as strong, as steady, as free, as the felt mastery both of death and of himself could make him. Figuring himself to himself, deliberately, as a grain of wheat falling into the ground to die, and so to live again more fruitfully, he settles calmly into his appointment, without misgiving or regret. Having also a great baptism, as he knows, to be baptized with, he is no wise appalled by the prospect, but only oppressed by the delay; exclaiming, "how am I straitened till it be accomplished." In all which we may see, that the highest nerve of courage, endurance, and resolute equability, may be set, only in the silence and solitude of a complete self devotion, never in the noisy tumult of commotions and great throes of public excitement. What other being among men ever graduated into such glory of public life as Jesus, when he came out of the desert and his forty days of silence!

I do not mean, of course, in hanging so much upon the temptation of the forty days, to say that Jesus was never tempted before, or after that time. All such temptations were casual, matters by the way, having a certain consequence, but no principal consequence in fixing the tenor of his life. But the forty days temptation had this distinction, that it took him at the point of crisis, so that every thing was turned by the settlement, and went with it. There could be only one such crisis, and the turning of it rightly was the grand inaugural of all that came after, in his wonderful and gloriously consecrated ministry.

In just the same manner, there is, I conceive, in the life of almost every Christian disciple, a crisis, where every thing most eventful, as regards the Christian value of his life to himself, and of his consecration to God, especially hinges, and where, as we may figure, his grand temptation meets him. Other temptations have gone before, others will come after, here is *the* temptation of his personal call, and opportunity. What it will be, or in what form it will come, can not of course, be specified; enough that it will commonly bring the strong present conviction with it of a great Christian crisis arrived, on which all the heaviest results of character and service done for God are depending. At such a time, there is to be no haste or precipitation. The time for a grand, practical, settlement of the life has come, and if the man has any gravity of meaning or high aspiration, he will meet the crisis practically, and if possible, understandingly. To let go society, pleasure, profit, and the table, nay, to get away from them, will be a kind of relief. Any thing, any campaign of prayer, and thought, and self-devotement, will be accepted heartily, and be long enough protracted to settle the result finally and firmly. One great reason, brethren, why we make so poor a figure of fitfulness and inconstancy, is that we go by jets of emotion, or gusts of popular impulse, or sallies of extempore resolve; we do not settle our question upon a footing of counsel, and inward consecration, and, in fact, do not take time to settle any thing; least of all, any such great crisis of life. Moses drew off into the wilderness and was there forty years, getting ready for the call that was already half uttered in his heart. Paul retired into Arabia, and was there three years, gathering up his soul and soul's fuel, for the grand apostleship of word and sacrifice. So the Christian, every Christian, who has come to his crisis, will take time for the settlement of his plan, and the equipment of his undertaking—if not forty days, then as many as are wanted.

Having this high work upon you, brethren, silence and solitude will be congenial, and the fasting of Jesus will be remembered by you with a strange sympathy—all in the endeavor to come out on your future, thoroughly consecrated to it, even as he was to his. Drawn to him in such profoundest sympathy with his temptation, O how tenderly and approvingly will he be drawn to you, pouring, as he best may, all the riches of his forty days struggle and consecration to sacrifice upon you. "For in that he himself hath suffered being tempted, he is able to succor them that are tempted." Any life is great and blessed, into which you are entered, upon this high footing with Christ your Master. You can not be worse handled by men, or by what is called fortune, than he was; can not be more faithful to God's high purpose in you, or more consciously great, and happy, and true; and that, if I am right, is the only kind of life at all worthy of you. And then, at the end, it will be yours to say, in the sublime confidence also of your Master—"I have glorified thee on the earth, I have finished the work which thou gavest me to do."

VI.

CONVICTION OF SIN BY THE CROSS.

"*Of sin, because they believe not on me. Of righteousness, because I go to the Father, and ye see me no more. Of judgment, because the prince of this world is judged.*"—JOHN, xvi. 9–11.

In the convincement of sin, the Holy Spirit is to be the agent, and Christ rejected the argument—so Christ himself conceives the promise of the Spirit which he is here giving. The convincing work is to be wrought by no absolute method of force, but by truths and reasons drawn from Christ's person, and the treatment he received from the world. "Of sin," he says, "because they believe not on me." The two other points that he adds—"Of righteousness because I go to the Father and ye see me no more; Of judgment, because the prince of this world is judged;"—appear to be only amplifications of the first, or points in which the guilty convictions of his rejectors will be raised to a higher pitch. Thus when he is gone out of the world to be seen here no more, gone up to the Father in visible divine majesty, they will begin to conceive who he was—the Son of God, the righteousness itself of God. He will be no more the man or the prophet, poorly apprehended, doubtfully conceived; all their opinions of him will undergo a revision, and their minds be quickened to a new sense even of what righteousness is; so, to a deeper more condemning, more appalling sense of their sin. Then again this conviction will be set home with a still heavier emphasis, by the fact made visible in his death and resurrection, that the "prince of this world is judged," and forever cast down. For if evil, when triumphant by conspiracy, still can not triumph, but falls inevitably doomed, how certainly doomed is every soul that meets the Just One it rejected, on its final day. When the bad empire called the world, is itself cloven down, visibly, by the rising and the over-mastering kingship of God's Messiah, the conviction of sin will be as much more appalling, as the general defeat and overthrow requires it to be.

It is then a fixed expectation of Christ himself, and that is the truth to which I am now going to call your attention—*that his mission to the world will have a considerable part of its value, in raising a higher moral sense in mankind, and producing a more appalling conviction of their guilt or guiltiness, before God.*

A widely different, or even contrary, impression appears to be generally derived from certain things said in the scripture, concerning the law; taken as they are, in a less qualified manner than they should be, or the facts of the gospel require them to be. Thus it is declared that, "by the law is the knowledge of sin." It is also described in its relation to the gospel, as "the letter that killeth," "the ministration of death," "the ministration of condemnation;" that on the other hand, being "the Spirit that giveth life," "the ministration of righteousness." On the ground of such representations, an impression is received, that conviction of sin is distinctively "a law work." As such it is specially magnified, and it is even abundantly insisted on, that the effective preaching of the law is the prime condition of all genuine success in preaching. The conception is that what is called "the law" is a certain battery side of government, before which guilty minds are to be shot through with deadly pangs, and then that the ministration of life, in Jesus and his cross, coming on the gentle side opposite, does a work of pure healing and life. On that side, all is condemnation. On this side, all is forgiveness. There is guilt, here is peace. Bondage only is there, liberty only is here.

Now this impression is so far true, that conviction of sin doubtless supposes the fact of some rule or law, broken by sin; and that, when such law is broken, it can, as law, do nothing more than condemn—can not help, or save. God only can do that, and that he does in Christ.

But, in a certain other view, there is more law in Christ, more, that is, in his character and life and doctrine, then there is in all statutes beside. The law of Eden is to the law of the sermon on the mount, as a jewsharp to an organ. The ten commandments, mostly negative, or laws of not doing, are not, all together, as weighty and broad upon the conscience, as Christ's one positive law, "Do ye unto others as ye would that others should do unto you." Not even the thunders of Sinai are any match for the silent thunders of Calvary.

Besides, it is not so much the question, where most law is given, as by what means the sense of law may be most effectually quickened, where before it slept. And here it is that Christ's great expectation hinges, when he says, "of sin," "of righteousness," "of judgment." For in him, the law is more than a rule, or than all rules—a person, clothed in God's righteousness, bearing God's authority, filling and permeating all human relations with an exact well doing, and with all most loving ministries, such as never before had been even conceived in these relations. How much then will it signify, when guilty minds are so painfully dazed by the glories of right in his person, that they can not endure the sight; conspiring even his death, and falling upon him in their implacable malice, to thrust him out of the world! Why, simply to have had such a being living in the world, doing his work, suffering his pains at the hands of his enemies and breathing out his pure untainted breath upon the poisoned air, changes it to a place of holy conviction, where sin must be ever knowing itself, and scorching itself in its own guilty fires!

Thus much it was necessary to say, in a way of general statement, or adjustment, as respects the relative agency of Christ and the law in the convincement of guilty minds. That Christianity was to have, and has had, a considerable part of its value, in this convincing, as well as in a forgiving and restoring agency,

I will now proceed to show, by arguments more special and positive. And—

1. Make due account of the fact, that conviction of sin is a profoundly intelligent matter, and worthy, in that view, to engage the counsel of God in the gift of his Son. If we have any such thought as that what is called conviction of sin is only a blind torment, or crisis of excited fear, technically prescribed as a matter to be suffered in the way of conversion, we can not too soon rid ourselves of the mistake. It is neither more nor less than a due self-knowledge—not a knowledge of the mere understanding, or such as may be gotten by philosophic reflection, but a more certain, more immediate sensing of ourselves by consciousness; just the same which the criminal has, when he hies himself away from justice; fleeing, it may be, when no man pursueth. He has a most invincible, most real, knowledge of himself; not by any cognitive process of reflection, but by his immediate consciousness—he is consciously a guilty man. All men are consciously guilty before God, and the standards of God, in the same manner. They do not approve, but invariably condemn themselves; only they become so used to the fact that they make nothing of it, but take it even as the normal condition of their life. Their sin gets to be themselves, and they only think as thinking of themselves. Living always in the bad element, they think it is only their nature to be as they are. Their consciousness is frozen over, so to speak, and they see no river underneath, but only the ice

that covers it. The motions of sins they do not observe, because the standards they have always violated are blunted and blurred by custom. They are only conscious, it may be, of a certain shyness of God, and they come to regard even that as being somehow natural. Hence it comes to be a very great point, in the recovery of men to God, to unmask them to themselves, to uncover the standards and reopen their consciousness to them; exactly what is done by Christ and his rejected Messiahship, inwardly applied by the Spirit of God. The result is conviction of sin; which is only a state of moral self-knowledge revived. Doubtless there is a pain in this kind of self-knowledge, but it is none the less intelligent on that account. The sense of guilt is itself a pain of the mind, just as light is pain to a diseased eye; but light is none the less truly light, and guilt is none the less truly intelligent, on that account. This returning of guilty conviction is, in fact, the dawning, or may be, of an everlasting and complete intelligence, in just that highest, moral, side of the nature, that was going down out of intelligence, into stupor and blindness. Is it then a severity in Christ that he is counting on a result of his ministry and death, so essentially great and beneficent?

2. It is quite evident that such a being as Christ could not come into the world and pass through it, and out of it, in such a manner, without stirring the profoundest possible convictions of character. If the divine glory and spotless love of God are by him incarnated into the world, the revelation must be one that

raises a great inward commotion. It should not surprise us that even the bad spirits were rallied, in that day, to a pitch of unwonted disturbance and malign activity, much more the bad mind of the race. The great standards of holiness, so fatally blurred as rules, will be all brought forth again, speaking in the doctrine, shining out in the perfect life. Every guilty mind will feel itself arraigned, and brought to know itself, that beholds, or looks into the perfect glass of history that describes this life. And above all when it is ended by such a death, inflicted by a world in wrong, who that knows himself to be a man, will not be visited by silent pangs, not easy to be stifled.

3. Christ was a being who perfectly knew the pure standards of character and duty, knowing, as well, just what sin is in the breach of them, and what man is in the sin. He also knows of course, exactly what is necessary to stir up the guilty consciousness of men; sometimes doing it by instruction, sometimes by acts of unwonted patience and beneficence, sometimes by terrible rebukes and lifted rods of chastisement, and more than once by a divine skill of silence—as when stooping down, once and again, he drew mystic figures on the ground; sending out thus one by one, condemned and guilt-stricken, the pretentious accusers of the woman; or when, scarcely speaking and urging no defense, he so visibly shook with concern, the guilty mind of Pilate, by the dumb innocence only of his manner. He knew exactly what to do on all occasions, and with all different classes of men, to put the sense of guilt upon them, and

we can see ourselves, that he has it for one of the great objects of his ministry; even as it was a great expectation, in the matter of his death, that all enemies and rejecters would discover, in bitter pangs of conviction, that, in what they have done upon him, they have only let their sin reveal its own madness. Let us turn now

4. To the scriptures and gather up some few of the tokens that Christ, before his coming, was expected to come in this character; and also of the declarations, by himself and his followers afterward, that he had, especially in his death, accomplished such a result.

"They shall look on me whom they have pierced," says the prophet, "and they shall mourn." Other expressions of the prophets correspond. Accordingly when the infant Jesus was brought to Simeon, by his mother, he said to her, "Behold this child is set for the fall and rising again of many in Israel, and for a sign which shall be spoken against, that the thoughts of many hearts may be revealed." His rejection was to reveal the heart of his rejectors. John the Baptist conceives, in the same manner, that he is coming with "the axe" of conviction, to be laid to the root of all sin, and "the fan" of separation, to winnow out the chaffiness of all pretense, so to unmask the secrecy of guilt and place it in the open light of conviction.

Christ himself also testifies that he has done it, saying to Nicodemus, "He that believeth not is condemned already, because he hath not believed in the name of the only begotten Son of God. And this the condemnation (how deeply shall the sting of it some time pierce the heart of my rejecters,)—this is the condemnation, "that light is come into the world and men have loved darkness rather then light, because their deeds were evil." On another occasion, he says, to the same effect,—"If I had not come and spoken unto them, they had not had sin, but now they have no cloak for their sin;"—they see now, by what they reject and hate, precisely what they are—"If I had not done among them the work which none other man did, they had not had sin, but now have they both seen and hated both me and my Father;" intimating clearly that their hatred of him, they will sometime see, is, at bottom, a hatred of goodness itself. On still another occasion, he brings out the same truth more argumentatively saying—"If God were your Father, ye would love me; for I proceeded forth and came from God. He that is of God heareth my words, ye therefore hear them not, because ye are not of God." Your rejection of me is nothing but an exhibition, without, of that rejection of God in which you inwardly live. The bitterness of their reply you know.

Take the trial scene of Jesus next, noting first, the bad spirit out of which it comes, and then the guilty conviction that follows it. What injury had Christ done to Caiphas and the managers of his party, that they should be so bitterly exasperated against him? There was never a more inoffensive being, save as goodness is itself an offense to sin. Hence the violence of their animosity; for no man is so violent and brutish in his animosities, as he that is storming against goodness, to drown the disturbance, and redress the guilty pangs it creates in an evil conscience. Hence the barbarous insults put upon the Saviour's person. If these great people of Jerusalem—high-priests, rabbis, scribes, and others—had been a tribe of Osages, or Dyaks, their treatment of Jesus would have been exactly in character. The slap in the face, the crown of thorns, the mock cries, the scourging, the spitting, the wagging of the heads, and the jeer "let him come down," connected with a visibly conscious disrespect to evidence and justice, and with outcries raised to stifle even the sense of justice; the malignity and spite of the punishment itself, a slave's punishment, a crucifixion put upon a man whose dignity and the power of whose words, —"speaking as never man spake"—had been a principal part of his offense—what does it mean that gentlemen, Jewish leaders of the highest standing and culture, are found instigating these low barbarities of spite and cruelty? What has he done to transform civilized men, into savages in this manner? O it is the offense of his character! He has raised up demons of remorse in the conscience of these men, by the luster simply of his good ness. This it is that rankles in their hatred, and hate, as against goodness, is a feeling too weak to suffer the assumption even of dignity. Hence the simply diabolical frenzy of their conduct.

Mark the result. The very moment after Jesus has commended his spirit to the Father and ceased to breathe, the conviction of crime begins to break through the enmity of his crucifiers. Their malignity is discovered, they could hate a living enemy, but the helpless body of a dead one over-masters their violence. Immediately the centurion himself glorified God, saying, "certainly this was a righteous man." "And all the people that came together to that sight, beholding the things which were done, smote their breasts and returned." This is the sign that was "to be spoken against," and now "the thoughts of many hearts" begin to be "revealed." "They look on him whom they have pierced," and they are pierced themselves.

Next we see the great principle of conviction—"of sin because they believe not on me,"—beginning to be wielded with overwhelming energy, by the apostles. This very truth charged home—you have rejected and crucified Christ—is the arrow of the day of Pentecost. "Therefore let all the house of Israel know assuredly," says Peter in his sermon on that occasion, "that God hath made that same Jesus whom ye crucified both Lord and Christ—he hath shed forth this which you now see and hear. Now when they heard this, they were pricked in their heart, and cried—'Men and brethren, what shall we do?'"

And the very next sermon of Peter hangs upon the same bitter truth of conviction. "Ye denied the Holy One and the Just, and desired a murderer to be granted unto you, and killed the Prince of Life, whom God hath raised from the dead, whereof we are witnesses."

And again, in the third sermon of the same apostle, he hurls the same arrow. "For of a truth against thy holy child Jesus, whom thou hast anointed, both Herod and Pontius Pilate, with the Gentiles and thy people

Israel, were gathered together."—all orders and nations, because all alike are sinners—"and now behold their threatenings and grant unto thy servants that with all boldness they may speak thy word." Whereupon the place is shaken again a third time. Under the first sermon, three thousand souls have the thoughts of their hearts revealed, and turn to seek salvation in Jesus Christ. Under the second, the number is swelled to five thousand. Under the third, the count ceases and the number becomes a multitude—"the multitude of them that believed."

So it was that Peter, in his preaching, charged home upon his hearers everywhere the rejecting and denying of Jesus the Saviour.

Paul too was traveling over all seas, and through all lands, telling the story of his remarkable conversion—how at first he disbelieved and hated the very name of Jesus, how he was exceedingly mad against his followers, and went about dragging them to prison, till, at last, on his way to Damascus, he was met by that word of irresistible conviction, which had been so powerful many times before—"I am Jesus whom thou persecutest." O what depths were opened now in the persecutor's heart! All his bitter wrongs and fiery inflictions flame back in that word—"I am Jesus whom thou persecutest!" showing him the madness that reigns within. Thus begins the life in Christ of this great apostle—itself an illustration how sublime of the Saviour's thought! "Of sin because they believe not in me." But there is a reason—

5. Back of this great fact, in the scheme of the gospel, in which it is grounded; viz., that a very bad act often brings out the show of a bad spirit within and becomes, in that manner, a most appalling argument of conviction. Hence the immense convincing power to be exerted on mankind through the crucifixion of Christ by his enemies. Even as a profligate, unfilial son, discovers himself as he is, and receives the true impression, for the first time, of his own dire wickedness and passion, when he looks upon the murdered form of his father, and washes the stains of parricide from his hands. In like manner Joseph's brethren, when he stood revealed before them, as the brother whom they cruelly sold, were struck dumb with guilt, and could not so much as speak to ask his forgiveness. So also Herod, haunted by the sense of his crime in the murder of John, imagined, in the wild tumult of his guilty brain, that Christ must be the prophet's ghost, returning to be avenged of his wrong.

The death, or public execution of Socrates affords, in some respects, a more striking illustration. His pure morality of life, his sublime doctrine of virtue, the discredit reflected on the gods of his country, by his belief in a supreme, all-perfect God and governor of the world, worthy of a better worship, raised up enemies and accusers, who indicted him as a corrupter of the youth, and a denier of the gods of his country. The people, artfully wrought upon, voted his death. Shortly after, the dead teacher rose upon them mightier even than the living, and a wave of conviction rolling back upon their consciences, filled them with bitter distress. They voted his innocence; they acknowledged the public misfortunes just then coming upon the state to be judgments of heaven upon their crime; they put to death Miletus his principal accuser, drove his subordinates into exile, and erected a brazen statue to his memory. So the Saviour says, "of sin because they believe not on me;" only the reaction of his cross begins more immediately and extends through all the coming ages of time. No sooner is he dead, than all the multitude present, not his accusers only and his executioners, but the lookers on, were pricked with heavy compunctions of feeling, and went home smiting their breasts, for anguish they could not repress. And with better reason than they can distinctly know; for it is the Holy one and the Just, the Perfect Son of God, whom they have seen put to death; nay worse who has not been permitted even to die respectably, but has been publicly stripped, gibbeted, exposed to shame, compelled to die slowly, like a slave, nailed fast upon a cross. He had come into the world on a mission of love from the world above, a perfect character, clothed in the essential glory of a divine nature, a being whom all the righteous spirits—angels, archangels, and seraphim—had been wont to magnify and adore—such was the visitant who lighted, for once, on the earth and the race of mankind could not suffer him to live, tore him away in their spite, from his acts of healing, and his gentle mercies even to themselves, and thrust him out of the world, in mockeries that forgot even the appearance of dignity.

I have spoken of this act, as the act of the human race, and such, in some true sense, it was; and as such has been ringing ever sense in the guilty conscience of the race; for it is, in fact, a proof by experiment, of what is in all human hearts. Thus, if there should come down from the upper sky some pure dove that has his home in that pure element, and the birds of the lower air should be heard screaming at all points, and seen pitching upon the unwelcome visitant and striking their beaks into his body, we should have no doubt of some radical unlikeness, or repugnance, between the creatures of the two elements. And this exactly is the feeling that has been forced upon the world's guilty mind, ever since, by the crucifixion of Jesus. It rolls back on our thought in a kind of silent horror, that will not always be repelled, that the manifested love of God, impartial and broad as the world, a grace for every hu man creature, is yet gnashed upon by the world and crucified. If we say that this act of crucifixion was not ours, it certainly was not in the particular sense intended, and yet in another and much deeper sense, it was; viz., in the sense that what it signifies was ours. It was done by mankind, as Christ was a Saviour for mankind, and we are men. It proves for one age all that it proves for another; proves for the lookers on all which it proves for the doers. In this manner it is yours, it is mine. I think it quite certain, sometimes, that I should have had no part it, and it may be that I should not. But again I sometimes shudder privately over the question, whether if such a being were to come upon the earth now, in my own day, one so peculiar, so little subject to the respectabilities and conventionalities of religion, doing such miracles, becoming an offense to so many religious schools and rabbis, charged so inevitably with being a wild impostor, I should not be quite turned away from him. Perhaps I should not join his crucifiers, but should I not as truly reject him as they? O shame to say it, but it fills me with pain, or even with a kind of horror, to conceive the possibility. Were not his enemies religious men in their habit, serious, thoughtful men, exact in the observances of their religion, many of them even sanctimonious in their lives? Had they not religious pretexts for all that they did? At any rate they had human hearts, and so have you and I. And will not what they show for their own heart, be as good a proof for us? So felt the multitude of spectators, and the feeling of the world has been the same.

Lastly there is another and more direct kind of argument, that I mean which we get from our own consciousness. I think I may assert, with confidence, that there is no man living, who is not made conscious, at times, of sin, as in no other manner, by the simple fact of his own rejection of Christ. Nor does it make any great difference, if his belief appears to be hindered by speculative difficulties. He may imagine, or distinctly maintain, that he rejects, or does not believe, on the ground of sufficient evidence. Still Christ is Christ, and the cross is the cross, and he can not so much as think of himself, before the merely conceived image of a goodness so divine—be it really historic or not—without a feeling of disturbance, in the not cleaving to the profound reality of the truth discovered in him. No matter what may be reasoned by infidels and Christian speculatists about, against, or for, the historic person of Christ; if he is a fiction only, or a myth, a romance of character gotten up by three or four of the most unromantic writers of the world, still he is the greatest, solidest, most real, truth ever known to man. The mere conception of such a life and character is inherently eternal—more indestructible, and so far more real than a mountain of rock. It affirms itself eternally as light, by its own self-evidence, and the soul of guilt trembles inwardly before it—trembles even the more certainly that it is a good approved, but not welcomed, or embraced. Enough that the Christ of the New Testament is the want, consciously or unconsciously, of every human heart, and that aching secretly for him, it aches the more that it has him not, and still the more that it will not have him. Who of you could ever think of him rejected without a pang?

But the most of you are troubled by no such speculative doubts; you are only selfish and earthly, want your pleasures, want other objects more, that must be renounced to receive him—meaning still, at some time, to do it, and become his disciples. Living in this feeble and consciously false key, your courage wavers, and self-rebuking thoughts are, ever and anon, making their troublesome irruptions upon you. When the Saviour says—"Of sin because they believe not on me," the very words sharpen guilty pangs in your bosom. Sometimes the question rises, distinctly why is it, that beholding this love, I still do not embrace it? why do I so profoundly admire this wonderful excellence and still suppress the longings I so consciously feel? And then the goodness rejected becomes a fire of Hinnom in your uneasy convictions. It is not any particular sins that trouble you thus; consciously it is *sin*—nothing else explains you to yourself. The conviction of it runs quivering along your feeling in sharp pangs of remorse, and you half expect to hear—"I am Jesus of Nazareth whom thou rejectest." Even his tenderest call comes to you, more as an arrow, than as a balm, and your heart is inwardly stung, pricked through and through, with the rankle of thoughts that are being revealed. How many have passed, or now are passing through just this struggle of experience. To many too it will have been, I trust, the gate of heaven.

But I must not close my argument on this great subject, without noting a common objection; viz., that all such phases of mental disturbance called conviction of sin, in the New Testament, are too weak for respect, and should not be indulged, even if they are felt. But if they are according to truth, if they are so far intelligent as to be modes of sensibility accurately squared by the fact of character within, then they are only a kind of weakness that is stronger to be allowed than stifled. They are however, in some sense, moods of weakness I must still admit; for they belong to sin and sin itself is weak. Nothing in fact is weaker. Courage, repose, equilibrium, strength of will, firmness of confidence—all these receive a shock under sin, and are more or less fatally broken. Were not all those Athenians weak who wept the death of Socrates, when they saw his place made vacant by themselves? But that weakness it was even honorable to suffer, because it was the very best thing left, after they had been weak enough to vote his death. So, when the Son of God is crucified and expelled to be seen no more, not the spectators only of the scene, but all we that pierced him by our sin were to be visited with guilty, soul-humbling pains in like manner—how much more that he is gone up visibly, as the wonderful Greek was not, to be stated in the eternal majesty of righteousness and judgment. All sin is weak, and the convincing cross must needs bring out the revelation of weakness, even as it did at the first. When the marshal's band, sent out to make the arrest, were shaken out of courage and strength enough even to stand, they fitly opened the scene that followed, by their backward fall and prostration. Was not Peter weak when he wept bitterly? Was not Judas weak when he cast down the money for which he sold him? Were not the priests and elders weak when they said "he stirreth up the people?" Was not Pilate weak when he was "the more afraid?" Were not the multitude when they went home smiting their breasts? Nay, were not the rocks themselves weak when they shook, and the tomb when it opened, and the stone when it rolled back? O, it was a mighty judgment day, that day of the cross; token visible, to you and to me, of that other, higher, judgment which our righteous Lord has gone up to assume! Hence the distress which rises in so many hearts before the cross, and which some can think of only with disrespect. Could they learn to disrespect the sin that makes it necessary, they might even honor it rather, as the sign, or beginning, of a return to righteousness and reason.

In what manner Christ was to convince of sin we have now seen, and no farther argument appears to be needed. But the subject can not be fitly concluded without noting a remarkable effect that has followed the cross as a convincing power on the world; viz., the fact that, in what is called Chistendom, there has been a manifest uplifting of the moral standards, and a correspondent quickening of the moral sensibilities, both of individual men, and of whole races and people. In the people of the old dispensation and of the great Pagan empires long ago converted to the cross, moral ideas have now taken the place, to a great extent, of force; the coarse blank apathy of sin is broken up; the sense of duty is more piercing; and it is even as if a new conscience had been given respecting the soul in its relations to God. It is as if men had seen their state of sin glassed before them, and made visible in the rejection of Christ and his cross. Jews and Pagans had before been made conscious at times of particular sins; we are made conscious, in a deeper and more appalling way, of the state of sin itself, the damning evil that infects our humanity at the root—that which rejected and crucified the Son of God, and is in fact, the general madness and lost condition of the race. Thus, immediately after the departure of Christ from the world, that is on the day of Pentecost, there broke out a new demonstration of sensibility to sin, such as was never before seen. In the days of the law, men had their visitations of guilt and remorse, respecting this or that wrong act; but I do not recollect even under the prophets, those great preachers of the law, and sharpest and most terrible sifters of transgression, a single instance, where a soul is so broken, or distressed, by the conviction of its own bad state under sin, as to ask what it must do to be saved—the very thing which many thousands did, on the day of Pentecost, and in the weeks that followed, and have been doing even till now. So different a matter is it to have rules in a book, or rules in the conscience, from having them bodied into power, through a person, or personal character; that character, hated, persecuted, murdered, by the public will and voice; that murdered one rising again to be glorified in the triumphant righteousness, of his life; that righteousness, after having cast down principalities and powers, installed in the judgment bench of the world. Hence an amazing accession of strength, in the moral standards and convictions of all Christian peoples. It is all from the cross; which has raised the sense of guilt in human bosoms to such a pitch, that even strong men weep, and groan, and tremble for their sin. Every sensibility that lies about the standards of the soul, and its fallen possibilities in defection from them, is amazingly quickened. And it is just this to which the apostle refers, when speaking to the Hebrews of "the word of God"—he means the new word of Christianity, that which we have now, and not the old word of the law—"For the word of God, is quick and powerful, sharper than any two-edged sword, piercing even to the dividing asunder of soul and spirit, and of the joints and marrow, and is a discerner of the thoughts and intents of the heart." Having this penetrating and convincing efficacy, the word of the cross is capable of a most faithful and deep work in the character; no gospel therefore of temporizing mercy, and slight healing, but a downright, thorough-going, radical, life-renewing energy—a power of God unto salvation. It bends to no false principle, deals in no mock sentiment, hides no point of exactness, spares no necessary pain. It applies to sin a surgery deep as the malady, it cuts the cancer clean out by conviction, that a genuine, true healing may follow. Just so much worthier is it of our confidence and respect. And what shall we do but open our heart to it, counting it even good to be condemned before a salvation so thorough, so deeply grounded in the unsparing severities of truth. But this condemnation, these unsparing severities, it behooves us to remember, will be not less piercing, when they cease to come in the hopeful guise of a salvation. Doubtless Christ rejected, will have a convincing power always, even in the future life. Moral ideas and standards will be raised, and moral sensibilities quickened still by the cross remembered. And the pangs of guilt will of course be sharpened still farther, by the barren regrets and the hopeless future of that undone state. O, that desert of guilt—to one that has journeyed long ages in its fiery and thirsty sands, how dreadful the words of the rejected Saviour still ringing and forever in his memory. "OF SIN BECAUSE THEY BELIEVE NOT ON ME."

VII.

CHRIST ASLEEP.

"*And behold there arose a great tempest in the sea, insomuch that the ship was covered with the waves: but he was asleep.*"—MATT., viii. 24.

Christ asleep—the eternal Word of the Father, incarnate, lapped in the soft oblivion of unconsciousness—a very strange fact, when deeply enough pondered to reveal its significant and even singular implications.

Where then do we go to look upon so great a sight, the sleep of God's Messiah? Is he royally bestowed in some retired hall, or chamber of his palace? Is he curtained about and canopied over on his bed of down, as one retiring into the deepest folds of luxury, there to woo the delicate approach of sleep? Must no doors be swinging, no feet of attendants stirring in the halls? Are the windows carefully shaded, lest some ray of moonlight streaming in may break the tender spell of the sleeper? No, it is not so that Jesus sleeps, or with any such delicate provisions of luxury to smooth his rest; but he is out upon the Gennessaret, in some little craft that his disciples have picked up for the crossing, and upon the short space of flooring, or deck, in the hinder part, he sinks, overcome with exhaustion, and is buried shortly in the deepest, soundest sleep. The open sky is over him, the boat swings drowsily among the waves, and the boatmen, talking over the miracles of the day, and all they have seen and heard, under the wonderful new ministry, continue on, as we may suppose, till by degrees the conversation lulls, the replies become slow and sepulchral, as if coming from afar, and finally cease. Meantime Jesus sleeps, fanned by the gentle breath of the night, rocked by the babbling waters, watched by the stars, that brighten seemingly to a finer purity, reflected from the sleeper's dreams.

By and by a change appears. A dark and ominous cloud, sailing up, shuts in the sky. The lightnings begin to fall, crashing on the head of Gerizim and Tabor, and very soon the tempest that was booming heavily in the distance, strikes the little skiff, dashing the waves across, and filling instantly the forward part with water. The little company are thrown, as it would seem, into the greatest panic and confusion, unable to manage the sinking vessel, and only mixing their cries of distress with the general tumult of the storm. Still Jesus sleeps, folded in that deep self-oblivion which no rage of the elements can disturb. "And behold there arose a great tempest in the sea, insomuch that the ship was covered with the waves: but he was asleep." Even so, no wildest tumult without can reach the inward composure of his rest. The rain beating on his face, and the spray driving across it, and the sharp gleams of the lightning, and the crash of the thunder, and the roar of the storm, and the screams of the men—not all of these can shake him far enough inward, to reach the center where sleep lodges and waken him to consciousness. It is as if both consciousness and soul were gone—gone up in holy dream, to bask in the divine peace, breathing airs of music, and wandering along the rivers of paradise, where angels moor their boats and watch the currents of eternity. Finally some one touches him gently and says, "Master;" whereupon he is roused instantly; for it is a tender word, spoken, too, distressfully, in a manner of appeal, and there is no softest call of compassion that is not louder in his ear than either tempest or thunder. So his sleep is ended, and the storm, in turn, is laid in a deeper sleep than he.

The sleeping of Jesus I believe is mentioned nowhere else in the gospels, and I do not recollect ever to have heard the subject presented as a topic of discourse, or even distinctly noticed—an omission the more remarkable that the theologic implications of the fact appear to be so important.

Sleep is a shadow that falls on the soul, as well as on the body. It is such a kind of state, or affection, as makes even the mind, or intelligent principle, unconscious. What could be more in point, then, for the speculative humanitarian, than to call this fact to his aid, by raising the question, what can be made of the sleep of Jesus, on the supposition that he is divine? Does sleep attack divinity? How can it be conceived that deity, or a nature essentially deific, sleeps, falling into the condition of unconsciousness? And then what next should follow, in the common way, but that such as think to maintain the divinity of Christ, only as they are able to explain it, will make answer, that it is the human nature of Jesus that sleeps and not the divine—giving up thus, for the time, the fact of the incarnation itself; which, if it is any thing, is the absolute unity of the divine and the human in one person.

It would carry me too far, to go into these questions here, taking me, in fact, quite away from my subject. I most readily admit that Jesus, being essentially a divine person, can not, in good logic, sleep; and just as certain it is that, if we proceed logically, he can not, as having a deific nature, be a man. And yet he both slept and was a man. As being God incarnate, the Word made flesh, the infinite in the finite, he is logically impossible. But God has a way of doing the impossible. In the communication of himself to men, he tears away the logical carpentry, refusing to put his glory into it. The truth is that our laws of thinking are totally at fault, in regard to subjects of this nature, speculatively handled. All that we can say of the personality of Jesus is that he is a being in our plane, and yet not in it—in it as a practical approach of God, not in it as being logically resolvable by our scientific, or speculative deductions. The very thing proposed in the person of Jesus is to make an approach transcending any possible explication by us; viz., to humanize divinity; that by means of a nature, fellow to our own, he may bring himself within our range, and meet our feeling by a feeling formally humanized in himself. And in order to this, there must be no doubt of his humanity; he must not be simply templed in a human body, but he must make his humanity complete by that last, most convincing evidence, the fact of sleep. If he were exhaustible only, or weak, or frail, as other men are known to be, but were never to sleep, we could scarcely feel that he is one of us; but beholding his intelligence close up, his consciousness fall away, and his prostrate body palpitating in deep slumber, we no longer question his humanity. Call Him the Word incarnate, the Son of God, God manifest: still he is none the less truly man to us, now that we find him asleep. No matter if we can not explain the mystery, or seeming contradiction, as we certainly can not. To say that only the human soul sleeps, explains nothing, and it signifies nothing more to us, if it does, than the sleep of any other human soul. To say that he is only human, is against the plainest declarations of scripture, and against all that we know of his more than mortal bearing, or character. All that we can do here is to confess that the incarnate Word is somehow man, even one of ourselves, receiving and embracing in him the eternal love, and fellowship, and fullness of God.

There is then a very great spiritual importance, in the fact that Jesus sleeps. In it we behold the divine humanity sealed or set in complete evidence. Divine he must be, for his character is deifically spotless and perfect; human he must be for he sleeps like a man.

O this Great Benefactor and World's Redeemer in his sleep! just to look upon him here, in this strange hour—the rain and the spray drenching his body, his hair and pillow of plank washed by the driving storm, his calm benignant face lighted by the glittering flashes that set the night ablaze—thus to gaze upon him, king of angels and men, descended to this mortal plight—how very nigh does it draw us to his humbled state, how closely, and by what easy ties of sympathy, knit us to his person!

And yet more nigh, by a sympathy more tender, when we go over the count of what he had been doing yesterday, and see how it was that he fell into a sleep so profound. The warrior sleeps returning spattered and spent from the bloody horrors of the field; the devotee of pleasure sleeps, because he has drunk the cup dry and would fain forget himself; one hasting to be rich, exhausted and spent by his overmastering cares, and the strain of his mighty passion, sleeps a hurried sleep, fevered by his price-current dreams; the hireling sleeps on his wages, gathering strength for the wages of to-morrow; Jesus sleeps, because he has emptied the fund of his compassions and poured himself completely out in works of mercy to the sick and the poor. His giving way to sleep is well accounted for, when we find him engaged the whole day previous, in works of teaching, advice, counsel, sympathy, consolation, healing, and rebuke, such as kept him in a constant expenditure of feeling and strain of attention, that no mortal strength could support. According to Matthew he heals the centurion's servant, and Peter's wife's mother, and continues at his work of healing, thronged by multitudes pouring in upon him, even till night. On the same day, according to Mark, he appears to have given the parable of the sower, and that of a candle hid under a bushel, and that of the earth as a harvest field sown by the owner, and that of the grain of mustard seed, with a discourse on hearing, and a private exposition of his parables to his own immediate disciples. It is also understood by some, combining what is given in the sixth chapter of Luke, and the third of Mark, that he was awake the whole night previous to this day, engaged in prayer; that he chose the twelve at day-break, and that coming down from the mountain, he was so thronged, at that early hour, that he could not so much as eat bread, and came near being trampled by the crowd; whereupon his friends laid hold of him to bring him off, declaring that he was beside himself; his mother and brethren also came to expostulate with him. However this may have been, it is at least clear that every moment of his day is a draft upon his physical resources, and the multitude are growing more clamorous for attention as their number increases, till finally, unable to bear the strain longer, he flies what he can not support. It even appears to be intimated by Matthew, that he was obliged to effect his escape, by hastening on board a vessel that lay near the place—"Now when Jesus saw great multitudes about him, he gave commandment to depart to the other side." The greatness of the multitude, and their pressing applications were rather a reason why he should stay, than why he should try to escape. They were only not a reason, when he was just ready to sink for exhaustion. Accordingly we see that, no sooner is he entered into the boat and cleared from the shore, than he drops on the deck of the skiff, apparently not minding the hunger of a whole day's toil unrespited, perhaps, by food, and is buried immediately in a slumber so profound that not even the hurricane wakes him.

In this sleep of Jesus therefore, as related to the works of the day, a very great mistake, into which we are apt to fall, is corrected or prevented; the mistake, I mean, of silently assuming that Christ, being divine, takes nothing as we do, and is really not under our human conditions far enough to suffer exhaustions of nature by work or by feeling, by hunger, the want of sleep, dejections, or recoils of wounded sensibility. Able to do even miracles—to heal the sick, or cure the blind, or raise the dead, or still the sea—we fall into the impression that his works really cost him nothing, and that while his lot appears to be outwardly dejected, he has, in fact, an easy time of it. Exactly contrary to this, he feels it, even when virtue goes out only from the hem of his garment. And when he gives the word of healing, it is a draft, we know not how great, upon his powers. In the same way every sympathy requires an expenditure of strength proportioned to the measure of that sympathy. Every sort of tension, or attention, every argument, teaching, restraint of patience, concern of charity, is a putting forth with cost to him, as it is to us. And yet we somehow do not quite believe it. We read that he goes long journeys on foot, but we do not conceive that he is weary and foot-sore as we might be. We read that he is actually "wearied with his journey," and sits him down by a well, while his disciples go into the town to obtain food, but we do not seem to think that he is really way-worn, or faint with hunger, in the proper human sense of these terms. We read that he actually "hungered," and that having no table, or supply, he went aside to explore a fig tree, and break his morning fast on the fruit, but we do not think that such a being as he could really care much for a breakfast any way. He declares his poverty and his outcast lot on earth, by protesting that he has not so much as a place for comfortable and protected sleep—"the Son of Man hath not where to lay his head"—but we think of him probably as meaning only to say, that he has no property; never as testifying his privation of comfort in this first article of civilized bestowment, a sheltered, in-door sleep—obliged, like the dumb animals, to sleep where he may; in the mountains, on the rocks, sometimes under the night rains, shivering often with cold.

Now all such miscolorings of his human experience take him, so far, out of our tier of life, and slacken proportionally our sympathy with him. And they are beautifully corrected in the night of the boat. Jesus had become so exhausted that he could not, in fact, support himself an hour longer, and dropped immediately down, mind and body together, into the profoundest sleep. Is it really no true sleep, but only a divine seeming? Is he conscious in it? Does he hear the storm? does he feel the rain? does the plunging of the boat startle him? Ah! there is reality enough here to make a sight how affecting.

Blessed be thy rough sleep, O thou great benefactor! thou that art wearied and spent by thy particular works and the virtues that have gone out of thee! What is it now to thee, that the waters drench thee, and the fierce tempest howls in tumult round thee! Sleep on exhausted goodness, take thy rest in the bosom of the storm! for it is thy Father's bosom, where they that are weary for works of love, may safely trust, and sink so deeply down into the abysses of sleep, that no thunder even may rouse them.

Notice more particularly also the conditions, or bestowments of the sleep of Jesus, and especially their correspondence with his redemptive undertaking. Saying nothing of infants, which in a certain proper sense are called innocent, there have been two examples of full grown innocent sleep in our world; that of Adam in the garden, and that of Christ the second Adam, whose nights overtook him, with no place where to bestow himself. And the sleep of both, different as possible in the manner, is yet most exactly appropriate, in each, to his particular work and office. One is laid to sleep in a paradise of beauty, breathed upon by the flowers, lulled by the music of birds and running brooks, shaded and sheltered by the overhanging trees, shortly to wake and look upon a kindred nature standing by, offered him to be the partner and second life of his life. The other, as pure and spotless as he, and ripe, as he is not, in the unassailable righteousness of character, tears himself away from clamorous multitudes that crowd upon him suing piteously for his care, and drops, even out of miracle itself, on the hard plank deck, or bottom, of a fisherman's boat, and there, in lightning and thunder and tempest, sheeted, as it were, in the general wrath of the waters and the air, he sleeps—only to wake at the supplicating touch of fear and distress. One is the sleep of the world's father, the other that of the world's Redeemer. One has never known as yet the way of sin, the other has come into the tainted blood and ruin of it, to bear and suffer under it, and drink the cup it mixes; so to still the storm and be a reconciling peace. Both sleep in character. Were the question raised which of the two will be crucified we should have no doubt. Visibly the toil-worn Jesus, he that takes the storm, curtained in by it as by the curse—he is the Redeemer. His sleep agrees with his manger birth, his poverty, his agony, his cross, and what is more, as the curse that is maddening in his enemies is the retributive disorder of God's just penalty following their sin, so the fury of that night shadows it all the more fitly, that what he encounters in it is the wrathful cast of Providence.

How fitting was it also, both that sleep should be one of the appointments of our nature, and that Christ should be joined to us in it. These rounds of sleep are rounds, in fact, of bodily regeneration, and there is no better possible type of the regeneration of a soul, than the recreating of a body, in the article of sleep. It was spent by labor. All the functions were subsiding unto weakness. The pulse ran low and slow, the gait was loose, life itself was ebbing consciously, and a general ferment of disability was, in every faculty, from the brain downward. The man said he was tired, and alas! he could do nothing in himself to mend his condition. No surgeon's or physician's art could put him up again equipped for action. But the silent new-creator, sleep, could do it. Taking down the spent subject of consciousness into his awful abyss of nihility and dark un-reason, he will decompose him, so to speak, and put him together again, all lubricated for new play, and send him forth to his old works, as it were with a new nature. We are made familiar thus with great internal changes and mighty new-creations, wrought by mystic powers, whose methods we can not trace. And Christ the great moral Regenerator goes the same rounds with us here; suffers the same exhaustion, sinks into the same unconsciousness, rising to the same newness of life—himself regenerated bodily with us, as he fitly should be.

But as I have spoken of the sleep, I must also speak of the waking; or at least I must so far note the manner of it, as to draw from it some deeper and more fit conception of the internal state of the sleep. It is a matter of common remark that one who goes to his night's rest charged with a purpose to rise at some given signal, or at some fixed hour, will catch the faintest notification, and will almost notify himself, by a kind of instinctive judgment, or sense of time kept ready for the spring, even in his unconscious state. So Christ, whose love is ready, and full-charged to catch the faintest note of human distress, sleeps on through all the commotion of the elements, undisturbed; but the first cry of panic, "Lord save us, or we perish"—louder to him than all the tumult of the sky and the waters—strikes his inward ear and brings him straightway to his feet. "Then he arose and rebuked the sea, and there was a great calm." The tempest met his sovereign look and fell abashed before him; type sublime of the diviner and more difficult calm that he will bring to the storms of the mind. "What manner of man," said they, "is this, that even the winds and the sea obey him?" A far more wonderful and greater, that he can speak to man's guilty feeling, and the turbulent storms of his remorse, and calm even these into peace.

But observe specially his manner when he wakes. It is as if the great commotion round him had been only a hymn lulling his slumber. He is not flurried or startled by the tumult, shows no sign of confusion, or alarm. If he sleeps, a man, he wakes, a God. You can almost see by his waking, that his dreams have been thoughts pure and mighty, coasting round the horrors of a guilty wrath-stricken world on errands of love and peace. Indeed if it has ever occurred to you to wish that you could once look in upon the sleep of Jesus, and distinguish accurately the dream-state of his thought, even this you may sufficiently guess from the manner of his waking. How majestic the tranquillity of it. The tempest roaring, the men screaming, the vessel just ready to go under—and yet, if his waking were the sunrise, it would not be less disturbed, or less flurried by excitement. Could any thing make it more certain that his sleeping mind has been flowing serenely, steadied and evened by a mighty peace. Internal purity, order, and harmony have been the paradise plainly of his rest. In all the wild confusion of the night and the sea without, his self-approving mind has been sleeping, as it were, in a chiming of sweet melodies. Thoughts vast, mysterious, merciful and holy, have been coursing through his unconscious humanity, as recollections, or recurrences of habit, from his august and supremely good eternity; so that when he wakes, at the cry of his disciples, it is only to say, "peace," to the raging elements, from that transcendent peace that was bathing his spirit within. It was no such waking as the bad and guilty mind, haunted all night by spectres, pursued by murderers, dropping into pitfalls, throttled by serpents round the neck, crushed by weights on the breast, scared by night-mare shapes in the air—it was out of no such element of guilt, or dyspeptic torment that Jesus waked. A sleep thus exercised prepares to fear and the wildness of panic—if the house be on fire, to leap into the fire, if the ship be sinking, to leap into the waters. A good pure mind sleeps goodness and purity, and wakes in peace; a bad sleeps painfully, conversing with internal horrors, ready, when it wakes, to meet the images it has seen.

Probably the sleep of a holy mind is even more destinct from that of a bad, than its waking state is, because, in sleep, the thoughts run just as the internal habit makes them; the superintending will-power that musters, and drills, and artificially shapes them, when awake, being now suspended. Hence the profound philosophy as well as the beauty of the poet's prayer—

> "Be thine the sleep that throws
> Elysium o'er the soul's repose,
> Without a dream, save such as wind,
> Like midnight angels, through the mind."

I am fully conscious, my friends, that I have been discoursing on this matter of the sleep of Christ, in a somewhat random way; for it is a specially intangible, unexplorable subject. Not an unimportant subject either in its theological implications, or its practical relations to our Christian life, but one whose value does not so much depend on our definite interior knowledge of it, as in the external and evident fact. It does not definitely, or conclusively teach, but it suggests many things, and things only suggested are often of as great consequence to us as things proved. Let us note a few of the points suggested. And

1. The possible, or rather actual redemption of sleep. Sleep is just as truly fallen as humanity itself. And who that knows the sleeping thoughts of man, as they are, can have any doubt of it? Nay, who that knows the waking thoughts of man, as they are, can be at all ignorant how they will run when he sleeps? Gnawed

by care, racked by ambition, bittered by the gall of envy, sensual, selfish, fearful, hateful, a prey to bad resentments, loaded and clogged by excesses, filled with hypocondriac terrors from nerves that are shattered by abuse, what can he be, in his sleep, but a faithful representative of what he is awake? And hence it is even one of the saddest known facts of the world, that it sleeps badly—one of the most grateful and most touching facts of the world, that Christ will even be the Redeemer of sleep. He does not of course offer himself to the state of sleep, for it would only be absurd; but he does undertake the regeneration of the soul in character, and that includes every thing; for when the soul's fearful stricture is taken off by love, when it is rested in faith, fortified by self-government, cleared by temperance and spiritual chastity, cheered by hope, it falls into chime, inevitably, with the divine order; so that, when the will is suspended, as in sleep, its internal movement flows on still in the divine order, meeting only grateful images and thoughts of peace. Hence partly it was that so much was made of their dreams, by holy men of old. It was no superstition of theirs—they had only come, so consciously, into the divine order of health and sanctity, that when they went to their sleep, they seemed even to be yielding themselves up to a sanctified flow of the mind, and to the unobstructed sway of a really harmonic movement with God. Nor is any thing more certain than that souls, advancing in holiness, will advance proportionally in the quality of their sleep. As they are being redeemed themselves, so it is a part of their divine privilege that their sleep is also. Accordingly it is often reported by such as have cleared the bondage of nature, and risen to a specially high pitch of intimacy with God, that they find a remarkable change in their sleeping thoughts. None but Christ can sleep the sleep of Christ, and they that are nearest to him in spirit will as certainly be most like him, in the peace of their unconscious hours. Their very redemption is, according to its measure, the redemption of their sleep.

2. It is another point suggested here, that there is a right and wrong sleep, as well as a right and wrong waking state. Sleep is the subsiding of soul and body into nature's lap, or the lap of Providence, to recruit exhaustion, and to be refitted for life's works. But what right has any one to be refitted for wrong; and above all refitted, by the help of Providence? Such sleep is a fraud, and the fund of new exertion obtained by it is actually stolen. Sleep was never appointed by God, to refit wrong-doers and disobedient children, and enable them to be more efficient against Him. Their very sleep they go to, therefore, as a crime, and the dark shadow of guilt curtains in their rest. O ye daysmen, that a few hours hence, when your fund is spent, will go to your sleep to be refitted for to-morrow, is it to be a lying down upon wrong, upon sin, or will it be upon right—there is a very serious meaning in the question. Will you suffer it to rise and be distinctly met, when your head meets your pillow? How very hard a pillow would it be to many, if they took it understandingly!

Observe, meantime, how free a guarantee Christ gives to sleep, when it is right sleep. There have been multitudes of devotees under the Christian name, that made a great merit of withholding sleep, in the rigid observance of long vigils; as if the reduction of the soul's quantity, and the obfuscation of its functions, were the same thing to God as advancing in holiness. These vigils are about the most irrational, most barren kind of fast, that was ever invented; for the reason that, instead of clearing, or girding up the mind, they even propose to make a penance of stupor and lethargy. It is a great mistake also of some that they are jealous of sleep, and have it as a point of merit to shorten the hours, by a regularly enforced anticipation of the dawn. Any such rule for the reduction of quantity is doubtful. A much better rule respects the quality. Make it your duty to prepare a Christian sleep; that kind which the exhaustion of a righteous, or right minded industry requires, and then you may know that Christ your master is with you. It is remarkable that he actually tore himself away from even his healings, and from vast multitudes of people crying piteously for help. He did not reason as some very good men often do, that he must go on, pressed by such calls of mercy, till he could stand no longer. He was famished with hunger, his strength was gone, and enough, to him, was enough. What merit could it be, if he should continue into the night, and falling at last on the ground for faintness, be carried off in that weak plight, to be himself commiserated in turn? He plucked himself away, therefore, fled to the boat, and casting himself down, fell, at once, into the soundest sleep. So when a man's capacity, full spent in good, comes to its limit, and conscience audits the reckoning of its hours, to fall back into God's sole keeping, and be recruited by unconscious rest in his bosom, is the true Christly sleep, at once a natural bestowment, and a supernatural gift. Be it in a palace or a hovel, be it on the land or on the sea, be it in outward calm or storm, be it with man's approbation or without, the resting place is glorious, the rest itself a baptism of peace—"God giveth his beloved sleep."

3. The associations connected with the sleep of Jesus induce a very peculiar sense of his nearness to us in it. Only to have slept in some fisherman's hut, or about some hunter's fire, in company with a noted or publicly known person, gives a certain familiar kind of pleasure to our remembrance of him. In the same way, when the Son of God is joined to us here in a common sleep, subsiding nightly into unconsciousness with us, under the same heaven, a most strange association of nearness is awakened by the conjunction. In our very proper endeavor to exalt God, and give him the due honors of majesty, we commonly push him away, just so far, into distance; we seat him on the circle of the firmament, we lift him, not above the clouds only, but even above the stars; scarcely content, till we have found some altitude for Him, higher than all points visible, and even outside of the creation itself. When, therefore he comes down, as the incarnate One, to be a man with us, tired and spent as we by life's toils, when he lies so

humbly down that even the waters of a lake some hundreds of feet below sea level, dash over him, and there sleeps, even as a soldier, or a sailor might, our feeling is in a strange maze of tenderness. Our God is so nigh, our glorious tent-mate in a guise so gentle, that we come to look upon him in his divine sleep, more tenderly than we could even in the waking mercies and charities of his life. The very heaven of sky and star, that ceils the august chamber of his sleep, is more sanctified from underneath, than before, it was from above. The world is another world—we are other ourselves. O this nearness, this daring familiarity, shall I say, of God! When he says so evidently in this dear, tender, mystery, "come," canst thou, guilty, fearing spirit, reject an approach so lowly and so lovely! And thou disciple too, whose faith is clouded, and upon whom the storms of the mind, as well as the less terrible storms of Providence, are loosed, think it not strange or disheartening, that thy Master sleeps—tender and great sign is it for you that he does—only go to him and say "Master I perish," and have it also to say, as the storm settles forthwith into peace, "What manner of man is this?"

Once more the analogies of the sleep of Jesus suggest the Christian right, and even duty, of those relaxations, which are necessary, at times, to loosen the strain of life and restore the freshness of its powers. Christ, as we have seen, actually tore himself away from multitudes waiting to be healed, that he might refit himself by sleep. He had a way too of retiring often to mountain solitudes and by-places on the sea, partly for the resting of his exhausted energies. Sometimes also he called his disciples off in this manner, saying—"come ye yourselves apart into a desert place, and rest awhile." Not that every disciple is, of course, to retire into solitudes and desert places, when he wants recreation. Jesus was obliged to seek such places, to escape the continual press of the crowd. In our day, a waking rest of travel, change of scene, new society, is permitted, and when it is a privilege assumed by faithful men, to recruit them for their works of duty, they have it by God's sanction, and even as a part of the sound economy of life. Going after a turn of gaiety or dissipation, not after Christian rest, or going after rest only because you are wearied and worried by selfish overdoings, troubled and spent by toils that serve an idol, is a very different matter. The true blessing of rest is on you, only when you carry a good mind with you, able to look back on works of industry and faithfulness, suspended for a time, that you may do them more effectively. Going in such a frame, you shall rest awhile, as none but such can rest. Nature will dress herself in beauty to your eye, calm thoughts will fan you with their cooling breath, and the joy of the Lord will be strength to your wasted brain and body. Ah, there is no luxury of indulgence to be compared with this true Christian rest! Money will not buy it, shows and pleasures can not woo its approach, no conjuration of art, or contrived gaiety, will compass it even for an hour: but it settles, like dew, unsought, upon the faithful servant of duty, bathing his weariness and recruiting his powers for a new engagement in his calling. Go ye thus apart and rest awhile if God permits.

But if you go to kill time, or to cheat the ennui of an idle life, or to drown your self-remembrance in giddy excesses, or to coax into composure nervous energies eaten out by the passion or flustered by the ventures of gain, there goes an enemy with you that will bitterly mock you, giving you the type, in what you seek but nowhere find, of that more awful disappointment that awaits the rest of eternity. What, in fact, are you dying of now, but of rest that is no rest—the inanity of ease and idleness, the insipid bliss of cloyed, overworn pleasures, nights that add weariness to the weariness of the days, sabbaths of God that are bores and not restings under the fourth commandment. O I would rather sleep in a fisherman's boat, in thunder and tempest and rain, exhausted by a day of useful, Christly work, only dreaming there of the good rest to come, than to never know the exhaustions of true industry, and spend life, lolling in equipages, and courting pleasures that will not come! For what too are such ready, dying in their pampered bodies and worn out splendors, but to turn away heart-sick, as here, from the golden sands of the river, and chill with nervous ague for the shades of the trees of life. Blessed are the dead that die in the Lord; for they rest from their LABORS. Blessed only they; for where there is no labor, spending life's capacity for God, there is, of course, no rest.

VIII.

CHRISTIAN ABILITY.

"*Behold also the ships, which though they be so great, and are driven of fierce winds, yet are they turned about with a very small helm, whithersoever the governor listeth.*" JAMES iii. 4.

The ships that were "so great" in former days, were, in fact, scarcely more than cock-boats, or small coasters, scraping round the shores of the inland seas; whereas, now, what we call the great ships are big enough to store in their hold, a whole armed fleet of the ancient time, vessels and men together; and these huge bulks strike out on the broad oceans defying their storms, yet still turned about, as before, with a very small helm, whithersoever the helmsman will. There he stands at his post, a single man, scarcely more than a fly that has lighted on the immense bulk of the vessel, having a small city of people and their goods in the world of timber under him, and perhaps with only one hand, turning gently his lever of wood, or nicely guaging the motion of his wheel, steers along its steady track the mountain mass of the ship, turning it always to its course, even as he would an arrow to its mark.

Dropping now the particular reference had by our

apostle, in his illustration, to the tongue, or the power of the tongue, I shall take it simply as an instance or exhibition of what is more general, viz., the fact—*That man turns about every thing, handles all heaviest bulks, masters all hardest difficulties in the same way; that is, by using a small power so as to get the operation of a power greater than his own.* He gets an immense ability thus, where his sufficiency is most restricted, and his Christian ability is of just this kind. We have no power to handle ships at sea by their bulk; as little have we to do or become, in the grand whole of character, what God requires of us. The soul is a magnitude more massive than any ship, and the storms it encounters are wilder than those of the sea. And yet there are small helms given us, by which we are able always to steer it triumphantly on, to just the good we seek and the highest we can even conceive.

In this mode of statement the very supposition is, you perceive, that we have no ability in ourselves, more than simply to turn ourselves into the track of another, more sufficient power, and so to have it upon us. Helms do not impel ships, and if there were no other kind of power moving on the sea, they would only swing dead-logged upon the waters, making never a voyage. So the power we have as persons, in religion, is not a power of self-impulsion, but only a steering power; though it is a very great power at that. For when we so use it as to hold ourselves fairly to God's operation, as we hold a ship to the winds, that is sufficient, that will do every thing, turning even our impossibles themselves into victory. Our inability to regenerate, or new-create ourselves can not be too strongly stated. As little can our ability, when regarding the fair adjustment and perpetual offering of ourselves to God's operation.

Glance a moment here at the analogies of our physical experience. Great, overwhelmingly great, as the forces and weights of nature are, what do we accomplish more easily than to turn about their whole body and bring them into manageable service?—doing it always by some adjustment, or mode of address, which acknowledges their superior force. We do not manage a horse by the collar, but by the bit. We do not raise the winds that serve us by blowing on the mill ourselves, but we let them blow as they list, only setting the fans of the wheel to get advantage of them. The cliffs of rocks we do not tear open with our hands, but we drill them and, by merely touching a little gunpowder with a spark of fire, as we know how, let that blow them into the air by a force of its own, repeating the operation till we have literally removed mountains. Our many thousand wheels of manufacture we do not turn by our arms, but we take the rivers, flowing as they will, and let them flow, only cutting sluices for them and setting wheels before them, or under them; whereupon they turn producers for us and even builders of cities. We have a way too of taking that most fierce and dreadful power called steam into service and management—doing it never by gathering it up into our arms and holding it in compression, but by raising it in heated folds of iron, and turning it through cocks and conduit pipes, into points of lifting or expansion, where it does the work of many winds and waters, conquering in fact both oceans and their storms. The lightnings we do not catch by the chase and whip into service, to be our couriers, but we just give them a wire and they run, of their own accord, upon our errands, true and swift as we could wish. We bring in thus all the great powers of nature and set them to doing almost miracles for us, by only just offering ourselves to them, in a way that steers them into our service. The great art now of all arts, that which is changing and new-creating the modern world, is, at bottom and in some real sense, a steering art. All our machineries—and where is the end of them?—are only so many adjustments, by which the great bulks and masses of force in nature are steered into methods of use. Even our rail roads, which are revolutionizing, in a sense, all the values and powers of the world, are in fact scarcely more than adjustments for the steering of motions and forces. The very skill we study most, and most continually practice is that of address to nature; finding how, or by what means and arrangements, we may get the forces of the creation to exert themselves in our behalf. Our ability thus amplified stops at almost nothing. Neither have we any difficulty in regard to this kind of ability, as if it were no ability at all. It is precisely that in one view, and in another it is all ability. Having got some force of nature, be it this or that, into use, we have it even as a property, we make real estate of it, buy it and sell it and, when we have it not, set our wheels of motion, raise our cylinders and fires, to obtain it. And it never once occurs to us that the weakness we thereby confess in ourselves is any real inability, or creates any shade of discouragement to effort. On the contrary we call it our great power over nature, and we have courage given us in it to attempt almost any thing.

Prepared by such analogies, our dependence, in the matter of religion, ought to create no speculative difficulty, and I really do not believe that it does, unless it be in some few exceptional cases. There used to be much debate over the question of ability and dependence, but as far as my knowledge extends, such difficulties are not felt any longer as they once were. And yet we seem to have as much difficulty as ever in making that practical adjustment of ourselves to God, which is necessary in any and every true act of dependence.

Thus a great many, admitting quietly the fact of some such ability as makes them responsible, take it really upon themselves to do, out and out and by their own force, all which they are responsible for. It is as if they were setting themselves to steady and move on the general bulk of the ship, seizing it by its body. What tremendous weights and fearfully complex forces the soul contains, and how many and fierce the storms may be that have broken loose in it, under the retributive damage of sin, they do not sufficiently consider, daring even to hope that they can gather it back into the sweet unity of order and health, by their own self-governing power. It turns out of course, since they can govern but one thing at a time, that while they are governing that one, a hundred others are breaking loose—and all these lusting, rasping, raging, tumultuous, wild, forces of evil, driving like fierce winds and tossing like mountain seas, are too much, of course, for any human power of self-government.

Besides we have no capacity, under the natural laws of the soul, as a self-governing creature, to govern successfully any thing, except indirectly, that is by a process of steering. We can not govern a bad passion or grudge by choking it down, or master a wild ambition by willing it away, or stop the trains of bad thoughts by a direct fight with them—which fight would only keep them still in mind as before—all that we can do in such matters, in a way of self-regulation, is to simply steer the mind off from its grudges, ambitions, bad thoughts, by getting it occupied with good and pure objects that work a diversion; and then the danger is—only working thus upon ourselves—that we shortly forget ourselves; when the sky is filled, again, of course, with the old tumult. We ourselves, acting on ourselves, institute harmony in the soul and establish heaven's order in its working?—why if all its many thousand parts and forces were put in a perfect military subjection to the will, we could not even then conceive the state of internal order and harmony accurately enough to command them into their fit places and functions.

Furthermore, if we could, our self-government would

not be the state of religion, or bring us any one of its blessed incidents. The soul, as a religious creature, is put in affiance, by a fixed necessity of its nature, with God. Having broken this bond in its sin it comes back in religion to become what it inwardly longs for—restored to God, filled with God's inspirations, made conscious of God. And this is its regeneration; a grand, all-dominating, change that supposes a new revelation of God in it, and is called, in that view, its being born of God. Can it then reveal God in itself by its own self-regulative force? Can it, in fact, accomplish any one thing that is distinctively religious—the state of peace, the state of liberty, the state of light, the state of assurance? "Impossible" is the word written over against every character and condition of good it can, as a religious nature, attempt. And yet these impossibles we can easily and surely master, by only bringing ourselves into the range of God's operations. The helm-power only is ours, the executive is God's. He can govern the soul, its grudges, lusts, ambitions, bad thoughts, all at once. He knows the state of harmony internally and can settle us in it as a state of rest. He has inspirations, when he gets into our love, that make all duty free. He can settle assurance and confidence in us. He can be peace in the sealing of his forgiveness upon us. Revealing himself in the soul, he can fill its horizon with light. He can be angelic perfection in us, he can be purity, heaven, in his own fit time and order.

What is wanted therefore in us, and nothing more is

possible for us, is the using of our small helms so as to make our appeal to God's operation. Self-impelling, self-renovating power we have none; but the helm power we have, and if we use it rightly, it will put us in the range of all power, even the mighty power of God. Hence the great call of the scripture salvation is, "come unto me," "come unto God;" because the coming unto God is the coming unto God's operation, and the receiving of what his divine power will work in the soul, when he is templed in it. Hence also the call to renounce our own will, to renounce the world, to renounce eternally sin; because whoever lives in his own will—lives for the world as his end, lives apart from all homage to God—can not be in God's will, or come at all into God's operation. In the same way there must be a clearing of a thousand particular and even smallest things that will steer off the soul from God. When the helm of a ship gets foul, or so tangled in ropes, or weeds, that it can not traverse freely, it will even steer the ship into wreck instead of holding it to its course. So exactly it is with the soul. An old grudge adhered to steers it forever away from God. Any mode of profit, whose fairness or beneficence to men we distrust, but will not give up, will do the same. Adhering only to a party that we begin to doubt the merit of, takes away the possibility even of confidence toward God. In the same way, the dread only of being singular, the going after popularity, the fear of men's opinions, the cringing of the soul to men's fashions—all these give over the helm of one's life to others, that they may turn it where they will—always away, of course, and still away from God. Every such thing must of necessity be renounced or even denounced, as we hope to come into God's operation, or come unto God. No soul is born of God till it comes into his very mind and offers itself, as a really transparent me dium, to his light. When the helm is practically set, honestly guaged for God, God will be a perfectly open harbor to it, but how can it think of entering either this or any other harbor, when it is really steering itself away?

Hence also that very positive matter called faith, or the fixed demand of it as a condition of salvation. The conception of it is, not that we are to do or attempt doing something great upon ourselves—regenerating ourselves, sanctifying ourselves. All that we can do is to simply trust ourselves over to God, and so to bring ourselves into the range of His divine operation. In one view, or considered as including what God does for it and by it, faith it is very true is every thing—the whole substance and bulk and body of holiness; but considered in a manner most analytical and closest to us, it is our act alone and a very small one at that, to be the determining helm of a new life. Doubtless faith, again, is some how wrought by God, but it is none the less acted by us, being the sublimest and completest mortal act of dependence possible; in which the soul, ceasing from itself, turns away to God—comes unto God. Whereupon as God meets it, accepts it, and pours himself into its open gates, it is filled with God's inspira-

15

tions and the working of his mighty power. Now the life proceeds again from God as it ought, being instigated inwardly, by his divine movement. Peace, liberty, light are its element; it is even conscious of God.

All human doings therefore, as regards the souls' regeneration, or the beginning of a new-life, amount to nothing more than the right use of a power that steers it into the sphere of God's operation. And the reason why so many fail here is, that they undertake to do the work themselves, heaving away spasmodically to lift themselves over the unknown crisis by main strength—as if seizing the ship by its mast, or the main bulk of its body, they were going to push it on through the voyage themselves! Whereas it is the work of God, and not in any other sense their own, than that coming in, to God, by a total trust in Him, they are to have it in God's working. Let the wind blow where it listeth—God will take care of that—they have only to put themselves to it, and the impossible is done.

In just this way also it is that so many miscarriages occur, after conversion. Nothing was necessary to prevent them, but simply to carry a steady helm in life's duties. Thus there will be some who get tired of the helm; to be always at their post, praying always, guaging their motions carefully to meet their new conditions, keeping their courses set exactly by their conscience, and allowing no slack times of indulgence, becomes wearisome as certainly as they lose out the Spirit that makes exactness liberty, and then they take away their hand, as it were to rest themselves. Some too will have a way of persuading themselves that the soul will get on well enough, at least for a time, by the impulse it is under already, and so far will consent to do what no sailor ever dares, let the ship steer itself; whereupon, when it begins to wheel, and plunge, and go just nowhere, as regards the voyage, they begin also to cry, "impossible!" "how can we stop it!" "how can we turn it back!" They imagine some great fatality, impossible to be controlled, when in fact the only fatality suffered is that of a ship that can not keep, or get back into, its course without being steered.

At the same time it must not be forgotten, that multitudes of disciples fall out of course, for no less positive reason than that they actually steer themselves out of God's operation. One goes into an employment the right of which he is not sufficiently sure of to have a good conscience in it. Another galls himself in a right employment, by the consciously wrong manner in which he carries it on. A third goes into company that consciously does him injury, yet still continues to go. A male disciple turns himself to the pursuit of honor, a female disciple to the worship of fashion; one to the shows of condition, the other to the more personal vanities of dress. Thousands again will let their lusts and appetites get above their affections, their bodies above their minds. Some are nursing their pride and some their envy, driven of fierce winds by the gustiness of one, eaten out and barnacled by the water vermin of the other. These now and such like are the small helms, which all you keep turning, who turn yourselves away. You ask why it is, half grievingly, that you fall away from God so often, and loose the savor of his friendship so easily? But the very simple fact, if you could see it, is that you really steer yourselves away; allowing yourselves in modes of life that even turn you off from God, as by your own act. You not only forget, or neglect, the small helms of guidance, but you actually turn them the wrong way—only making now and then some clumsy effort, as you wake up in pauses of concern, to do some mighty thing by your will; in which you virtually attempt to handle the ship by its body—sighing piously in mock resignation, as you fail, over the inevitable fact of your dependence! O, if you could but use your dependence rightly, finding how to really and truly depend, what power and victory would it bring! The very steering power you have, which is the highest power God has given you to wield, is nothing but a way of depending; that is of right self-adjustment to the gales of the Spirit and the operating forces of God. How certainly too and tenderly would your God be drawn to you, putting all his power upon you, if he only saw you carefully guaging your small duties so as to guide yourselves into his help. Remember his promise, "he that is faithful in that which is least,"—nothing draws the heart of God like that.

Now it is very true that a man who is tending the small helm of duty with great exactness may become painfully legal in it—a precisionist, a Pharisee. But it should not be so, and never will be, save when the precision is itself made a religion of. That precision which is only a way of steering the soul, precisely and faithfully, into God's inspirations, is but the necessary condition of liberty. No man ever keeps the way of liberty in a heedless, hap-hazard life. Mere strictness is only a mode of pain, but the strictness of a delicately faithful and punctual address to God, has God's witness and free blessing always upon it. Such a disciple consciously means to be faithful and, as certainly as God is God, he will somehow have God's power upon him. A very nice way of application, a steady, sleepless watch of the helm, turning it moment by moment, by gentle deflections—this navigates the ship and keeps it bounding on, as in the liberty of the sea! No Christian is ever driven loose from his course, when he holds himself up to God, in the adjustment of a careful trust.

Now in all that I have said, thus far, in the unfolding of this very practical subject, I have been preparing a more distinctly Christian view of it, that could not otherwise be given—this I will now present, and with this I close.

I have been showing what power accrues, or will accrue, as we keep ourselves in, or bring ourselves into, the range of God's operation; and this word *operation* has been taken probably as referring only to the omnipotent working of his will, or spiritual force. But there is a power of God which is not his omnipotence, and has a wholly different mode of working; I mean his moral power—that of his beauty, goodness, gentleness, truth, purity, suffering compassion, in one word, his character. In this kind of power, he works, not by what he wills, but by what he is. What is wanted, therefore, above all things, in the regeneration of souls, and their advancement toward perfection afterward, is to be somehow put in the range of this higher power and kept there. And here exactly is the sublime art and glory of the new divine economy in Christ. For he is such, and so related to our want, that our mind gets a way open through him to God's divine beauty and greatness, so that we may bring our heart up into the transforming, molding, efficacy of these, which we most especially need—need even the more imperatively, that our very conceptions of God, under the lowness and blind apathy of our sin, are so dull, and dim, and coarse, as to have little value and power.

The infinite perfection, or unseen beauty of God—how could we so much as frame a notion of it, when even the being of God, as an unseen spirit, has so little reality to our coarse and fearfully demoralized apprehensions? Therefore understanding well our utter inability to so much as conceive the perfect good in which we require to be fashioned, or the moral excellence of God whose image is to stamp itself upon us, He has undertaken to put even this before our eyes. To this end he becomes incarnate in the person of His Son. As the incarnate Son, He is God in the small, God in humanity, the Son of Man, bringing all God's beauty and perfection to us in a personal being and life akin to our own—powerful on our own, by the tragic tenderness of his cross; so that if we simply love and cleave unto his human person, unto his cross, we embrace in him all that is included in God's infinite feeling and character. In this view it is, that he says, "I am the door;" for he is just that opening into the infinite beauty that brings us to the sense of it, and puts us in the power of it. Just this too was his meaning when he said, "he that hath seen me hath seen the Father"—he has seen a man simply, in one view; yet, in another, he has seen even God, in all those distant, impossible glories and perfections, he otherwise could not conceive. This too was what he had in thought when he said—"He that believeth on me believeth not on me, but on him that sent me. And he that seeth me seeth him that sent me." The omnipotence of God works absolutely, the moral power of God by being seen, and Christ makes it seen. By which means, as an apostle conceives, he becomes the power of God—"Christ the power of God and the wisdom of God." In short this exactly is Christianity—this thought labors all through—that Christ in humanity is God humanized, divine feeling and perfection let down into the modes of finite sentiment and apprehension. In his human person, and the revelation of his cross, he is the door, the interpreter to our hearts, of God himself—so the moral power of God upon our hearts. It is not necessary that we should so much as frame the intellectual idea of God's perfection from him, which multitudes could never do—we have simply to love him and cleave to him as to a human person, and we have the very excellence of God framing itself into us, by a most naturally relational, humanly real, sympathy; the power, that is the moral power, of God is upon us, and revealing itself in us with all needed efficacy.

Christ then as the Son of Man, is that small helm put in the hand, so to speak, of our affections, to bring us in, to God's most interior beauty and perfection, and puts us in the power of His infinite, unseen character; thus to be molded by it and fashioned to conformity with it. And so we have nothing to do but to keep his company, and watch for him in faithful adhesion to his person, in order to be kept in the very element of God's character, and have the consciousness of God, as a state of continually progressive and immovably steadfast experience. The moral power of God and God's glory is mirrored directly into us, to become a divine glory in us. Beholding, as in a glass, the glory of the Lord, we are changed into the same image from glory to glory. This it is, working in our sin, that clears it all away—the power of God unto salvation.

What now brethren and friends, is our conclusion? What have we seen but that all condolings with ourselves, all regrets of failure, turning upon the fact of our weakness, all protestations of inability, all sighs and suspirations ending in the word "impossible," are without a shadow of reason—utterly groundless. We can do and become just all that we ought, and without so much as one strain of self-endeavor. It is very true that God has not made us omnipotent—we can not manipulate ourselves into holy character by our will, we can neither regenerate, nor make free, nor purify, nor keep ourselves. And just so we can not do any thing in the world of natural experience, without making our address to the powers of nature. Do we mourn over this in listless impatience, and call it our dreadful inability? Does the man who can not navigate a ship by its body, or drag it through the sea by its beak, set himself down upon the word impossible, and desist from the voyage? No, but he takes the very small helm, heading bravely out into the storms, compelling the huge bulk, in that easy manner, to go where he sends it, dashing on still on, by night and by day, and week after week, and month after month, till he has taken it possibly clean round the planet he lives on, and brought it quietly in to the haven for which he was set. Here, just here, is the mighty power of man, that he can steer! Weak in himself, as regards most things, able to do almost nothing in the gross, he can yet do almost any thing by only steering it into the lines of forces that will do it for him. And the same holds true exactly in religion. No man here is called to do some great thing which he can not do. Nothing is necessary for you, in becoming a Christian, or maintaining a triumphant Christian life, but just to stay by the helm, and put yourselves in where the power is—then you have all power, and every mountain bulk goes away at your bidding! Come unto God, unite yourselves to God, and the doing power you have is infinite!—and is none the less yours because it is His. Trim your ship steadily to the course, and God's own gales will waft it. If you want success enough to set yourselves for it, and guage your courses accurately by a strict application, infallible success is yours. Or, better still, if your mind is dark, if you do not even know how to guage any movement rightly, or even what the words mean that speak of it—then come to the man Jesus, your blessed, all perfect brother, ask him to let you go with him and keep him company, cling fast to him, and all the transforming moral power of God shall be with you. To investigate much and know many things, is not necessary. Only to love Jesus and adhere to him faithfully, knowing simply him, is wisdom enough.

He will be the door, so that your heart will pass in, where your understanding can not reach. No matter how weak you may seem to be, or how many impassable mountains to be before you, or how many fierce storms to be raging round you, still you will go over mountains beaten small as chaff, on through tempests that have heard the word "be still." You will never fail or fall. Stay by your love to Jesus and the power of God's infinite will is with you, and the still mightier, more inconceivable, power of his greatness upon you. O this glorious fact of our dependence—if we speak of ability, we have all utmost ability in it. We come to no bar in it, brethren, as many are wont to speak. If only we can rightly depend, we come into all power rather, and are able to do all things! Here it is that so many of God's mighty ones became mighty—Moses, Elijah, Paul, Luther, Cromwell—all those efficient and successful ones that we ourselves have met, wondering often how they got such emphasis of action, such resistless sway. They were men who kept company with God, and lived in the powerful element of his divine operation. Here is the only way of success, whether of single men, or of churches. How can a church get on in any great concern of religion, when it is out at sea, beating about as it is driven, and steering just no whither. Nor is it any better if we take the ship into our own hands, to do all for it ourselves. Let us come into God's operation, and God will know how to open a way for us. He will lead just where we most want to go, and send us every gift even as he gives us a gospel. So if we are baffled personally, in all our Christian aims and doings, losing ground, weak and growing weaker, unhappy, dissatisfied, hopeless of good—out upon this wild and dreadful sea, and driven by all fierce winds and storms of the mind, we have only to steer ourselves on, by the steady helm of dependence, and our way is clear to the harbor.

IX.

INTEGRITY AND GRACE.

"*Judge me O Lord according to my righteousness, and according to mine integrity that is in me.*"—Ps. vii, 8.

A truly noble confidence!—and yet many of our time would call the language very dangerous, or scarcely Christian, language, if it were spoken by any but one of the scripture saints. What can be a slipperier footing, they would say, for any sinner of mankind, than to be appealing to God in the confidence of his own righteousness; or, what is even worse, in the confidence of his mere integrity? What does it show but a state of egregious, fearfully overgrown, spiritual conceit, coupled with a prodigious self-ignorance? And what could evince a lower sense of God and religion? We shall see whether it is so, or must needs be so in all cases or not.

It may not be amiss to note that some Unitarian teachers, on the other hand, charge it as a fault in our doctrine of salvation by grace, or justification by faith, that it lets down even the standards of our morality itself; making grace a cover for all defections from honor, truth, honesty, and whatever belongs to the outward integrity of our practices; allowing us to be selfish, heartless, perfidious, crafty, cruel, mean, and all this in good keeping, because it is a part of our merit under grace, to have no merit.

Let us pursue this subject, and see if we can find the true place for integrity under the Christian salvation. And we shall best open the inquiry, I think, by noting—

1. How the scriptures speak of integrity; how manifold and bold the forms in which they commend it, and how freely the good men of the scripture times testify their consciousness of it, in their appeals to God. The text I have cited does not stand alone. In the twenty-sixth Psalm, David says again—"Judge me O Lord; for I have walked in mine integrity." And again—"But as for me, I will walk in mine integrity." The Proverbs testify in language still more unqualified,—"that the integrity of the upright shall preserve them," "The just man walketh in his integrity." In the same view it is, that good men are so often called "the upright" and "the just"—"Mark the perfect man and behold the upright," "The way of the just is uprightness, thou most upright dost weigh the path of the just." They are called "righteous" too and "right" in the same manner, and it is even declared that they "shall deliver their own souls by their righteousness." And lest we should imagine that the integrity, honored by so many commendations and examples, is only a crude and partial conception, belonging to the piety of the Old Testament, the Christian disciples of the New

are testifying also in a hundred ways, to the integrity, before God and man, in which they consciously live. They dare to say that they have a conscience void of offense, that they serve God with a pure conscience, that they count it nothing to be judged of man's judgment, when they know that God approves them. They rejoice in the confidence that they are made manifest unto God, and tenderly hope that they may be made manifest also in the consciences of men. They are so assured in the sense of their own integrity, as followers of Christ, that they even dare to exhort others to walk as they have them for examples. And this holy consciousness of being right with God, of being wholly offered up to him, of wanting to know nothing but Christ, of losing all things for his sake, appears and reappears in as many forms as language can possibly take. They spend their life, as it were, in the testimony that they please God. Making the strongest confessions of ill desert, and resting their salvation everywhere on the justifying grace and righteousness of God, they still are able, somehow, to be free in professing their own conscious integrity in their discipleship, and the sense they have of being right and true—whole men, so to speak, in the service of their master. Whether we can explain the riddle, or not, so it is. But the explanation is not difficult, and, before we have done, will be made sufficiently clear. Consider then—

2. What integrity means, or what is the state intended by it. As an integer is a whole, in distinction from a fraction, which is only a part, so a man of in-

tegrity is a man whose aim, in the right, is a whole aim, in distinction from one whose aim is divided, partial, or unstable. It is such a state of right intention as allows the man to be consciously right-minded, and to firmly rest in the singleness of his purpose. He is a man who stands in the full honors of rectitude before his own mind or conscience. It does not mean that he has never been a sinner, or that he is not now, as regards the disorders and moral weaknesses of his nature, but simply that whatever may have been his life, or the guilt of it, he is now turned, as regards the intent of his soul, to do and be wholly right; firmly set, of course, to receive all the possible helps in his reach, for maintaining a life wholly right with God and man.

But we must not pass over the distinction between what is called commercial, or social integrity, and the higher integrity of religion. This commercial integrity which is greatly affected and much praised among men, relates only to matters of truth and personal justice in the outward affairs of life, and becomes integrity only because it is measured by a partial and merely human standard, viz., the standard of the market, and of social opinion. Such a character is always held in high respect among men, and, what is more, it should be. It is really refreshing in this selfish, scheming, sharp-dealing world, to meet an honest man. Whether he be a Christian or not, we love to honor such a man. It will also be seen that he is a man who means, at least so far, to honor himself. But it does not follow that such a man's integrity is complete enough even to give him a good conscience. He is, after all, it may be, no such integer in his confidence, or the approbation of his own mind, as he consciously might be. His intent is not really right, that is to accept the principle of right doing in its breadth, as the arbiter of all action, and do and be all right and forever. All that can be said of him, all that he will say for himself, is that he has had it for his law to speak the truth, fulfill his promises, and deal fairly by his fellow men. Still it is not, and has never been his aim, or object, to do what is right to God; and that if I am not mistaken, is a matter of much higher consequence and more necessary to his real integrity. God is a person as truly as men are, more closely related to us than they, a better friend, one who has more feeling to be injured than they all, claims of right more sacred. What then does it signify that a man gives men their due, and will not give God his? Does it give one a title to be called humane, that he will not stick a fly with a pin because of his tenderness, and yet will stab, in bitter grudge, his fellow man? Does it fitly entitle one to the name of a just man, that he is honest and fair with men of one color, and not with those of another, honest and fair on three days, or even five days in the week, and not on the days that remain? What then shall we think of the mere commercial integrity just described, taken by itself? Calling it integrity, it is still integrity by halves, and, of course, without the principle; integrity by market standards only, and not by any standard that makes a real integer in duty. Real integrity begins with the principle, meaning to give every one his due; to be right with God, as with men, right against popularity as with it, right everywhere, wholly and eternally right.

You perceive, in this manner, how easy it it is for a man to be in great repute for this virtue, and yet be wholly uncommitted to principle in it. Nay, he may even be a very bad man. Examples of the kind will occur to almost any one. I knew in college, and afterward in a remote part of the country, a man of such repute now in the law, that he was said to have made the greatest argument ever presented before the Supreme Court at Washington, whose reputation, as a kind of Cato in this matter of market integrity, was scarcely less remarkable. He had more than once kicked a man out of his office, who had come to engage him in a case plainly tainted with fraud, and would never allow himself to gain a point, by the least deviation from truth. And yet he was a man of many vices, and a man, withal, of such infernal temper, that his wife and children knew him only as a tyrant scarcely endurable. Getting exasperated almost to the pitch of insanity, by what he conceived to be a base attempt of his law partner to jew him, for he was a Jew, in a matter of business, he drew off in disgust and anger from his practice, determined to add nothing more to the profits of the concern, where before he had, in fact, brought all. As the contract still existed in law, the right of his proceeding might be questioned, but his almost overgrown sensibilities to points of honor would no longer suffer him even to look upon the face of such a man. Still he would not so far disrespect the contract as to open a separate and rival office, but hired himself out as a common laborer in unloading coal from one of the ships in the harbor. While at work there, smirched and grimed by coal-dust, there came to him, in a few days, a client who wanted to engage him in a great cause involving the title to a vast property. Inasmuch as he must live, apart from all profits, he finally consented to undertake it, on condition that he should receive only a small day-wages allowance. He won the cause. And then, five or six years after, when he had his family with him, and was known to be short in the means of living, his old client, whom he had made a rich man, sent him a present of twenty thousand dollars. He was rather offended than pleased—as if he would do so mean a thing as to cover up the fact of a fee, under the semblance of a stipulation for day-wages! Forthwith he returned the present, and when it was renewed as a present to his wife, he required her also to send it back. If his partner had seen fit to raise a legal claim for the money as a fee, he might easily have been quieted by half the sum, but rather than consent to enrich a knave by that amount, he preferred to rob his family of the same.

Now this man, so keenly sensitive to the matter of honor in business, as to be well nigh demonized by it, was not even a virtuous man. He was, in fact, the most magnificently abominable man I ever knew. And he died as he lived. The steamer on which he was a passenger sprung aleak at sea, and when they called him to the pumps, protesting, with an oath, that he would do no so mean thing as to pump for his life, he locked himself up in his state-room, and there he stayed, like a tiger in his cage, till the ship went down.

Was he then a man of integrity? In one view he certainly was, and that was his reputation. Still he was a man false to every right principle, both of God and man, but just one; an example in which any one may see how little the boasted integrity of commercial honor and truth may signify, when taken alone.

I could easily have given you a thousand nobler and more beautiful examples of integrity, in the spheres of business, and before the human standards of commercial obligation. I give you this, just because it is so nearly repulsive; showing, in that manner, how little true merit of character belongs to this kind of virtue, when it stands by itself. How far off is it then from being any true equivalent for that broad, universal, radically principled, integrity that includes religion. Whoever is in the principle of right-doing, as a principle, will be ready to do all right, always, and everywhere—to God as to men, to men as to God. This it is and this only that makes a genuinely whole-intent man, thus a man of integrity.

There is, then, a kind of integrity which goes vastly beyond the mere integrity of trade, and which is the only real integrity. The other is merely a name in which men of the market compliment themselves, when they observe their own standards; though consciously neglecting the higher standards of right as before God.

This higher, and only real, integrity, is the root of all true character, and must be the condition, somehow, of Christian character itself. Let us inquire—

3. In what manner? Christ, we say, does not undertake to save men by their merit, or on terms of justice and reward, but to save them out of great ill desert rather, and by purely gratuitous favor. What place have we then under such a scheme of religion, for insisting on the need of integrity at all. Does it not even appear to be superseded, or dispensed with?

I wish I could deny that some pretendedly orthodox Christians do not seem, in fact, to think so. It is the comfort of what they call their piety, that God is going to dispense with all merit in them, and this they take to mean about the same thing as dispensing with all the sound realities of character—all exactness of principle and conduct. They are sometimes quite sanctimonious in this kind of faith. Cunning, sharp, untruthful, extortious, they look up piously still, at the top of what they call their faith, and bless God that he is able to hide a multitude of sins—able to save great sinners of whom they are chief! Submitting themselves habitually to evil, they compliment themselves in abundant confessions of sin; counting it apparently a kind of merit that they live loosely enough to make salvation by merit impossible. Ten times a day they declare that they will know nothing but Christ and him crucified, and lest they should miss of such a faith, they do not spare to crucify him abundantly themselves!

It can not be that such persons are not in a great

mistake. Any scheme of salvation that undertakes to save without integrity, has, to say the least, a very poor title to respect. And it ought to be evident beforehand, that Christianity is no such scheme at all.

Yes doubtless, it will be said, there must be such a thing as integrity—that is, commercial integrity—in Christian men, else they would bring very great scandal on the cause. Is it then permitted that, if they will be just and true in trade and in society, they may safely consent to be out of integrity with God? Looking at the principle of things, for there is nothing else to look at here, it would seem that the Great God and Father of us all is certainly as much entitled to consideration from us as we are from each other, and how can there be any genuine principle at all in a disciple, who is not in that higher integrity which includes doing justice to God—being right with God?

There must then be some place for the claim of integrity in our gospel, even though it be a scheme of salvation by grace. Nor does the solution of the matter appear to be difficult. Integrity, we have seen, is wholeness of aim, or intent; but mere intent of soul does not make and never could complete a character. It is even conceivable that a soul steeped in the disorders of sin, might take up such a kind of intent, on its own part, and, acting by itself, be only baffled in continual defeats and failures to the end of life. There is no redeeming efficacy in right intent, taken by itself—it would never vanquish the inward state of evil at all. And yet it is just that by which all evil will be vanquished, under

Christ and by grace, because it puts the soul in such a state as makes the grace-power of Christ, co-working with it, effectual. Conscious of wrong, for example, and groaning under the bitterness of it, I take it up as my intent to be and become wholly right. Then I find Christ near me—O how near!—yielding me his divine sympathy, and pouring his whole tenderness into my feeling. As regards the guilty past, he will justify me freely, and hold me to account no more. As regards the future, he will take me as a friend, raise my conceptions of what is good by his own beauty, ennoble my feeling by society with him, draw me up out of my lowness and my weak corruptions, by his character great in suffering, and so enable me to conquer all my evils, as he conquered his. As certainly then as I come into right intent, I shall come into faith, and trust myself to him, as a means of becoming what I have undertaken to become.

Here then is the place of integrity. It is even presupposed in all true faith, and enters, in that manner, into all true gospel character. It does not exclude the grace of Christ, or supersede salvation by grace, but on the human side moves toward grace, and is inwardly conjoined with it, in all the characters it forms. The sinning man, who comes into integrity of aim, is put thereby at the very gate of faith, where all God's helps are waiting for him. Now that he is so tenderly and nobly honest, there is no grace of God, or help of his merciful spirit, that will not flow into him as naturally as light into a window. By this grace, in which he will now trust, his whole being, feeling, aspiration, hope are invested, and the light of God, the brightness of salvation, everlasting life, is in him—he is born of God.

His integrity, therefore, his new and better aim, is not any ground of merit, or title of desert, which dispenses with faith, but his way of coming into faith—thus into the helps, inspirations, joys and triumphs that Christ will inwardly minister—in one word, into the righteousness of God. And accordingly the scriptures formally condition all such helps, on the integrity of the soul that wants them. "Ye shall seek me and find me, if ye search for me with all your heart—that is with a whole and single aim." "If I regard iniquity in my heart, the Lord will not hear me." "If thine eye be single, thy whole body shall be full of light." The scriptures, we may thus perceive, have no difficulty in finding how integrity is needed in a way of salvation by grace, and there is, in fact, no such difficulty, save as we make it ourselves.

Having discovered, in this manner, what, and how great a thing integrity is, and the necessity of it on strictly Christian grounds, let us note in conclusion, some of the practical relations of the subject. And

1. Consider what it is that gives such peace and loftiness of bearing to the life of a truly righteous man. What an atmosphere of serenity does it create for him, that he is living in a conscience void of offense. And when great storms of trouble drive their clouds about him, when he is assailed by enemies and detractors, per-

secuted for his opinions, broken down by adversities, thrown out of confidence and respect even, as will sometimes happen, by false constructions of his conduct and malignant conspiracies against his character, still his soul abides in peace, because he justifies himself and has the witness that he pleases God. These clouds that seem to be about him do still not shut him in. He sits above with his God, and they all sail under! Such a man is strong my brethren—how very strong! There is no power below the stars that can shake him! The steaming vapors of a diseased body can not rise high enough to cloud his sun. He is able still and always to make his great appeal and say—"Judge me O Lord, according to my righteousness, and according to the integrity that is in me." Who can understand like him, the meaning of that word—"And the work of righteousness shall be peace, and the effect of righteousness, quietness, and assurance forever." Here too—

2. Is the ground of all failures, and all highest successes in religion, or the Christian life. Only to be an honest man, in this highest and genuinely Christian sense, signifies a great deal more than most of us ever conceive. We make room for laxity here that we may let in grace, and do not hold ourselves to that real integrity that is wanted, to receive, or obtain, or be in, that grace. O how loosely, irresponsibly, carnally, do many Christians live—covetous, sensual, without self-government, eager to be on high terms with the world, praying, as it were in the smoke of their vanities and passions, making their sacrifices in a way of compound-

ing with their obligations. Little do they conceive, meantime, how honest a man must be to pray, how heartily, simply, totally, he must mean what he prays for. Perhaps he prays much, prays in private, prays in public, and has it for a continual wonder that he gets on so poorly, and that God, for some mysterious reason, does not answer his prayers! Sometimes he will even be a little heart-broken by his failures, and will moisten his face with tears of complaint. He has made great struggles, it may be, at times, to freshen the fire that was burning in him, and yet, for some reason, he is all the while losing ground. His faith becomes a hand, as it were, without fingers, laying hold of nothing. The more he pumps at the well of his joys, the drier he grows. It is as if there were some dread fatality against him, and he wonders where it is. Commonly it is here—that he wants rectitude. He is trying to be piously exercised in his feeling, when he is slack in his integrity. He has been so much afraid of being self-righteous, it may be, that he is not righteous at all. When he is loose at the conscience, how can he be clear in his feeling?

Perhaps he has conceived a higher standing in religion, a state of attainment where his soul shall be in liberty, and has tried for whole months, possibly for years, to reach it, and yet he finds it not. He begins to imagine, not unlikely, that no such thing is for him—God's sovereignty is against him, and he must be content to stay in that lower plane that God has appointed him. "God never means," he will say, "that

I should be much of a Christian—that is given to others that have a higher calling." Now strange as it may seem, here again is the root of his difficulty—that his projected attainments are clear ahead of his integrity. Some traitor is hid in his soul's chambers that is kept there, and carefully fed. What is wanting is the integer of a clear, undivided intent. Honesty! honesty! O that Christian men, saying nothing of others, could understand how much it means, and the wonderful power it has! We connive at evil and do it so cunningly that we do not know it. Our eye is evil, we regard iniquity in our heart, therefore do we fail in our prayers, therefore do we lose ground, therefore are we baffled and floored in all our attempts to rise. But it is not so when we have the single eye. Such power is there in this integrity, when it is real, that, making faith real, it makes all gifts attainable. God loves the honest mind, hears the honest prayer, pours all his fulness into the honest bosom. No great flights of ecstatic feeling are wanted, frames carry nothing, but that silent, sound, integrity, which poises the soul on its pivot of truth and self-approbation, is so mighty that it wins its way to God through all obstacles. Here is the secret after all, of the true success in every case. Success is the fixed destiny of any soul that has once reached the point of whole intent. No one need be troubled about his frames, or fluctuations, or even what appear to be his losing moods, if only he can stay by his conscience firmly enough to say, "Judge me O Lord according to mine integrity." Here then, brethren, is the spot where you are to make your revision, find what your intent is, whether it is honest and whole and clean, warped by no ambiguities, divided and stolen away by no idols. Here the Achan will be hid, if any where. Make sure of his dislodgment, and your way is clear. Then your faith will be faith, your prayers will be prayers; every thing will have its genuine meaning, and God will be revealed in every thing you do. I proceed now

3. To another very important deduction, viz., that every man who comes into a state of right intent, or is set to be a real integer in the right, will forthwith also be a Christian. There is apt to be much pride in men not religious, on the score of their commercial integrity. They will find, if they search more narrowly, that they still have no right conscience in it. They feel themselves to be inwardly wrong. They live in a state of conscious disturbance. They are often consciously disingenuous, as regards the truths and claims of religion. They have consciously a certain dread of God which harrows their peace. What I mean to say, at present, is that whoever gets a clear perception of the state of wrong in which he lives, and comes back into a genuinely right intent, to be carried just where it will carry him, sacrifice what it will cost him—any thing to be right—in that man the spirit of all sin is broken, and his mind is in a state to lay hold of Christ, and be laid hold of by him, almost ere he is aware of it. Nor, when I say this, do I throw discredit on the common modes of expression; for this exactly is the point to

which every converted person comes, though he may not so conceive at the time. One may tell of his convictions, another of his fears, another of his unspeakable wants, one of the prayer that he made thus or thus, another of the restitution or acknowledgment he made to some one he had wronged, many of their deep sorrow that melted into joy, many others of the despair they came to in their struggles, under which they fell off helpless in the hands of God's mercy, and behold it was deliverance itself. But whatever may have been the form of exercise, this most assuredly is in it always, consciously, or unconsciously present, that there is a coming somehow into a state of pure intent, a mind to receive all truth and do all right forever. And no man ever came to this, who did not find himself, at once, all over in the faith of Christ, a consciously and strangely new man.

Let me give you a case, in which this particular point, in the matter of conversion to God, will be clearly distinguished. There died, in the city of New York, about ten years ago, a distinguished merchant, and much more distinguished saint of God, whose conversion was on this wise. He was born and brought up in the island of Santa Cruz, belonging to a wealthy and gay family, in which he received no religious instruction at all. He had a naturally gay, light, forceful character, and scarcely a religious idea. One Sunday, when the family and their guests went out for a ride, he remained at home. Going to the library for something to read, his eye fell on a book labeled "*The Truth of*

Christianity Demonstrated." He took it down, saying as he looked on the back of it, "The truth of Christianity demonstrated—the truth of Christianity demonstrated—well if it is, I ought to believe it and live it, and—I WILL. Let me try the book and see." Sitting down, at that point, he opened the book and began to read, and though it was an argument only, giving no particular appeal to feeling, he was surprised to find a strange brightness of light on the words. Holy conviction flowed in upon him, a wondrous love waked up in his feeling, a still more wondrous bliss dawned upon his love, and in a very few minutes, it seemed that the helm of his nature was somehow taken by a mysterious power he could not resist. The joy of the change, which he did not understand, or conceive, was so great as to prove its reality; he could never, from that moment, shake off the conviction of his being quite another man. What it was to be a Christian he did not know, but he knew that he was something, which to lose, or cease to be, he could as little think of as losing his life. When the riding party came back, he began forthwith to let out his joy, tell his wonder, testify of Christ, just as he would of any good, gay time he had had before. They were astonished, some of them doubted whether he was not somehow beside himself. But there was no slack in his flame, he went on like the just, growing brighter and brighter. There was no appearance of sanctimony, no cant, he was the same outspoken, social, manly youth, that he had been. Hungering finally after some religious society, he managed to remove to Philadelphia, where he found teaching and sympathy, and great works of duty. He went once to the theater, once to a ball, having no scruples about the right of it, and scarce knowing that he could have. But he never went again, simply because it did not meet his feeling, and gave him no pleasure. He finally came to a settlement in New York, where he was known many years as a man of dignity and power, nobly free and joyous, fond of the young, and open to all humblest minds wanting counsel, the most distinguished mark, and brightest ornament ever known in the churches of that great city. From first to last his Christian life was but a hymn.

At what point now did this remarkable servant of God pass his conversion? Not when he was reading the book, but when he was looking on the back of it; for there it was, in that little deliberation on the label, and the nobly honest conclusion he accepted concerning it, that his soul took hold of integrity, and sin was all reversed! The mere resolve to accept it, if true, decided all. And therefore it was that Christ met him in the book, with a revelation so blessed. Doubtless it was the Spirit of God, working unseen, that drew him out in the previous parley on the label; and every step of the change, nay, of his whole life, was in some sense, worked by a power superior to his own mere will. And yet he had a will, by that consented to believe what is true, and live it in his life.

Now there is no man in this audience, however remote he may have been from the thought of being a

Christian, when he came into this place of worship today, who has any thing more to do, in order to be one, than to just come into the same really honest mind. You can not will to believe what is true, and do all right, as fast as you can find it and forever, and go out hence in your sins. Are you not ready my friends for this new and nobler kind of life? Can you lie down tonight and sleep outside of this blessed integrity? How can you think of yourself with respect, as not being a Christian, when that which is demanded of you is only what you think you are demanding of everybody. True, this integrity we speak of is of a higher kind, and more real; is it therefore less to be honored, and less promptly chosen?

And now in conclusion of my subject, I will only lay down God's indorsement upon it and upon all that I have said, in a single, but remarkable sentence of scripture. I wish it might be remembered, and stay by you always, even from this hour till your last—"For the eyes of the Lord run to and fro, through the whole earth, to show himself strong in behalf of them whose heart is perfect toward Him." This "perfect heart" means a right conscience, a clean, simple intent. And the substance of the declaration is, that God is on the look-out always for an honest man—him to help, and with him, and for him, to be strong. And if there be one, that God will not miss of him; for his desiring, all-searching eyes are running the world through always to find him. And when he finds him, he will show himself to him in the discovery even of his strength.

I believe that he has sometimes found such a man, even in the depths of heathenism, and to him been discovered as the helping and strong friend he longed for. Many a skeptic has he flooded with light, because he saw him willing, at last, to be right, and hungering for something true. This perfect heart, this soul of integrity, my friends—O if we had but this, what else could we fail of? I repeat the word thus explained—put it down to be with you, in your struggles with sin, your sickness, your poverty, your Christian defects and drynesses, all the mind-clouds, all the guilt-clouds, of your mortal state—"For the eyes of the Lord run to and fro through the whole earth to show himself strong in behalf of them whose heart is perfect toward him."

X.

LIBERTY AND DISCIPLINE.

"*As long as they have the bridegroom with them, they can not fast. But the days will come, when the bridegroom shall be taken away from them, and then shall they fast in those days.*"—MARK ii, 19.

It is one of the honorable distinctions of Christ's doctrine that he is never one-sided; never taken, as men are, with a half-view of a subject, or a half-truth concerning it. If there is, for example, a free side, or free element, in Christian life and experience, and also a restrictive side; conditions and times of not fasting, and conditions and times of fasting; he does not fall to setting one against the other, but he comprehends both, and holds them in a true adjustment of their offices and relations. John's disciples come to him in the question, why he does not put his disciples to fasting, as their own great prophet and the Pharisees do theirs? But instead of making light of fasting, and calling it an old, ascetic practice, now gone by, as many human teachers would have done, seeing only half the truth, and rallying a party for the part they see, he simply replies—"every thing in its time; the attendants of the bridegroom will, of course be wholly in the festive mood, while the wedding is on foot, but when it is over, they will fall into such other key as their personal condition requires. My disciples can not fast while I am with them. But when I am taken up they will turn themselves to such ways of fasting as their deprivation, or bereaved feeling requires."

His answer, taken more spiritually, amounts to this: that when the love is full, and the soul is consciously gladdened by the present witness and felt impulse of God, any kind of restrictive, or severely self-compelling discipline is inappropriate or uncalled for, and is really out of place; but that when there is a failure of such divine impulse, when the soul is losing ground, brought under by temptation, groping in dryness and obscurity of light, then some sharp revision of the life, some new girding up of the will in sacrifice and self-discipline, is urgently demanded, and must not be declined. In other words, let there be liberty in God while there may, girding up in ourselves, by forced exercise and discipline, when there must; let the soul go by inspiration when the gale of the Spirit is in it, and when it has any way stifled or lost the Spirit, let it put itself down upon duty by the will; when the divine movement is upon it, let it have its festal day with the bridegroom, and when the better presence fades or vanishes, let it set itself to ways of self-compulsion, moving from its own human center.

Much the same general truth though differently conceived, is taught by Paul when he represents the Christian soul as a coin having two seals or mottoes, on the two sides; on the obverse, or face—"The Lord knoweth them that are his;" on the reverse, or back—"Let every one that nameth the name of Christ depart from iniquity." It is as if divine calling, endowment, and help were on one side; self-discipline, watching, mortified lusting, and steady resolve on the other.

Liberty and discipline, movement from God's center and movement from our own, sanctified inclination and self-compelling will, are the two great factors thus of Christian life and experience. We may figure, in a certain coarse analogy, that we live in a city having two supplies of water for its aqueduct; one upon high ground back of it, whence the water runs down freely along the inclinations of the surfaces; and the other in some lake or river on its front; whence, in case that fails, or the ducts give way, a supply is to be received by forcing, or the dead lift of the pump. The water, however, is not created in this latter case, you will observe, by the enforcement, but is taken, as in the former, from the general supply of nature's store. So there are ways of Christian living, where every thing goes by impulse, and a gracious inspiration, flowing in, as it were, by its own free motion; and other ways and times, where a self-compelling discipline of sacrifice and painstaking are wanted to regain the irrigating grace that was practically lost or shut away, by moods of inconstancy and mixtures of subjection to evil.

It is very obvious that both these conceptions may be abused, or pushed to excess, as in fact they always are when they are taken apart from each other, and made a religion of. Thus we shall have, on one side, just what has many times appeared in this or that variety, a school of enthusiasts, living only in frames and for them, flighty, rhapsodical, ecstatic, moving in the upper air on wings, till such time as they get weary of their thin element, and consent, for comforts' sake, to light upon the ground; when, of course, they do as the prophet's living creatures did—"when they stood they let down their wings." Perhaps they will spread them again, and perhaps not. They are all for inspiration, or the state of divine impulse, and nothing else is to be much accounted of. To be in this elysian state is piety, and if they chance to fall out of it, or sink away, flagging and spent, as regards their good excitabilities, they have no way of going on foot to think of, that will prove their fidelity, and put them in a sober way of blessing. They have no conception of a walking with God that is not flying with him, and their high movement commonly ends, where dissipation must, in a state of loose keeping, disability, and general collapse.

On the other side, where every thing takes the shape of will-work and discipline, the result will commonly be quite as bad. Sometimes the word will be *activity*, and a general campaign of doing will set every thing in a way of tumult, and aggressive motion. Responsible only for action, action will come to be just the thing most irresponsibly done. Hard, graceless, censorious, denunciatory, sometimes wild, and always unchastened by the love it magnifies, it keeps the conflagration up till the combustible matter is burned away, and then the fire goes out of course. Sometimes the word is *sacrifice*, and then comes on the dreary train of penances, vigils, vows of celibacy, mendicancy, and the pallid funeral hosts marching out alive to be entombed in cells. All these, making up a religion by their will, and the drill of their passionless obedience, agree, in fact, to make as hard a time of it as possible, and they will most fatally succeed; for it can not be long, ere the discipline they covet as a religion, breaks down both will and principle together, and shows them, alas! too perfect in the training of uncharity, mendacity, sensuality, and lust.

I ought also, perhaps, to name two counterfeits that cover the ground of both these particular excesses. Thus, on one side, the argument will be, "why should I do, or attempt to do in religion, what I can not do in liberty, or from inclination? When I am not inclined to prayer why should I pray? Why cross myself in duties which I only dislike? Why put myself under service by rules that only annoy me, and do not bless me? How can I imagine that God is pleased with me, when he finds me doing by compulsion, what he knows I distaste, and have really no heart to?"

The assumption is, in this way of speaking, that when there is real inclination to the thing done, there is even something a little remarkable in it; a kind of superlative, or superfine, merit, such as discharges all thought of obligation respecting duties where such inclination fails. And yet the supposed inclination, having so great value as to excuse all responsibility for inclination where there is none, is even understood to be nothing but an occasional glow of sentiment or desire, in the plane of nature; not any really divine or supernaturally inbreathed impulse. It is not of the bridegroom, raises no thought of any festal flow, in which Christ bathes their feeling. It is even the end of the law, without Christ, in a much more summary and complete sense that Christ himself could be; for it not only discharges all obligation, but forbids any farther command—how can God command what one is not inclined to already? and what he is inclined to needs, of course, no command.

The counterfeit upon the other side, is that self-reliant morality, which counts it a sufficient, or even a rather superlative religion, to live in correct practice under rules, and makes nothing of receiving from God, or being in any consciously restored relationship with him. Christ is engaged as a Saviour, I conceive, to connect human nature with God, according to its normal idea, and have it regenerated, as by God's restored movement in it—born of God. He wants to raise again the very plane of our existence, lifting us up out of mere self-hood into a state of divine consciousness and beatitude. This to him and this only is religion. The beaver is not more certainly below humanity, than the footing it along by mere rules, is a kind of life below the grade of religion, or concourse with God. That high world of blessing too, for which Christ has undertaken to prepare us, is not a world of good morals, but of godly affinities and free inspirations, moved, and lifted, and wafted, and glorified, and always to reign in God.

We have then two conceptions of Christian life and experience, which Christ holds comprehensively together, but which his disciples are often trying to hold separately, making a whole religion of either one or the other; and then we have a counterfeit of each, contriving how to make a religion of each, without the reality of either one or the other. Let us see now if we can bring ourselves back into the conception of Christ, and find how to hold with him both the two sides at once; setting both in that genuine mutual relationship that belongs to them. There is then

I. A ruling conception of the Christian life, which is called having the bridegroom present; a state of right inclination established, in which the soul has an immediate knowledge, or consciousness of God, and is swayed in liberty, by His all-moving, supernatural, inspirations. This kind of state, if it were complete, as it never is in this world, would, of itself, be the all of perfection and of blessedness. The whole aim of Christianity is fulfilled in this alone. No other kind of service, taken by itself, at all meets the Christian idea. Self-compelling ways of discipline, resolve, self-regulation, body-government, soul-government, carried on by the will may be wanted—I shall presently show in what manner—but no possible amount of such doings can make up a Christian virtue, and, if such virtue were perfect, they would not even be included in it. Every thing in genuine Christianity goes for the free inclination. Here begins the true nobility or princely rank of God's sons and daughters, and they will be complete, when their inclination is wholly to good and to God. They strike the point of magnanimity, when they do the right, as God does, because they simply love the right—bearing burdens, because it is the nature of love to bear them, making sacrifices, never from fear, interest, self-consideration, always for God's great ends of mercy and blessing. The bridegroom joy is now upon them, because their duty is become their festivity with Christ. Perfected in this duty and joy, they are complete in God's everlasting beatitude; for there is no wear of friction in such duty, but eternal liberty and play rather. What then

II. Is the place, or office, or value of that whole side of will and self-discipline, which Christ himself assumes the need of, when the bridegroom is to be taken away? Here is the main stress of our subject, and upon the right solution of this point, its uses will principally depend.

There is then, I undertake to say, one general purpose, or office, in all doings of will, on the human side of Christian experience, viz., the ordering of the soul in fit position for God, that he may occupy it, have it in his power, sway it by his inspirations. No matter what the kind of doing to which we are called, or commanded; whether it be self-government, or self-renunciation, or holy resolve, or fasting, or steadfast waiting, the end is one and the same, the getting in position for God's occupancy. As the navigator of a ship does nothing for the voyage, save what he does by setting the ship to her course, and her sails to the wind, so our human doings in religion, those I mean, which make up our self-compelling, self-adjusting, self-constraining discipline, are all to be concerned in setting us before God, in the way to receive the actuating impulse of his will and character. We are not called, of course, to work a religion thus, ourselves, or by our own will. Setting sails to the wind does not propel the ship, or give it the least onward movement, as regards the voyage; and yet, without such holding of it in position, the voyage could never be made. So also a seed must have position, else it can not grow; if it is laid on a rock, or buried in sand, or sunk in water, or frozen up in ice, it will be inert as a stone; but in good warm soil, and sun, and rain, and dew, it will quicken easily enough, because it is in position. A tree will die out of position, a clock will stop out of position, a plough wants holding, a saw wants guiding, a compass wants setting; nothing in the world works rightly that has not position given it. And the reason is that every thing to be operated upon must be fitly presented to that which operates; telescopes to their objects, mills to water-falls, and souls to God.

And here is our particular human part in religion—all that we can do is summed up in self-presentation to God, or the putting of ourselves in position for his operation. Hence the call to salvation is "come," and the complaint is, "ye will not come to me that ye might have life." So also, when the casting down of pride and self-will is required, the forsaking of all things, the yielding up of life and whatever is most dear, these ways of self-renunciation are only the taking down of bars that fence away God's entrance and free movement from the soul. Faith again is made the condition of salvation, in just this view, and no other; because, when a sinning soul trusts itself up to Christ, to be cared for, regenerated in good, and saved by his mercy, it is put in exactly the position toward God that is most open, and admits him most freely; even as the brazen serpent, lifted up before Israel, was to be effective in their healing, when looked upon. Out of position, with their backs toward it, there was no virtue to be received from it, because there was none expected or admitted.

So it is in the matter always of conversion, or the beginning of a new life—it is always begun, just as soon as the subject comes into position far enough to let it be. And then the same holds true of all proper Christian doings afterward—they are all summed up, either in keeping position toward God, or in regaining it after it is lost. Thus, if by reason of a still partially remaining subjection to evil, the soul should be stolen away from its fidelity and the nuptial day of its liberty should somehow be succeeded by a void, dry state, without any proper light or evidence left, then the disciple has it given him to recover himself, by getting himself in position again before God. He will take time by forcible resolve, and gird himself to a careful revision. He will set himself upon his idols to clear them away, take up his cross invoking sacrifice itself to be his helper, rectify his misjudgments, make good his injuries, slay his resentments and grudges, mortify his appetites, crucify his bosom sins, tear open all the subtleties of distemper and treason—watching all the while his new beginnings, saving carefully his little advances, doing first works humbly and tenderly, and by this drawing into position, will, if possible, make ready for the festal coming of his Lord, and the restored liberty of a son.

In this kind of struggle the disciple will get on most effectively, when for the time, he is much by himself, and much apart from the world, and even its pleasurable scenes and gifts. In one view, there will be a certain violence, or desperation sometimes in the fight of his repentances. "For behold what carefulness it wrought in you; yea what clearing of yourselves; yea what indignation; yea what fear; yea what vehement desire; yea what zeal; yea what revenge." By these stern rigors of will, these mighty throes of battle, the disciple out of liberty will in fact be only putting himself in position to recover it. He takes himself in hand in fiery self-chastening, and rigidly enforced subjection, that he may prepare himself to God's help. He gets confidence in this manner, by his thoroughness, to believe that God accepts him, and has the testimony given him that he pleases God. Restored in this manner to his liberty, the enemy that came in at the postern goes out at the front, and God again will have his full dominion.

Neither let any one object that all such stresses and strains of endeavor must be without merit, because they are forced and are, in one sense, without inclination. Such kind of endeavor God honors because it is practical, and not for the merit of it. What should he more certainly honor than the true endeavor of souls to present themselves to him, and get position for the complete admission of his will. If these struggles of enforcement do not belong to the perfect state of good, it must be enough that they are struggles after that state. God is practical, and without prudishness; if nothing is really good to him that is not from the heart's inclination, he will yet be drawn to such struggles against inclination, as he is to the cries of the ravens, and will put his benediction upon them, under that same fatherly impulse, if no other.

Holy scripture has no such dainty way of reasoning in this matter, as they give us, who, by affected reverence, excuse themselves from all rough discipline, because they have no inclination for it. It even commands us to serve, when we are not in a key to reign. "Mortify therefore, your members which are upon the earth"—do men mortify themselves by inclination? "Ye have crucified the flesh with its affections and lusts"—do we this self-crucifying by inclination? "Deny thyself, take up thy cross"—do we deny ourselves by inclination, or take up the cross for inclination's sake? When Christ again, to get a certain rich moralist or formalist into position for God, bids him sell all that he has and give to the poor and come and follow—whereupon he "goes away sorrowful"—does the sad questioner sorrow because he is required to have his inclination? The Saviour too has even a more cutting requirement than this—"And if thy right eye offend thee pluck it out; if thy right hand offend thee cut it off." Is there any thing in which we are farther off from inclination, than in plucking out right eyes and cutting off right hands? What in fact is the very point of the Saviour's meaning here but to say, put your will down upon whatever is hardest and most against your inclinations—any thing for position.

How feeble, superficial, sophistical, and withal, how very like to a practical mockery of all deep movement in religion is that word so often ventured, and of which I have already spoken—"Why should I pray when I do not feel inclined to it? Why should I go to church, why should I read the scriptures, why should I give alms, why should I hold myself to observances, all which I am weary of, and in fact really dislike? If I can not offer God from the heart, what better is my offering given than withheld? Just contrary to all such feeble platitudes Christ, we have seen, appoints a grandly rugged, thoroughly real, massive, discipline, by which souls, at best only half inserted into good are to hold on their way, and press themselves down upon the constancy their fickle hearts would fly. Filling them to the full, if he possibly may with holy inspirations and loving impulses, he counts even this a gospel on one foot, if he may not also put them every man to a hard fight of discipline, and watch, and drill and resisting even unto blood. When the inspiration is upon them, he will let the festive movement flow in its liberty. And when the grace-power lulls or is gone, he will have them take their turn of discipline, to gather up by their will, and bring into position for God's occupancy, all their vagrant and unsteady functions; so to strengthen the things that remain and are ready to die. These two things, in fact, he will hold, if possible, at all times, to a close and practically guarded comprehension, the festive and the restrictive, the movement of love and the self-girding watch.

But I should not produce any just impression of the immense reach of this very practical matter—the so ordering of our life, on the side of self-discipline, as to be always squaring ourselves to God, and holding true position before Him—if I did not specify some of the humbler and more common matters in which it is to be, or may be, done.

Order, for example—how great a thing is it for a Christian, or indeed, for any one, to keep his life and practice and business in the terms of order? Holding himself steady, and squaring his habit thus carefully by system in God's will, his very order is itself position—the orbit he traverses having God to traverse it with him; and the worlds of the sky will not be more surely and steadily moved in their rounds, than he by God's impelling liberty. Fallen out of this order into all disorder and confusion, how can he ever be in position for God, till he comes back into the exactness and true discipline of the same?

A responsible way has the same kind of value. An irresponsible man has no place for God or God's liberty. But a soul that stays fast in concern for all good things—responsible for the church, for the brethren, for the welfare and salvation of perishing men, for the vices and woes of society, for the good of the country—is just so far in position with God, and ready for his best inspirations. God loves responsible men, and delights to keep them in the full endowment of strength and liberty.

Openness and boldness for God, the readiness to be found on God's side in the full acknowledgment of his name and people, is an absolute requisite, as regards the effective revelation of God in the soul. Whoever will not thus acknowledge God, in a bold commitment of himself before the world to his cause, wants the firm courage and manly truth of feeling which puts him in position. Real and bold devotement is magnanimity, and where there is nothing of one, there is nothing of the other—as little receptivity therefore for God. God loves to be trusted, and loves the men that can boldly take their part with him. When they stand openly for his name, he stands by them, and puts his might upon them.

Descending to what is in a still humbler key, let me speak of honesty—how a large and faithfully complete honesty puts every soul in true position before God. A single eye—that is honesty; and "if thine eye be single, thy whole body shall be full of light." But the honesty of which I thus speak, is more and higher, you will observe, than mere commercial honesty. That will do justice to customers and laws of trade, but not to enemies, and least of all, to God. There is no reality in it therefore, more than there would be in doing justice to customers of one country, or color, and not to those of another. Called honesty in the market, it still may, and, many times, certainly is, hypocrisy and a lie. Real honesty takes in principle, engaging to do justice every where, every way, every day, and specially to God's high truth and God. O, what a presentation that to invite the incoming of God! Who is in position for God but he that will clear himself, thus impartially, of every wrong and injury; and how certainly will God's spirit flow into such a bosom, in how full a tide of liberty! How completely open here is the gate of possibility for all greatest and divinest things!

I could speak of things yet humbler and more common; such, for example, as dress and society. These are matters which we commonly put even outside of the pale of religious concern, or responsibility. And yet there is how much in them to fix the soul's position toward God. How perfectly evident is it that one may dress for the Holy Spirit and the modest opening of the soul to God's manifestation; or so as to quite shut away any possible visitation from the divine. In the same way, society may be observed in such a way of sobriety and grandly true hospitality, that angels, much more Christ and God, will gather to it unawares; or in such a way of ambition, flashiness, and worldly assumption, that the Holy Spirit can not get room in it for any smallest dispensation of his gracious impulse. I speak not here for any sumptuary, or morbidly scrupulous, restriction. I only say that there may be enough, in the modes of dress and society, to quite settle the matter of the soul's position toward God.

Not pursuing these illustrations further, it must be enough that we have found, and practically verified two elements in Christian life and experience, liberty and discipline, God's free movement and our own self-constraining will. That is the heavenly state of blessing and perfection; this our human concern to get, as in conversion, recover, as in dryness and decay, or keep, as in all most ordinary goings on of life, the position toward God that commands his bestowment of the other.

But what, of fasting? the very thing about which my text is itself concerned, and about which I have said as nearly nothing as possible. In one view it is even so; in another I have been speaking of nothing else; for the whole course of argument pursued has been tracing its fit place and relationship, as an integral part, or factor, of the true Christian discipline.

Are we then to allow, some will ask, that fasting belongs to Christianity? I certainly think so. Did not Christ himself declare that his disciples should fast after he was gone? Did he not also begin his great ministry, by a protracted fast, which duly considered, and rightly conceived, constitutes one of the grandest and most impressive chapters of his story? It is easy, doubtless, to assume, in self-compliment, that we have now come to an age of maturity that permits us to conceive the Christian grace more worthily; but no such assumption will be very impressive as against the example of Christ himself! Some will also maintain, more argumentatively, that fasting is a bodily penance, excluded by the genius of Christianity; but when Christ is heard, in his great, first, sermon, discoursing of it just as he does of prayer and of alms, and giving it exactly the same promise of reward, the conclusion appears to be not far off that, either they do not, or Christ did not, understand Christianity!

It is a great mistake of many, in our time, that they are so easily carried by a certain half-illuminated declamation against asceticism. Let us have nerve enough to withstand the odium of a word, and be less superficial, and just as much stronger in our practical life. For there is—I put the issue boldly that it may not be missed—a good asceticism that belongs to Christianity, as a worthy and even rationally integral function; the same which an apostle describes when he says, "I exercise myself (ασκω) to have a conscience void of offense." By which he means that he puts himself to it by the direct training of his will, even as a rider trains a horse by the rein.

In this good asceticism, we take ourselves away purposely, when it seems to be needed, from society, from gain, and from animal indulgence, that we may assert, with more emphasis, the principle of self-subjection to God, or gird ourselves anew to the divine keeping. Thrusting down a whole side of our nature that habitually assumes to be uppermost, we get in this manner a powerful shove of reaction; for the great law of action and reaction holds universally, both in the worlds of matter and mind. In this manner painstaking itself is a great element of success; not because it is the taking of so much pain, as if there were some merit in that, but because the mind gets a confidence of honest meaning in it, such as nerves the soul to sacrifice, and gives it assurance with God. Christianity, as I have shown, takes in this element. Filling us with great inspirations, it puts us to a stout self-discipline also, that we may get position for still greater, and a still more victorious liberty.

Over against this good asceticism, there is also a false and a bad, as already intimated. It makes a virtue of self-torment, contrives artificial distresses to move on God's pity, or pacify his resentments, or purchase his favor. It macerates the body to make the soul weak and tender. It dispenses, in fact, with faith itself, and even thinks to square its account with God, by a due contribution of bodily pains and privations.

This bad asceticism we exclude, the good we accept. And in this, we shall train ourselves, sometimes even naturally, by a fast. If we are mortified by the discovery that the body is getting uppermost, if our Sundays are choked, our great sentiments stifled, by indulgences of the body we meant not to allow, we shall turn upon it in this good asceticism, and say to it, with a meaning—"I keep under the body." In the same way, if we can not find how to bear an enemy, if we recoil from sacrifices that are plainly laid upon us, if we have no great courage to meet a great call, we shall emulate the example of Cromwell's soldiers, who conquered first the impassive state, by their fastings and prayers, and then sailing into battle as men iron-clad, conquered also their enemies; or better still, we shall emulate those martyrs, who could sing in the crisp of their bodies, because they had trained their bodies to serve. So again if we are losing ground, getting under the world, heated by prosperity, soured by disappointment, bittered by resentments and grudges, we shall do well to seek the wilderness, taking our temptation with us to be mastered. So again if we have some great crisis upon us, even as our Master had, some turn of life to settle that will settle every thing; or if we have great endowments coming upon us, or coming out in us, that we must be responsible for—property, place, eloquence, fame, beauty, genius—what a girding do we need to meet our occasions, or even to effectually stifle the nonsense of pride and foolish suggestion. O, if we could set ourselves in position thus for God's call and his Christly inspirations, how cheap the discipline would be.

Observed on occasions like these, a fast will sometimes wonderfully clear the atmosphere of the mind. The sentiments will be quickened in their play. The imagination, which is a great organ for religion, will get a more reverberative ring. The conscience will become at once more rigid and more tender. All the powers will be girded up, and God will have the soul in position, waiting to be filled with his eternal life and vigor.

No such good results of fasting will follow, or will be expected, where it is improperly observed. No one should ever go into a fast, when he has the bridegroom consciously with him. Such fasting is untimely. Turning sunshine into night, and making misery *gratis*, when we are not miserable, is any thing but Christian, though alas! some very good people do sometimes make a merit of it.

Some persons, who are not practiced in the art, so to speak, of fasting, complain that they are only troubled and mentally confused by their hunger, and get no advantage from it. But when they have learned the way to set their mind facing Godward, instead of facing the body, and moving in the low range of the gastric energy, it will not be so—they will even forget to be hungry. It might be well for such to begin with a prolonged half-fast, or Lenten reduction, instead of abstinence. Feeding the body circumspectly thus, as between cage bars, they may still the growling of nature, and learn, at last how to get a spring of reaction for the mind. A prolonged bridle check upon the body is good both for it and for the rider; for what both most especially need is to get accustomed to the rein!

At the same time, fasting should always be a reality, never a semblance. To pretend a fast, when all the routine of table, office, and shop, is still going on as usual, is to make a cheat of it; such as takes away the mind's honor, and leaves a most sorry conviction of hypocrisy in place of any benefit. But let no one make the fast excessive under pretense of making it real. It should never amount to a maceration of the body; though sometimes the benefit gained by a disciple will even tempt him to make a luxury of it. Let it be a rule that the fasting should never be more frequent or more stringent, than is necessary to maintain, for the long run of time, the very clearest, strongest, healthiest, condition both of mind and body. For the digestive function wants its Sabbaths, just as truly as any other, and will keep the soundest health when it has them.

Instead of recoiling now, my brethren from this more rugged kind of discipline, there ought even to be a fascination in the severities of it. As it is profoundly real and earnest, it will also make us strong. How often are we oppressed with the feeling that our modern piety wants depth and spiritual richness. It is as if it were in the skin and not in the heart—thin, flashy, flavorless, destitute of the heroic and sturdy qualities. It never can be otherwise, till we consent to endure some hardness, or at least to find some way of painstaking. The gymnastic we are in must be strong enough to make muscle, else we shall not have it. Hence the profound necessity, as I conceive, that there should be an ascetic side or element in this free salvation, where the disciple "exercises himself," as the apostle has it, putting himself in training and self-chastening for success. For as the competitors in games of wrestling, and rowing, and racing, do not despise the toughest severities of training for the victory, no more should the Christian repel that nobler discipline that is to be the girding of his character. It would not do, for a way of grace, to only fondle or codle us, in tenderings of favor and soft mercy and overflowing bounty; we could not be floated into the heights of character by any such gentle tide-swing as many look for, and conceive to be the grace offered to their faith. Such a kind of treatment qualified by nothing more sturdy and severe, might even soften the brain of our piety. No, there must be an ascetic self-girding for us, as well as a gracious impulsion, something which is more than fasting, but of which that is a type. There needs to be a side of tough endeavor, in which we undertake a mighty becoming, even punishing ourselves, so to speak, into right position for God. We must come into the vise of a rugged and fiery self-discipline, where, if we wince for the severities suffered, we still forbid our cowardly, soft, nature to yield. If there is to be any fibre in our character, there must be a Spartan discipline to make it. There was never a strong Christian, or a Christian hero, that did not put himself to being a Christian with cost. To be merely wooed by grace, and tenderly dewed by sentiment, makes a Christian mushroom, not a Christian man. It is even difficult to conceive, how those angels that excel in strength, and are called the charriots of God, ever got their vigor without some fit training; nay, it is most certain that they never did. So much meaning has our master, when charging it upon us, again and again, without our once conceiving possibly what depth of meaning he would have us find in his words—Deny thyself, take up thy cross and follow me.

XI.

CHRIST'S AGONY, OR MORAL SUFFERING.

"*And being in an agony he prayed more earnestly, and his sweat was, as it were, great drops of blood falling down to the ground.*"—LUKE xxii, 44.

What Christian has not many times wished that he could lay hold of the precise condition and feeling of Jesus, in this very remarkable scene or chapter, commonly called his agony? And yet a suspicion may well be indulged that we not seldom push it quite away from us, and make it unrealizable, by dogmatic solutions that rather confound than solve it. Mystery, in some sense, it certainly is, and must be; for the person itself of Christ is, internally viewed, a mystery, and the what and how, of his personal pains, in what part they affect him, under what laws of intensity, and by what internal force he is able to support them, we can never know, till we understand his psychology itself—as we certainly shall not here on earth.

Still the agony is given us, because it can somehow be seen to be for us; yielding impressions of Christ and of God, manifested in him, which it is important for us to receive. And to receive these impressions from it is, at least so far, to understand it. All the more to be regretted is it, if we interpose theologic constructions that make it impossible to all receptive sympathy. Thus if we conceive, or dogmatically assume, that Christ is in this hour of distress, because the sin of the world is upon him, to be punitively treated in his person; that God withdraws judicially from him, to make him suffer, and that the "cup" over which he groans is the cup of God's eternal indignations; may it not be that we ourselves so far violate the subject matter, as to make it an offense to our most inborn convictions of right, and raise up mutinous questions that even forbid the discovery of its meaning to our hearts?

A much less artificial, tenderer, and, I think I shall be able to show, truer and more affecting conception of the agony is, that it rises naturally out of the perfect feeling, and the personal relations and exigences of the sufferer. Such a being, on such a mission, meeting such objects of feeling, at such a crisis, will have just this agony, without any infliction to produce it.

The facts of the scene briefly and freely related are these. The Saviour, attended by his disciples, goes up into a dell on the slope of Olivet, and enters a certain garden or olive yard, where he had often before communed with them apart. He requires them to sit down. But there is something peculiar in his manner. A feeling of depression makes him droop in his action, and gives a drooping accent to his voice. He signifies to three of their number that he wants their company while he goes forward a little way, to pray. Heretofore he has commonly sought to be alone in prayer, going apart at dead of night, and ascending this or that high mountain top, there to be closeted with God in solitude. The depression that before appeared now becomes a crushing weight upon him. In the language of the narrative, he begins to be sorrowful and very heavy. He speaks too, unable to suppress his feeling—"My soul is exceeding sorrowful, even unto death." And then he adds what indicates even greater anguish, such as almost takes away his self-possession—"do not leave me, do not sleep, stay here and watch with me!" He goes forward a few steps, falling upon his face, which is the eastern posture of extreme sorrow and despair, and there he cries aloud—"O my Father, if it be possible, let this cup pass from me." He rises and turns back to his friends, but the weight is still heavy on his heart, and he throws himself again upon his face. And he does it again, even a third time. There is also given us, in the narrative made out by Luke, the pathology of his feeling—"And being in an agony, he prayed more earnestly, and his sweat was, as it were, great drops of blood falling down to the ground." Which is the same as to say, that the agony of feeling he was in was so intense that, under the laws of bodily affection, there were forced out, through the pores of the skin, large drops resembled to blood. An ancient writer reports the fact of a bloody sweat, or a sweat exceeding like to blood, produced by the bite in India of a poisonous serpent, and the same thing is reported, I believe, as a result of certain bodily diseases that produce very intense suffering. But the symptom is none the less peculiar here, since it is not the effect of any poison, or physical pain, but of a purely mental anguish.

Thus far, as relates to the agony, or crisis of pain itself, reported in the narrative. Other points relating to his conduct in the scene, will come into view as we inquire into the causes of the agony, and need not be recited. Whence and why, this very strange crisis of mental anguish? According to a very common impression, as already intimated, the suffering has a judicial character, and is to be taken as a theologic factor, in a scheme of retributive justice. The conception is that Christ has somehow come into the place of transgressors, to receive upon his person what is due to them, and that God, accepting him in that office, launches upon him the abhorrence or displeasure, that is due to them; inflicting upon him, as it were, deserved pains, by withdrawing from him and letting fall upon him the horror of darkness under which he groans. The facts of the narrative have been so frequently, or even habitually, submitted to this construction, that our first concern will be to make a revision of the facts, ascertaining how far they give it their support.

Thus it is alleged, as a striking peculiarity of the scene, that the suffering appears, on a merely human footing, to be out of place. Before the arrest, in a quiet place out of the city, at a still hour of the night, when he has all his friends about him, and judging by outward tokens, has far less reason to apprehend violence from his enemies than he has had many times before—such is the time and place, where Jesus falls into his dreadful agony and great horror of distress. In which he certainly appears to be exercised in a way that is not human, invaded by a suffering that can not on mere human principles be accounted for. And this fact favors the conviction, it is imagined, that he suffers because some mysterious judicial infliction is descending upon him, from a source invisible. But such a conclusion is rather made up theologically for the scene, than drawn from the facts themselves. No single intimation of any such thing is, either contained in the facts, or given out by the narrative.

Again his language, in the figure of the "cup"—"if this cup may not pass away from me except I drink it"—is taken as favoring the idea of some suffering, in the nature of infliction. But do we not use the same kind of language ourselves, having still no such thought as that the cup of anguish we speak of, or pray to have taken away, is a judicial infliction? This figure too of the cup is used, in scripture, for all kinds of experience, whether joyful, or painful. Thus we have the "cup of salvation," "the cup of consolation," "the cup of trembling," "of fury," "of astonishment," "of desolation." Whatever God sends upon a man to be deeply felt, and by whatever kind of Providence, whether benignant, or disciplinary, or retributive, is called his cup. How then does it follow, when Christ speaks of his cup, that it is a cup of judicial chastening? Besides, does he not say to his followers—"ye shall indeed drink of my cup;" and is any thing more fixed in this penal view of Christ's agony, than that no human being can, at all, participate in such matter of atonement? And, that being true, his cup, as he himself speaks, can not, in this particular instance at least, have reference to any penal suffering, and probably has not in any other.

Again the agony is accounted for as having been caused by the judicial withdrawment of the Father; leaving him to feel the weight, in his human person, of that displeasure which is due to the sins of the world, now upon him. There is no intimation whatever, to this effect in the narrative, but his exclamation afterward, in the scene of the cross—"My God, my God, why hast thou forsaken me,"—is carried back to the agony to fix this construction upon it. But there is not the least reason to suppose that Christ means literally to say, in the exclamation referred to, that God has forsaken him. Did he not comfort himself but a short time previous, in the assurance—"therefore doth my Father love me, because I lay down my life for the sheep?" how then can he imagine that God is forsaking him, in just the sacrifice for which he loved him? Nay it was only an hour ago that he was saying, in the dearest confidence, and in tender appeal even to the Father—"I have glorified thee on the earth, and now I come to thee." Besides it is represented by Luke, in his account of the agony itself, that an angel is sent unto him to strengthen him; does God then send his angels to support whom he himself forsakes? And again, when he says in his prayer, three times repeated —"Not as I will but as thou wilt," what does he indicate, according to all human methods of judgment, but the dearest present confidence in God and repose in his favor? It must also be noted, again, that, between the agony and the crucifixion, and even before he leaves the garden, he formally declares just this confidence, saying—"Thinkest thou that I can not now pray to my Father, and he shall presently give me more than twelve legions of angels?" The whole account in short, is crowded full of the most decisive proofs that he does not himself imagine any such thing as that he is forsaken of God and judicially given up to suffering. Let it also be observed, that when he utters the cry, "why hast thou forsaken me," he is just reeling out of life; requiring his outcry therefore to be taken as a mere interjectional utterance of distress. Nothing could be further from him than to be protesting God's severity thus, in the article of death.

But he does it nevertheless, some one will say; for if we take his words interjectionally, why should he vent his sufferings by the outcry of what is not true? Because, I answer, the not true is often the most vehemently, best uttered truth. Thus when Jonathan and his armor bearer broke into the camp of the Philistines, the wild commotion, or panic, they two raised in the army, and the garrison, and all the people, is described by saying, "and the earth quaked; so there was a very great trembling." Does any one suppose that the earth really quaked on that occasion, or is it said only to set off the trembling? So when Paul, in the shipwreck, says, "not one hair of your head shall perish," it is not impossible that a good many hairs of the multitude were lost in their drifting ashore. He only said there should not, as a way of promising the safe landing more emphatically. Outcries too, of this kind are always to be taken freely, as the utterance of tragic feeling, or suffering, not as the language of historic allegation. Exactly so Zion cries in her distress, "the Lord hath forsaken me;" when immediately God answers, "I have graven thee upon the palms of my hands." It will be a great day, I must add, for the scriptures, when the dull soul of dogmatism has done with its undiscerning inflictions; when poetry is taken for poetry, passion for passion, and the hyperbolic intensities of interjection, never again for propositional statements.

I will further add what ought, by a short method, to finish the argument, apart from all criticism on the terms of the narrative, that the absolute morality of God makes any such withdrawment of the Father impossible. That eternal goodness should forsake goodness in suffering, and even to make it suffer, in a way of gaining ulterior ends or advantages however merciful, is to pawn the eternal chastities of character for ends of beneficence; which, as certainly as God is God, will never be done.

Dismissing now this artificial, over-theological, way

of conceiving the agony as a judicial infliction, let us endeavor

Secondly to find the spring of it, in a way that looks to the simple character and conditions of the sufferer himself. I greatly mistake, if it does not so become, at once, more intelligible, and as much more effective on our feeling, as it is closer to the range of our human sympathies.

That it is not resolvable into fear is, I think, sufficiently evident. It is quite incredible that a character of such transcendent worth and majesty should be thus appalled, thus miserably shaken, or dissolved, by fear of any kind. Besides, in fear the blood flies the skin, rushing back upon the heart, and leaving a deadly pallor over the whole exterior aspect; while here we have a kind of agony that racks the soul, in some way, at the very center of life, forcing the blood outward and driving it even through the skin. In which we may see as conclusively as possible, that fear, the common human weakness, had nothing to do with his suffering. It must also be noticed that the account given of his agony does not call it fear. It simply declares that he was sorrowful, "exceeding sorrowful," a state which has nothing to do with fear.

And yet he is shaken, somehow, in a degree that would not be considered honorable in a man of ordinary spirit, when about to die. Not only does the very great and wise man Socrates surpass him in the noble composure of his last hours, but thousands of malefactors even have received the sentence of death for their crimes, with a better show of serenity and self-possession.

We have a great matter then to account for, viz., that Jesus Christ, the incarnate Word of God, a being who has never had to acknowledge a sin, or had the feeling of it, a perfect character who has confronted every sort of peril in his works of mercy, one who shows the most perfect confidence in God and the final success of his cause, is yet somehow shaken by the most dreadful agony—rent as it were asunder, by his agitated sensibility—when he meets the prospect of death.

The first thing that occurs to us is that this agony can not be simply human. It visibly exceeds, in its degree, all that we know of human sensibility. Calling it then divine, if only we could think it possible for the divine sensibility to be a suffering sensibility, the question would begin to open. That this suffering sensibility should not fearfully wrench, and burden even to crushing, the human vehicle it occupies, is scarcely credible. A suffering that exceeds the proportions of the vehicle must needs appear by violent symptoms—even as a powerful engine in a frail, light-timbered vessel, must needs make it groan heavily, or shake it even to wreck.

What then is the fact? Is there any sensibility in God that can suffer? is He ever wrenched by suffering? Nothing is more certain. He could not be good, having evil in his dominions, without suffering even according to his goodness. For what is goodness but a perfect feeling? and what is a perfect feeling but that which feels toward every wrong and misery according to its nature? And thus it is that we freely impute to him, whether we observe it or not, every sort of painful sensibility that is related to bad and suffering subjects. We conceive of him as feeling displeasure, which is the opposite of pleasure. We ascribe it as one of his perfections that he compassionates, which means that he suffers with, the fallen. We conceive that he loathes what is disgusting, hates what is cruel, suffers long what is perverse, grieves, burns, bears, forbears, and is even afflicted for his people, as the scripture expressly declares. All which are varieties of suffering. We also ascribed it to God, as one of his perfections, that he is impassible; but here, if we understand ourselves, we mean that he is physically impassible, not that he is morally so. Moral impassibility is really to have no sensibilities of character, which is far as possible from being any perfection. Indeed there is a whole class of what are called passive virtues that can not, in this view, belong to God at all, and his perfection culminates without including more than half the excellencies demanded even of us, in the range of our humble, finite capacity.

There is then, we conclude, some true sense, in which even God's perfection requires him to be a suffering God—not a God unhappy, or less than perfectly, infinitely, blessed; for, though there be many subtractions from his blessedness, there is never a diminution; because the consciousness of suffering well brings with it, in every case and everlastingly, a compensation which, by a great law of equilibrium in his and all spiritual natures, fully repays the loss; just as Christ, assailed by so many throes of suffering sensibility—in the temptation, in his ministry, in the garden—still speaks of his joy, and bequeathes it as a gift most real and sublime to his followers.

Now it is this suffering sensibility of God that most of all needed to be revealed, and brought nigh to human feeling, in the incarnate mission of Jesus; not being revealed in any sufficient measure through nature and the providential history of men. It was necessary for us to feel God in his feeling, to know him in his passive virtues—his patience, forbearance of enemies, compassion, pity, sympathy, and above all, his deep throes of love, agonizing for the salvation of transgressors and wanderers from his fold. This, accordingly, is just what we are to look for in the agony so called, viz., a true discovery to our hearts of God's intensity and depth, in those suffering virtues by which his transcendently sovereign nature is exercised.

Christ then, we shall expect to find, suffers in his agony, not because it is put upon him judicially from without, but only as his better nature should and must in the crisis that has overtaken him. Not to particularize further, two great sources, or causes of anguish open upon him at once; firstly the chastity of his pure feeling recoils, with horror, from the hell-gulf of wrong and wild judicial madness into which he is now descending; and secondly the love he has for his enemies brings a burden of concern upon his heart, that oppresses and, for the time, well nigh crushes him. Of these two modes or kinds of anguish I will speak in their order.

Christ, is a being of unsullied innocence, or even of divine purity, though incarnated into the corporate evil and retributive disorder of the world, to bear its liabilities and be himself a part of it. This retributive disorder of the race is what is called in scripture "the curse;" and, being himself a man, he is just so far in it as he is human. In all his previous ministry—in his temptation, in his healings, in the arts of hypocrisy and the cruelties of wrong he has encountered, he has been struggling often with the sense of recoil, or even with pungent visitations of horror difficult to be suppressed. But now, as he nears the great crisis of his life, he beholds the corporate evil, or curse, gathering itself up to a deed upon his sacred person, that will display just all that is most horrible in it. He is not afraid, but his pure feeling shudders at the madness which is ready to burst upon him—shudders even the worse that it is to be judicial madness. For, though God is not going to deal judicially with him, he does perceive that the rage of sin, ordinarily restrained and graciously softened by God's Spirit, is now to be let forth in his betrayers and crucifiers, in just the madness that judicially belongs to it—so to glass itself before conviction, in a deed of murder upon the only perfect being that ever trod the world, nay a deed of murder upon divine love itself! This it is that, in sad note of warning, he testifies, when his enemies come shortly after, to arrest him—"For this is your hour, and the power of darkness." He refers to no power of darkness, as many contrive to understand, upon himself; it is darkness upon them, his enemies—judicial darkness, the full, unmitigated, natural curse of wrong. This is "the cup" over which he groans, and which he is now to drink; the wormwood and the vinegar of the world's wild malice. The suffering and death are penal upon him, only in the sense that all martyrs suffer penally, when the corporate judgments of God upon their wicked times and wicked fellow-men, infuriate and even dehumanize their natural feeling. But the martyrs are sinners, suffering as such at the point of their faith; he is the sinless, suffering at the point of his innocence. They suffer as men, still bronzed in their susceptibility, by the old demoralization of sin; he as the celestial one, and as a pure superhuman feeling must. The recoil of his horror is dreadful, quite unimaginable probably by us, and his poor human vehicle breaks under the shock, even as a stranded ship under the heavy blows of the sea. He groans aloud, falls upon his face, calls to his friends to stay by him, utters anguished cries to God, shows discolored drops resembled to blood exuding from his face—suffers in a word more incontinently, a great deal, than either soldier, philosopher, or man of spirit should, nay than many a malefactor would! And so, it truly seems to me, that he ought: for who of all mankind had ever a tithe of his sensibility to evil. Indeed one of the most difficult things for us mortals is to be duly shocked by wrong and feel a just horror of its baseness. Impassive to fear, even as God himself, he is yet wrenched all through, in every fiber of sensibility, by the appalling and practically monstrous scene before him—human creatures!—creatures in God's image!—going to crucify their Divine Friend from above!—God's messenger and their Saviour! By their bloody hands he is himself to die! Verily it is given unto men to die, but ah! it was not given unto him. Death has no rights against him. Nothing but the corporate liability of his incarnation puts him under it. He shudders in throes of recoil, even as God's pure angels would, meeting such a death; nay more and worse, as he has a vaster nature, and a deeper sensibility, with only a human apparatus to support the shock!

Now this suffering of the agony is the suffering, in one sense, of justice, answering doubtless many of the uses conceived by those who contrive to make it a suffering divinely inflicted. It is a suffering that he undergoes in God's retributive order. In one view it is the curse that murders him, being that power of darkness and corporate evil that has come upon the world, as disordered and shaken out of God's harmony, by the recoil of transgression. His very incarnation had put him into or under it, and he would not even by the power of miracle push the liability away; for it was one of his purposes to offer such a tribute of respect to God's retributive order, as would sanctify it in the feeling, and fix it in the convictions of mankind. Thus, by his power of miracle, he could have made to himself a *testudo*, so to speak, of inviolable protection against the rage of his enemies, but he preferred instead to suffer just what men are suffering, in that penal disorder and social dislocation, which God, in judgment, has appointed for the fact of sin. It was in his heart to let God's justice have its due honors, breaking out, at no one point, from the fiery liability into which he had come, in becoming a man. He consented thus to let the hell which scorches wrong scorch him too, claiming no exception even for his innocence. Behold, he would say, O man, God's sacrament of wrath that is on thee, revealed by the wrath its poison stirs within thee; and because it is the ordinance of his justice, bear witness that I spurn it not, neither ask that my integrity excuse me from it! Sacred it shall be because it is right; and being for man as man, a power of darkness for all sin, I will take the bitter cup for thy sake! Only this be noted, since the malediction working in thee will not suffer even goodness to live, how certain it is that blindness, madness, murder, all that is called hell, goes with thy sin, whose eternally just and sufficient penalty it is that it shall live in its own fires, and be itself!

After such a tribute paid to the instituted justice of God, who will imagine that the forgiveness of penitent souls will loosen the joints of governmental order? By this submission of Christ to man's curse or lot of penalty—penalty in no other sense to him—an impression will be made for God's justice, and a sting of conviction sharpened against sin, that will even start a new sense of his law, and the penal order of his rule in the hearts of all mankind. Even as Christ himself anticipated when he said—"Of sin because they believed not on me." Also as it was anticipated for him that under and by his suffering mission, "the thoughts of many hearts should be revealed." And again, still further back, in the ancient prophecy—"They shall look on me whom they have pierced." All which was to be signally proved by the result of his crucifixion—"And all the people that came together to that sight, beholding the things which were done, smote their breasts and returned." When had they ever felt the horrible nature and the justly damning power of their sin as now?

It remains to speak of yet another and very distinct kind of suffering included in the agony, viz., the suffering Christ bore on account of his love. As he recoiled in horror from the spirit and deed of his enemies, so he was oppressed by his anguish of concern for the men. He had come into the world, in the fullness even of God's love, to unbosom that love to the sight and feeling of mankind. As respects all enemies and rejectors, it had been a suffering love even from eternity, and it will be none the less a suffering love that it has taken humanity for its vehicle. Every sort of love connects some kind of suffering greater or less—desire, concern, affliction, anguish. A bliss in itself, it is even a bliss intensified, by the burden it so willingly or even painfully bears. Thus it is that friendship, charity, motherhood, patriotism, carries each its burden, light or heavy, according to the nature and degree of its love and according to the want, or woe of its object. What then must the feeling of Christ be, when he looks upon his enemies in the near prospect of death at their hands—death horrible to him, and a sacrilegious murder in them. If the great liberator Moses, discouraged and crushed in feeling by the perversity of his people, cried —"I am not able to bear all this people alone, because it is too heavy for me, and if thou deal thus with me kill me;" if Paul, himself a man, was constrained, by the burden of a man's love, to say—"I have great heaviness and continued sorrow in my heart; for I could wish that myself were accursed from Christ, for my brethren, my kinsmen according to the faith;" who shall wonder at the anguish of Christ's burden, when he bows himself under it to the ground, when he calls it his "cup," when he cries, "my soul is exceeding sorrowful even unto death?" If the love of a human benefactor will sometimes beget anguish, what will the love of God do less than to create an agony?

And yet how little will our dull-hearted world bronzed in evil, habitually unloving, unvisited or seldom visited, by a consciously tender compassion; how little, indeed, will the most unselfish, or even beneficently Christian of us, conceive this agony of the divine love for men! Our hearts make feeble answer to it at the best; so feeble that there even seems to be a kind of overdoing, or overfeeling in it. Indeed we are even wont ourselves, for dignity's sake, to halve our own little emotion; and we do the same unconsciously for the emotion of God; halving it also again, by the consideration here let in, that his love is only love to transgressors and enemies. Ah! if we could think it, that is just the fact, in which God's love becomes an agony; leaving, as it were, the ninety and nine of his friends, to go after that one who has gone astray, and rejoicing more over that, as he has felt the loss with a more painful concern. God's love has no burden of pain for the good; it sharpens to a pain only when it looks upon the evil. And here precisely is the stress of Christ's agony.

When I consider thus who Christ was, what the love he bore, what the crime his enemies were going to perpetrate, invoking, in horrible delusion, his blood upon themselves and their children; I seem to get some little, dim, conception of his anguish for them, in this dreadful hour. I can not go to the depth of it, I can not ascend to the height of it, but I can perceive why it should transcend my feeling and even the possible reach of my conceptions. It is even the more credible too that its tokens do so plainly exceed all human demonstrations. The most adequate and complete thing we can say of it is, that it reveals the Suffering Holiness of God.

The reason of the agony then—this is our conclusion—lies in the facts themselves; in the sensibilities of the sufferer and the causes acting on those sensibilities. No theologic reason, such as makes him suffer by infliction, or by the judicial forsaking of God, has even a tolerable pretext, aside from the theory that makes up such a construction for its own sake. Even the justice of God is more adequately impressed and set before the world more convincingly, without any so revolting conception, than with it. Never was there made before such an expression of God's abhorrence to sin, as in this recoil of Christ's agony from it; never such honor put upon God's instituted justice, as in Christ's submission to the corporate woe and penal madness of it. Never was the horrible nature of sin so revealed to human conviction, as by this agony of compassion, on one side, met by such judicial blindness and even phrenzied malice, on the other.

Can there now my friends, be any thing more strange than that multitudes of you, having had full time to ponder this scene, and take its meaning after the fact, should still adhere to your sin, nay should even be quite insensible to it and the feeling of God concerning it. Beholding this immense sensibility of God, you still have none! O it is even appalling! Rightly conceiving such a fact, you would even start from yourself! Were you called by some angel, in the brightness of the sun, or by voices of thunder in the clouds, it would signify much less; but that you should not feel the silent call of God's feeling ought to make you think even with dread of yourself. When the Christ of Gethsemane meets you bathed in the sad drops of his divine sorrow, there certainly ought, if there be any feeling left, to be some answering sorrow in you. Is there still none? What a relation this between your sensibility and goodness—functional death, lying as a rock in

Gethsemane, feeling as little that horror of sin, softened as little by that sorrowing love! O thou highly gifted creature, what kind of attainment hast thou made!

The lessons derivable to us, my brethren, from this subject are many; I can only call attention specially to this one, that as Christ suffers in his agony, not by the forsaking of God, not by any kind of infliction making compensation to eternal justice, but naturally, because of his character, and the crisis into which he has come, so there will be times and conditions where we shall suffer in like manner, according to our measures, and the degree of our likeness to him. Purity in us will shudder, love in us will bear its burden of sorrow. It is no presumption or profanation for us to think of being with him in his passion, we shall even require it of ourselves, as a necessary Christian evidence. Even as he himself declares—"ye shall indeed drink of my cup." Not that we are to be as deep in the pains of holy sensibility as he—that is impossible. Not that we are to make a point of suffering much, and be always talking of some dreadful burden that is on us, and having it as a point of merit to be always in a groaning testimony. Christ did not make a three-years' funeral of his ministry. Once he had a heavy struggle of temptation, telling never a word about it but the close. Once, and again, he wept. Once he declared that his soul was troubled. Once he fell into an agony, and was very soon through with it. It was never his way to suffer more than he must, or to call for sympathy by a show of his sorrows. On the other hand, no disciple is to make a merit of being always floated in a luxury of bliss, as if the gospel had no purpose more rugged and practical than simply to beget an elysian frame. Much less may a disciple think it well that he suffers nothing, or is never overcast in his feeling, when the simple reason is that his soul is cased in the indifference of sloth and worldly living. No pangs of life are suffered by the dead! As certainly as your Master's love is in you, his work will be upon you. His objects will be yours, and also his divine burden. And sometimes that burden will be heavy. If your heart grows pure, it will just so far be shocked and revolted by the wrath and wrong of evil-doers. As certainly as you have feeling, you will have the pains of feeling. Expect to have your part then with Jesus in his Gethsemane. Come in freely hither, tarry ye here and watch. Out of his agony learn how to bear an enemy; what to do for your enemies and God's. If your intercessions sometimes turn to groans, if you sometimes wonder that being a Christian you are yet so heavily, painfully, burdened, almost crushed with concern for such as you are trying to save, let your comfort be that so you drink indeed your Master's cup. If your love is repelled with scorn, and your good work baffled, and your heart grows heavy under sorrow and discouragement—ready to sink under its load—come hither and pray with Jesus in his sweat of blood, "let this cup pass from me." If wickedness grows hot in malice round you, if conspiracy and violence array themselves against you, go apart into this Gethsemane of your

Lord's troubles, and be sure that some good angel shall be sent to strengthen you; is not Christ's heart wringing for you more bitterly than yours for itself—tarry ye here and watch. If some demon of impatience whispers, here or there, "why not give it up?" behold the agonizing obedience of Christ, faithful unto death, and say, with him, "not as I will but as thou wilt." Look for no mere holiday of frames, but for such kind of joy as a heart may yield that is many times broken by sacrifice. Behold your Master prostrate on the ground, and by his agony and bloody sweat, be girded for a passion of your own. Consent with Christ to suffer; and when having gotten his victory, he says "rise, let us be going," go, not faltering, even though he lead you to the cross.

XII.

THE PHYSICAL SUFFERING, OR CROSS OF CHRIST.

For it became him, for whom are all things, and by whom are all things, in bringing many sons unto glory, to make the captain of their salvation perfect through sufferings.—HEB. ii, 10.

It is a fact worthy of distinct notice, that our apostle is here making answer to the very same question that Anselm propounded for settlement, a thousand years afterward, in his very famous treatise, the *Cur Deus Homo?* And despite of the very great admiration won by this treatise, I feel obliged to suffer an impression, that the apostle has greatly the advantage; writing out his answer with a freer hand, and a far more piercing insight, and presenting, in fact, the whole subject more adequately, in a single sentence, than the much venerated father was able to do in the high theological endeavor of his volume.

In the verse previous to this sentence, which is my text, finding Jesus made a little lower than the angels, and, for the suffering of death, crowned with glory and honor, it is as if his mind began to ask, even as

Anselm did, why should he suffer thus, or come, in the way of suffering, at all? why could not God, the Almighty, strike out the needed salvation by a shorter method, without suffering, viz., by his omnipotent force? Whereupon he makes answer, virtually, that force is out of the question; because the needed salvation is a purely moral result, which can be accomplished only by moral means and motives—"For it became Him"—it was even a fixed necessity upon Him, the Almighty—"for whom are all things, and by whom are all things, in the bringing of many sons unto glory, to make the captain of their salvation perfect through sufferings."

The words *bringing* and *captain*, here occurring, have a relationship in the original, which would not be suspected, and which disappears in the English; as if we should read—"in the bringing on of many sons unto glory, to make the bringer on" &c. There is no importance however in this reading, such as might be supposed, for a captain is a leader and bringer on of course; only we conceive the passage more fitly, if the family relationship of the two words is understood. The declaration is, and that is the matter of chief importance, that God, the Almighty, must needs work morally in such a case, and not by force: and that Christ, the leader, is made perfect, or perfectly competent, as regards the moral new creation, or bringing up unto glory, by his cross and the tragic eloquence of his death.

That we may fully develop the apostle's meaning in

this general announcement, and verify it in the orderly exposition of the points included under it, let us begin at the question where he appears to have begun himself; viz., *why should Christ, in the redeeming of souls, and bringing them unto glory, subject himself to physical suffering?—what, in other words, were the necessities and uses of that suffering?*

I confine the question here, it will be observed, to his physical suffering. He encountered two distinct kinds of suffering, as we commonly use the term, viz., mental suffering, and bodily suffering; that which belongs to burdened feeling and wounded sensibility, and that which is caused by outward privation, or violence done against the physical nature; that which appears more especially in the agony, and that which appears in the death of the cross. The former kind of suffering I believe is never called suffering in the New Testament, but a being *grieved;* a *bearing*, or a *burden*, as in sympathy and loving concern; a being *troubled in spirit*, or *very heavy; sorrow; agony.* The word *suffering* is applied, meantime, I think, only to physical suffering; and was doubtless used by the apostle, in the present instance, as relating to Christ's physical suffering only.

It is obvious enough then, at the outset, and as the first thing to be noted, that physical suffering, taken by itself, or as being simply what it is in itself, is never a thing of value. On the contrary it is, so far, a thing on the losing side of existence, a subtraction from the general sum of good. It will not help a friend, or feed an enemy, or stop a fire, or cool a fever. To the sufferer himself, looking never to any thing beyond it, or consequent upon it, but simply at what it is, it has no inherent value, like wheat and wool, and no market value, like gold. It is not, in fact, a commodity of any kind, exchangeable or not exchangeable, but a simple incommodity—a quantity purely negative and a worse than worthless fact.

And the same exactly is true of Christ's suffering. Taken as physical pain simply, nothing is to be made of it. All the worse and more deplorable is the loss or negation of it, that it is a suffering which has no relation to personal desert; and still more deplorable in the fact that, regarding the divine order of the sufferer, it is even a shocking anomaly, which reason can not comprehend and faith only can accept. God certainly did not want it as wanting to get so much suffering out of somebody. He does not exact a retributive suffering, even in what is called his justice, because he wants so much in quantity to even the account of wrong, but only that he may vindicate the right and testify his honor to it by a fit expression. Nothing could be more horrible, or closer akin to blasphemy, than to say that God wants pain for his own feeling's sake; or because he is hungry for that particular kind of satisfaction. We have it as a proverb, that "revenge is sweet;" but I recollect no proverb which avers that justice is sweet; because the mind of justice is a right mind, as the mind of revenge is not; and, being right, no pain is sweet to it, not even that which chastises injustice and sin. Besides, there is, it is agreed, no justice in the pains of Christ, as being due on his own account; and it ought to be as well agreed that God could not take them as compensations on account of others. That would be taking them as actual somethings, or quantities having value in themselves, when, in fact, they have, as we have seen, no value at all. Nay worse, if God takes them, he gets only incommodities for his satisfaction, and makes a gain that is purely harm and loss.

But some one will object in the question—are not the physical sufferings of Christ what are called, in the scripture, his sacrifice for sin? and what is the use of sacrifice but to atone God's justice? I do not understand the scripture to speak of suffering and sacrifice in that manner. Thus we hear an apostle say—"made perfect through sufferings"—for what made perfect? for the satisfying of God's justice? No, but "to bring many souls unto glory?" "Lamb of God that taketh away"—what? the pains of justice? No, but "the sins of the world." "Who his own self bare our sins in his own body on the tree"—for what end? that God might be satisfied with his pains? No, but "that we being dead unto sin, should live unto righteousness;" "By whose stripes"—what of the stripes? do they pay off the release of ours?—"by whose stripes ye were healed." "For Christ also hath once suffered for sins, the just for the unjust"—in what view? to satisfy the justice of God? no, but "to bring us unto God." All the lustral figures—those of washing, purging, sprinkling, purifying, cleansing—set forth the sacrifice in the same manner, not as a way of reconciling God to us, but of reconciling us to God. And so universally—I do not know the instance where Christ's cross and physical suffering are conceived as a making satisfaction to God's justice.

Regarding Christ's sufferings then as having no value in themselves, on the ground of which they may be accepted as compensations to justice, we must not leap to the conclusion that Christ could do nothing in a way of bringing men to God, without such sufferings. He could even have been incarnated into the world, in such a way as to involve no physical liability at all. He might even have been incarnated, I suppose, into the family of Cæsar, and strid into his mission, as a prince iron-clad, in all the dignities and immunities of the Empire. He might have taught the same doctrine, omitting only his call to take up the cross, which he taught as the son of Mary. He might have healed as great multitudes, with as kind a sympathy. He might even have been followed, if he chose, by trains of great people, as he was by the humble and the poor, dining at their tables, lodging in their palaces, receiving all the while the highest honors of genius. Or if it should be imagined that, teaching faithfully the same principles, and rebuking the same sins, and offering himself to men as the incarnate Word and Lord, he must of necessity provoke the hatred of enemies, and stir up powerful conspiracies of violence and bigot zeal, what suffering could they bring upon him, armed as he was with miracle, strongly enough even to have routed the Roman army? As the *posse* that went out to arrest him could not strengthen their knees to stand, or their hands to seize, but fell backward on the ground even as moths fall off from flames they attack; as the money-changers and trafficking priests fled away before him, taken by a strange panic that no single man ever raised before; so he could have withered Caiaphas by a look, and dashed his accusers away, as a rock tosses off the sea; making Pilate's wife dream a great deal worse dreams than she did, and causing the poor servile magistrate himself to be a good deal "more afraid" than he was; and as to being gibbeted on the cross, if the conspiracy could have gone so far, he probably enough could have changed the wood into water, as he did the water into wine. There was, in short, no necessary condition of physical suffering implied in his Messiahship. He probably could not have been as complete a Saviour without physical suffering, but he could have been a wonderfully great character and beneficent teacher, as clear of spot or stain, as true in his truth, as wise in his wisdom, as evidently, and some would say, a great deal more evidently, divine.

If then Christ's physical sufferings, taken as such, had no value, and if he could have been incarnated in the human state without suffering—doing and teaching, to a great extent, the same things—why did he come under conditions of suffering, what uses did he expect to serve by it, such as would compensate the loss? It was done I answer, that he might be made perfect by such suffering—perfect, that is, not in his character, but in his official competency; perfect as having gotten power over men, through his sufferings, to be the sufficient bringer on, or captain, he undertakes to be, in bringing many sons unto glory.

Does he then, it may be asked, undertake the suffering as having that for his object or as consenting to it for effect's sake? He of course knows that he will suffer, and how, and when, and by whom, and with what result, but he does not fall into the weakness of those partly fanatical martyrs who undertook the particular merit of being somehow murdered. Coming down to do a work of love, he simply took the liabilities of a human person doing such a work. He was not ignorant of the immense value or power of a right and great suffering, as regards the possible effect of it, and as sin would certainly be exasperated by his goodness, and drag him down to suffering, he meant beforehand to make it a right and great suffering, and so to win dominion by it. He suffered understandingly, therefore, as the Lamb that was slain from the foundation of the world, though not as aiming to get himself afflicted, or to make an ostentation of being wronged.

What, then, we have now to look after, is the manner and degree of that power over men's convictions and feelings, which Christ obtained by his physical suffering. And the points to which I call your attention are such as these.

1. The manner in which, by his physical suffering, he

magnifies and sanctifies the law in men's convictions. This in fact was a kind of first point to be carried in getting the necessary power over fallen minds. The speculation that requires him to suffer in a way of helping God to justify himself in the forgiveness of sins, before certain great judicial minds in other worlds and spheres, is a speculation that to say the least travels far, and the scripture gives it no help. The true Christian idea appears to be that Christ is magnifying the law, and making it honorable, not before the remote altitudes, but before the sinning souls of this world by whom it has been trampled. How else shall they ever be regained? God is an essentially practical and not a romantic being. He will not concern himself about the figure he makes in the forgiveness of sins, before the outlying populations of his realm, if only he can bring transgressors down to ask forgiveness here on earth, by making the pinnacles of order smoke before their guilty consciences.

See then how he does it in the matter of Christ's physical suffering. He came into the world with a perfect right to be exempted from such suffering. There is nothing in his character to require this kind of discipline, or even to make it just. He also had power to put all suffering by, and sail over the world as the stars do, in a region of calm and comfort above it. He could have exorcised the wild hate of his enemies, as he did the poor lunatics of the Gergesenes. By his power of miracle, if not without, he could have driven Pilate and his accusers out of the judgment-hall into the street, passing intact through all the conspiracies of his enemies, even as Moses passed through the sea. But he would not so far infringe on the penal order of God's retributions. Looking on society, in its madness against him and against the truth, as grinding in God's mill of retribution, swayed, and rent and tortured by exasperating causes in the guilt of its own transgression, he refuses to take himself out of the general torment. Having taken humanity, he takes all the judicial liabilities of human society under sin, preferring, in this manner, to submit himself to the corporate order of God's judgments, and testify in that manner, his profound homage to law and justice. He will not so much as parry any one of the bad causations loosened by sin. He will let the world be to him just that river of vinegar and gall which its sins have made it to itself. So he bears the world's bitter curse, magnifying, even by his pains, the essential sanctity of law and justice.

He suffers nothing as from justice to himself, and therefore makes no satisfaction to the justice of God. But he powerfully honors that justice in its dealings with the world, by refusing to let even his innocence take him out of the murderous and bloody element it mixes. Hence the marvelous, unheard of power his life and gospel, and especially his suffering death, have exerted in men's consciences. His suffering has this wonderful divine art in it, that it sanctifies both forgiveness and justice, and makes them common factors of good, in the conscience of all transgression.

2. The physical suffering of Christ has an immediate value, under that great law of human nature, that ordains the disarming of all wrong, and the prostration of all violence, by a right suffering of the evils they inflict. Nothing breaks the bad will of evil so completely, as to have had its way, and done its injury, and looked upon its victim. And if the victim, suffering even the worst it could do, still lives unvanquished, the defeat is only a more absolute and stunning paralysis. Thus in the bitting of horses, the animal champs the bit as if he would crush it, and throws himself on the rein as if he would snap it, till finding that he only worries and galls himself, he at last gives way to what has not given way to him, and so is tamed, or, as we say, broken to the rein. So when the wrath of transgression hurls itself upon the Lord's person, sparing not his life, nor even letting him die easily or in respect, the bad will is only the more fatally broken that, accomplishing so much in a way so dreadful, it has yet accomplished nothing. It has mocked him, tortured him, thrust him out of life, only to find him still alive and see him go up to reign! In one view it has succeeded against him, and he has been seemingly crushed under the heel of its malignity. It has pierced the noblest heart and seen it bleed. It has finished the worst, most shocking, deed of murder ever conceived, And yet that murdered one still lives and loves! How dreadfully crest-fallen now and weak is that bad will, how nearly slain itself by what it has done! Nay, to have only spent so great malignity, and come to the

point of exhaustion, would produce a nearly mortal weakness. Suffering kills, how often, the wrong-doing that inflicts it. The man of blood who looks upon his murdered enemy is disarmed by the sight. Even if there seemed to have been some provocation, how tender, and soft, and low-spoken, how visibly gentled in feeling is he, standing in the room where his lifeless adversary lies! That dead face looks imploringly up to him, and his fire is extinguished by natural relentings. How much more when the murdered one is a friend inherently good, bearing a much honored name and great; how much more, if he is the incarnate Son of God; still more, if he is not only killed, but crucified, hung up thus to be looked upon depending from his cross—sad, broken flower, which the spite of so great beauty has plucked! O how weak, irresolute, guilt-broken, now, is all sin, when confronted by that suffering goodness which reveals at once, both its spite and its impotence! "I am Jesus of Nazareth whom thou persecutest"—How piercing is the word!

3. The sublime morality, or moral worth of Jesus, could never have been sharply impressed, except for the sensibilities appealed to by his physical suffering. If he had come as one born of a good family, if he had been a considerable owner of real estate, if he had made his journeys in a chariot, lodging, at night, with distinguished senators and persons of consideration, if he had been a great scholar among the Rabbis, or had been familiar to the people in the livery of a judge, or a priest, winning great popularity by the profuseness

of his charities, and exciting even applause by his attention to low people and his tender ministry to their diseases; dying finally by some of the modes that are common, to be followed to his burial by multitudes that come to weep their loss at his grave—if, I say, he had lived in condition, and died as one admired for his excellence, the real depth of his virtue could never even have been conceived. He would only have been looked upon as fulfilling the type of a graciously benevolent gentleman, and described as the John Joseph Gurney of his time. No, it was only as he waived the honors of condition in his birth, and the comforts of property in his life, became a footman, hungered often, slept under the sky shivering with cold, spent himself daily in exhausting sympathies and got almost no sympathy in return, met the looks of crafty messengers and spies on every side, and scarcely found a place, except in the lone recesses of the mountains, where his ear was not all day, perhaps all night, saluted by the carping sounds of bigot voices quarreling with his doctrine, ending finally his hunted, hated, weary life, by a slave's death on the cross—this too, even for enemies, as truly as for his friends—it is here that we begin to really look down into the deeps of his great bosom, deeps holy and divine, that no mortal plummet has sounded! And so he is made perfect through sufferings, able to wake a sense in our bosoms of what love is, quickening thoughts in us that are new, opening sensibilities never before consciously opened. All the most effective powers, in short, of moral impression, contained in his character, would have been wanting, if he had not borne the lot of wrong and bitter suffering.

4. It is only by his suffering in the flesh that he reveals or fitly expresses the suffering sensibility of God. As certainly as God has any sensibility, such as belongs to a perfect mind and heart, that sensibility must be profoundly moved by all misery, impurity and wrong. Impassible, physically speaking, he is not impassive to evils that offend, or grieve, his moral perfections. Indeed his vast and glorious nature is, in this view, nothing but an immense sensibility, whose dislikes, disgusts, indignations, revulsions of pity, wounded compassions, afflicted sympathies, pains of violated tenderness, wrongs of ingratitude, are mingling and commingling, as cups of gall, for the pure good feeling of his breast. So far he suffers because he is a perfect being, and according to the measure of his perfection. Why if he could not hate what is hateful, pity what is pitiful, mourn for the hopeless, burn against the cruel, scent the disgusts of the impure—if all bad things and all good were just alike to him, what is he better than granite or ice? No, the glorious, all-moving fact is, that there is a great sensibility at the head of the worlds, and a mental suffering as great, when the worlds go wrong!

This accordingly it is, that we, as sinners, need most of all to know and to feel, and this that Christ, for our salvation's sake, has taken the flesh and suffered even death, to impress. Nature, in her scenes and objects, had no power to express this moral pain of God's heart.

The ancient providential history was trying always vainly to elaborate the same; testifying, in almost every chapter, of God's sorrows, griefs, repentings, loathings, displeasures, and his afflictions over the afflicted. Nothing could ever express it but the physical suffering of Jesus. Here, for the first time, a vehicle is found that will sufficiently bring home to our guilty feeling God's wounded feeling, and put us in real acquaintance with that suffering state of love, which his unseen goodness feels.

And every thing turns here, you will perceive, on the matter of physical suffering; for, to our coarse human habit, nothing else appears, at first, to have much reality. In the agony, for example, the real suffering is mental, and the great struggle, a struggle purely of feeling. But if it were not for the physical symptoms attendant, the prostrations, the audible groans, and above all, the body dripping, in blood-like drops, forced through the skin by the pains of the mind—were it not for these physical tokens we should get no impression of a suffering sensibility, that would be of much account. We should only look on drowsily, doubting probably how much, or what kind of, reality there may be in this rather dull scenic of the gospels!

And here is the precise relation of the agony and the cross. One is the reality, the other is the outward sign or symbol. Having all the mental sensibility Christ has regarding our sin, and shame, and wrong, and fearfully lost state, he still needs to be made perfect through physical sufferings, or by these to have his higher sensibility brought forth into power. He is perfect before, in all the pains of his perfect sensibility, but to our coarse, sensuous, undiscerning habit, there is nothing of much meaning in him, till we watch him undergoing his murder! This physical suffering we can understand; the other is a great way off and very dim.

In one view it is even a scandal that we make so much more of the cross than we do of the agony. And yet the cross was appointed for the culminating point of the gospel, partly in a way of condescension to our lowness and the want of our coarseness, and is really the greater for that reason. The grand thing to be revealed is that which stands in the agony; and the superior value of the cross, or physical suffering, lies in the fact that it comes to us, at our low point, speaking to us of the other, in a way that we can feel. When we look on Jesus suspended by nails through his hands and feet, and set up to die a slow death, in delirium and thirst and fever, we do have raised in our bosoms a little natural sensibility. And, taken hold of by that, our apprehensions will perhaps be sufficiently fixed, at last, to let us in where that deeper, and warmer, and more agonizing, sensibility heaves unseen in the mental compassions of God!

Let us not be too much taken, my friends, by the typology in which our gospel is here and there so feebly and pretensively dressed—the low perceptions, and the short culture, always putting their cheap honors and ornaments upon it. I speak not here of the cross set up as a symbol on our peaks of architecture, worn upon the person, painted on the banners of the religion itself; but I speak of the crucifixes, and the carefully carved distresses of the dying Lord, the droppings of blood, the contortions of form, the pallors of death so elaborately painted, and the generally overdone studies of art, by which Christ's dying woe is magnified as being, not the sign, but the all of his suffering. The very shallow, feeble, look of such art, the want of all high insight in it, is abundantly mortifying. There is scarcely a doubt that Christ suffered more intensely in the agony, where the pain was wholly mental, than he did upon the cross. Even the external signs appear to indicate as much. In the same way too, his chief suffering, on the cross, was probably mental and not bodily. For some reason, his suffering on the cross was so much more severe than that of the malefactors crucified with him, that he died whole hours before them; not because they did not suffer as great physical pain as he, but because he had a moral sensibility so vast, a horror of wrong so deep, a concern of love for his enemies so wrenched with agony, that his heart broke and his breath stopped, as it were before the time. This now—would that we could think it—was the real suffering to him! and the physical suffering of the cross was probably a matter of consequence to him principally in the fact that, considering our low, dull, habit, there might be force enough in it to initiate, or prick in, as it were, some faint impression of the other. And this it is, this only, that makes it a salvation. It is a cross before the eyes, for beings that live in their eyes, and are too coarse to apprehend the spiritual things of God in a spiritual manner—in that way a type of the more wondrous and tremendous cross that is hid in God's perfections from eternity. O, it is for this, to make sin feel this unseen, tender, sensibility, this pain of goodness, this fatherhood of sorrow—this it is that Christ has undertaken to impress, and for this end he is made perfect through sufferings. Once more—

5. It was necessary that Christ should suffer in the body, and get power over men by that kind of suffering, because the world itself is put in a tragic economy, requiring its salvation to be an essentially tragic salvation. God has made the world, we all agree, for the great sentiments it will organize and bring into play, and souls themselves to be lifted by that play, in those great sentiments. Hence the wonderful affinity of our human nature for the tragic exaltations.

There may have been a prior necessity that a free moral kingdom should include peril, disorder, suffering, great struggles to escape great woes, sacrifices in the good, wrongs suffered by the good, to regain and restore the evil; in other words, there may have been a prior necessity that the plan of God's moral universe should be essentially tragic in the cast of it. But, whatever may be true in this respect, we can see, every man for himself, that so it is. No merely fine sentiment, or morally high, is quite sufficient for us. The festive, the gay, the triumphal, the melo-dramatic tenderness, the pastoral sweetness, the flutes of domestic arbors, the gongs of public liberty—none of these quite satisfy, not even the mighty love-passion strikes our highest cords of tension till it draws blood! Blood! blood! we must have blood! Human history therefore moves on trailing in blood, tragic in its characters, and scenes, and its material generally.

The great crimes are tragic, and the great virtues scarcely less so. The tribunals sprinkle their gate-posts with blood. The stormy passions, honor, jealousy, and revenge, are letting blood in all ages; and the little ones of trust, and truth, and worth, do the bleeding. And then all the epics and romances, and a great part of the world's poetry go on to add imaginary pangs and troubles, and torture us still more with bloody felicities that are fictitious. Practically the world has a general fashion of suffering. Right is trampled everywhere, goodness fights with wrong, nations fall, heroes bleed, and all great works are championed by suffering. Some Prometheus, torn by his eagle, bleeds painfully on every rock waiting to be loosed from his chain. So if Christ will pluck away eternal judgment for the world, he must bleed for it. So great a salvation must tear a passage into the world by some tragic woe—without shedding of blood there is no remission.

This blood—O, it is this that has a purifying touch, working lustrally, as the divine word conceives, on all the stains of our sin, washing us, making us clean, sprinkling even our evil conscience. This tragic power of the cross takes hold, in other words, of all that is dullest, and hardest, and most intractable, in our sin, and moves our palsied nature, all through, in mighty throbs of life.

And this is Christianity; meeting us just where we most require to be met. Christ is a great bringer on for us, because he suffers for us. Christianity is a mighty salvation, because it is a tragic salvation. Why my friends, if it were not for this generally tragic way in things about us, and especially in religion, I fear that we should have a more dull time of it than we think. Indeed I suspect that even the same is true of the general universe—it probably is and is forever to be an essentially tragic universe. With a fall and an overspreading curse at the beginning, and a cross in the middle, and a glory and shame at the end, where souls struggle out, through perils, and pains, and broken chains, or bear their chains away unbroken still and still to be—how moving, and mighty, and high, must be the sentiment of it! O how grandly harrowing is that joy, how tremulous in tragic excitement is that song of ascription, roaring as a sea-surge round the throne—"unto him that loved us, and washed us, from our sins in his blood!"

Concluding at this point, my brethren, the exposition I have undertaken, you will not fail to note how it gathers in its force upon this table and rite of communion before us. These symbols, bread and wine, body and blood, represent exactly what is most physical in Christ's suffering. But they do not stop in that, as if there were a value in the pains. They are even a language, as that was, bearing an impression of something higher. They say "made perfect through sufferings;" calling up to be thought, and received, just all that I have here been trying to unfold, of the power which our Master was obtaining, by his dreadful cross and passion.

Back of the wood and the nails, back of the suffering body, there was another cross, another suffering, even that of God's deep love, struggling out through the blood and the pain, to make its revelation felt in us. And this for what? To bring many sons, that is to bring us all, unto glory.

Suffering and glory! even so; in that tragic copula, the gospel stands, and it is remarkable how many times it recurs. "Ought not Christ to suffer these things, and to enter into his glory?" "For the suffering of death, crowned with glory and honor"—"The sufferings of Christ and the glory that should follow"—"A witness of the suffering of Christ, and a partaker of the glory that should be revealed"—"Who hath called us unto eternal glory, by Christ Jesus, after that ye have suffered awhile"—responses all, as it were, to the word—"made perfect through sufferings in bringing many sons unto glory."

Here, too, as you have noted, Christ's sufferings for us, and ours for him, and his glory, and our glory, are blended all together, heaving in a common passion, shining in a common glory. And thus it is, my brethren, that our ascended Master, by these communion tokens, pledges us to-day our right to suffer with him, and to be strengthened with him according to his glorious power. And what we call his glory, is, if we rightly understand, but this same glorious power, or powerfulness of glory—no phantom of display, or dazzling crown, conferred by servile worshipers wanting a hero, but that most solid kind of merit which is an element and power of day, on all who are blessed in the sight. When Christ was transfigured in the mount, the shining as the sun, the glistering whiteness, which are called "the excellent glory," were yet but a surface glory in themselves, and were only good as types of that inherent, practical glory, that belonged to his nature, and was just now dawning on discovery in his suffering sacrifice. The immense power he gets in being made perfect through sufferings, is itself his glory. And so the state of glory in us is the solid power that we are to obtain, by following in our Master's steps, by suffering patience and sacrifice. When Christ says, "the glory which thou gavest me I have given them," that glory is the sense we have in them, as God's martyrs and servants, of a somehow divine brightness and transforming luster. There is something felt which yet we do not see, and we call that invisible something, glory. It is splendor of soul, or the halo that is on it, when the blur and disorder and opaque mixture of wrong are all gone bye; or it is the state of perfect strength, concord, liberty in good, freeness of knowledge, purposes eternally set, great sentiment hallowed by great principle, and uttered by and through great action, when Christ, who is himself the glory of the Father, has put himself fully upon us, and when so the divine splendor and power, and truth, and righteousness, are become our eternal investiture. And therefore it is, that the very state of glory for which we hope is set forth as a daylight element, bathing holy minds forever, whose sun is the Revelation of God by suffering—"For the Glory of God doth lighten it and the Lamb—is the light thereof. O, thou divine Lamb; suffering symbol in the flesh, of God's suffering love in the spirit, what shall be the light of our seeing forever, but that which may shine out from thee!

XIII.

SALVATION BY MAN.

For since by man came death, by man came also the resurrection from the dead.—i. Cor. xv. 21.

It can not, of course, be the apostle's meaning, that mankind are going literally to raise themselves from the dead. When he says "by man," he mentally refers to Christ; only taking advantage of the fact that, since Christ the Son of God incarnate, is become a proper man, a member of the race, it is therefore permitted us to regard the whole remedy of sin, or power of salvation, as being included in humanity itself. Redemption, life, resurrection—all are, in a sense, being and to be, by man. When we say *humanity*, there is inclosed and, as it were, closeted in it, all the inspiration all the light, all the life-impulse of the divine man, and so all the supernatural, resurgent powers of a complete salvation, even up to the resurrection force itself. It is not as if God had called us here from a distance or had sent his Son to sit upon the circle of the heavens and lecture us from those supernal heights, but he has gotten him into the race by a birth, and has entered, in that manner, a corporate grace of life into the race itself.

What I propose then at the present time, is the practically important fact that Christ is not so much to be thought of as a being external, or as dispensing salvation from above, as a second Adam in the race itself; a regenerative and redemptive power, so inserted into humanity as to be in a sense of it. Just as the apostle's language intimates—"For since by man came death, by man came also the resurrection from the dead." For this word "*since*" is a word of rational connection, supposing an impression felt of some inherent fitness, requiring the corporate disadvantage of the fall, to be made good by a corporate remedy. Consider then—

1. The antecedent probability of such a remedy, indicated by familiar analogies. It is not God's manner to work all remedies in things from without, but to make them largely self-remedial, when attacked by damage, or disorder. Thus all creatures of life, all substances above the range of mineral substance, are endowed by him with recuperative functions for the repair of their own injuries. The bush that is bent to the ground does not require some other bush or even tree, to come and lift it up, but, no sooner is it let go, than it springs up suddenly by an elastic force within. Cut it down, as it begins to be a tree, and it will set new growths to pricking through the hard bark even of its stump, and so, by a newly begun architecture it will go on to build

the tree it was beginning to build at the first. Every animal body has a distinct self-medicating force in its own vital nature, called by physicians and physiologists the *vis medicatrix*. When, therefore, it is attacked by disease, or hacked by violence, the qualified physician, knowing how it will rally its own hidden force and put its own mysterious self-medications at work, will simply endeavor, on his part, to clear the way, and supply the needed stimulus of action, till the subtle, inborn physician, wiser and more sovereign than he, has mended the break, or completed the cure. The same is true as regards all defections of honor or character. If the man himself does not return to himself, and repair his losses by a process of recovery undertaken by himself, there is no recovery for him. The whole world toiling at his vices and dishonors, could not repair one of them. He alone has power to win the first inch of recovery. On a larger scale the same is true of society. Broken down by oppression, desolated by conquest, rent by faction, weakened by every sort of incapacity, it finally gets clear and rises, by reactions from within itself—just as Italy is rising now. The rational resurrection comes by man—man, that is, grown manlier, as God prepared him to be, by his own great struggles of devotion.

We see, in this manner, on how large a scale God contrives to incorporate powers of self-recovery in things. What then shall we expect, when humanity is broken by the irruption, or precipitation of sin, but that if he organizes redemption, he will do it in a way to have it appear as a redemption from within, executed in a sense by man.

I do not mean, of course, when I speak in this manner of "self-recovery," and "salvation my man," that the recovery and salvation are not by God. There is exactly the same propriety in this kind of language that there is in speaking of a harvest, or a voyage, as being by man—it is never such in the sense of excluding God and his natural agencies. Indeed the recovery and salvation of souls are more properly by man, because the agency of God is here incarnated and works in the race by a man thus inserted into it.

2. It is another point to be observed, that we not only want a supernatural salvation (for nothing less than that can possibly regenerate the fall of nature,) but in order to any steady faith in it, we must have it wrought into nature and made to be as it were, one of its own stock powers. It does not meet our intellectual conditions, till it satisfies, in a degree, the scientific instinct in us, and becomes rational and solid, by appearing to work inherently, or from within, as by a certain force of law. Moving on the soul and society, as from a point above and without, it would be here, and there, and nowhere, flitting as it were apparitionally, breaking out now as from behind the moon, and vanishing next, as our faith reels away, in we know not what spaces of the air, or abysses of the sea. What we want can be seen, at a glance, from the eagerness that hurries such multitudes of our time after the doctrine of progress. We love to look on education, political liberty, personal culture,

and the sway of moral ideas, all as advancing under fixed laws of progress. This doctrine of progress is even a better kind of gospel to many, and more rational. And yet if we speak of a strictly natural progress, under natural laws, there is no fiction more utterly baseless: for after the fact of sin, or moral evil broken loose in the race, the progress of society must be inevitably downward from bad to worse. Just that too which ought to be true is true, many of the proudest, most historic races drop into extinction; and many others exist that we call savage races, just because they make no such progress, more than the animals, from age to age.

And yet we want a salvation that is to us all which this doctrine of progress pretends to be, and God defers to our want, by contriving a gospel for man that is to be, in form, by man; giving us to see the general humanity so penetrated and charged with the supernatural, by Christ living in it, as to be, in a sense, working out redemption naturally from within itself. We call it the progress of society, and such it really is, and yet, solid and scientific as we think it, all the reality it has comes of the incorporated, incarnated grace, in Jesus Christ, which is countervailing always the penal disorders of nature, and setting continually on, as by a destiny itself, the rising fortunes of the race. Our gospel is a cause, in this manner, among causes; a real calculable force, the confidence of which can be held with a steady assurance. Is any-thing more rational than to believe that goodness and truth are bound to master all things by their own everlasting necessary laws? No matter from what sphere they come, natural or supernatural, getting into man, into the race, they will as certainly master man at last, master the race, as gravity will master a stone. Exactly this confidence God therefore means to give us—no visionary confidence but a rational, that of a banker whose fund is in; for God has put the stock functions of his own everlasting kingdom into humanity itself, and by man He must reign. Meantime—

3. We shall see that, if it were possible to restore the fall of our race, by any kind of agency, or operation, wholly external, supposing no recuperative forces and concurrent struggles operating from within, it would reduce our character and grade of significance to a virtual nullity. Dismiss the grand world-honoring fact of the incarnation, conceive that the Jehovah angel, or some angelic messenger comes to us, not humanized in sympathy or in order, but having a plastic power to work on us from without and sway us to good, by his own methods of divine magic, apart from our consent; this would settle us, at once, into a state of cliency both dangerous and humiliating. We should probably begin, at once, to pay him the honors of idolatry; for the manly consciousness in us will be taken away, and we shall be to ourselves a kind of second rate interest in God's kingdom; just that which the incarnation, begetting a new divine power in the race itself, contrives to avoid with a skill so beautiful.

Or we may suppose that God was able to put the

physical world into such a state of divine glow, showing forth, in its objects, such radiances and miraculous revolvings, such glorious apparitions of truth, such faces of goodness, that men should have their bad will quite taken away by the magical sceneries they live in. But the transformation they undergo in this manner would have little dignity in it, because their manhood is unexercised in the change. It would be a kind of vegetable conversion, not a kindling of God's fires in the soul's aspirations and choices.

So, if the race were to be recovered in any way that includes no struggle of self-recovery, no power within striving toward recovery, it would almost take away the sense of our personality. We should be ciphers to ourselves, not men. Exactly contrary to this, it is the very great merit of the incarnation, that it brings help in a way to make it valuable. God could easily help us in a way to crush us, just as many human helpers will really make nothing of their beneficiaries, by allowing them to make nothing of themselves, and be nothing for themselves. The very thing wanted here is to get power into the fallen race, and put it striving upward; to raise a ferment of recuperative energy, feeling, aspiration, choice, and whole right working in humanity; exactly what the nearness and high sympathy of God in the incarnation must inevitably do. The Saviour being, or becoming man, the salvation dignifies and raises man even before he receives it; giving him the right to feel, that, coming verily as an approach of God, it is none the less a power in the race itself, a salvation by man.

4. Since it is continually assumed by the scripture that we fall by race, or as a corporate whole, we naturally look for some recuperative grace to be entered into the race, by which so great disadvantage may be repaid or overcome. Thus, if we say "as in Adam all die," we want also to say, "so in Christ shall all be made alive." Or if we say that "through the offense of one many be dead," we want also to say, "much more the grace of God, and the gift by grace, which is by one man, Jesus Christ, hath abounded unto many." In this manner it is that Christ is conceived to be a "second Adam," a kind of new progenitor, such that we get in him, as it were, a new descent from good.

But we are born of Adam physiologically, it will be remembered, and so we go down with him as a race by physiological consequence, while we are not thus born of Christ the second Adam. He only comes into the race at a given point, just as we do, and communicates nothing by descent to persons collateral, any more than we do to persons collateral to us. How then, being no progenitor, does he become any proper Adam at all? how get himself into the race, in any such general way, as to become a new headship of life?

To this I answer, that we must not press the correspondence too closely; it is not understood to be literal, or to hold in any but a general and qualified way. Let it be enough that as the sin abounded, so the grace much more abounds, only not in exactly the same manner. Adam is our head physiologically, Christ is our head by the head influences he inaugurates, by the authority, sympathy, beauty, of his suffering goodness—a power that propagates across all the lines of generation, as efficiently as if it traveled by descent—a new regenerative power incarnated into the race as such, there to work, running down through all descent, as a redemption of man executed in the large view by man.

Observe too this very striking distinction, that good souls have a power to get into the race by collateral propagations of their goodness, when bad souls have almost no such power at all. The bad impregnate human feeling through falsities, and lies, and oppressions, and combinations of interest, or at best through the dazzling exploits of ambition. But there is a short run to such kind of power. Deep in evil, the world is yet naturally shy of evil, and begins very soon to get away from it. No bad character propagates long, as by character. Even bad writings drop out soon and die, as it were, of their own poison. On the other hand it will be seen that good and great souls have a destiny of headship, propagating side-ways, and every way, till they become Adams in the sublime fatherhood of their power, and that so completely as to finally reach, and take headship of the race. Thus we think of Socrates, for example, as a kind of progenitor in good for his people; a man whose ideas, principles, sacrifices, entered him into the whole Greek race, and more and more widely into the general life of the world. So of Washington. Dying childless, he had yet many children, and his large posterity still multiplies more and more rapidly, in every part of the world. Aaron Burr was a man of greater splendor, but he never got into the world's life and feeling at all, and never became progenitor of any thing. He was dropped instinctively even out of the world's thought. But Washington goes on to be, not father of his country only, but world's father also; inserting his grand fatherhood into kings, emperors, peoples, and laws, accepted more and more reverently, by the compulsion of good in his life, and reigning, in fact, as a kind of civil-state Messiah, that has come to propagate his sway in human laws and liberties. The civil capacity even of the world, is increased by the august propagations of his example and sentiment.

And so it is, illustrating the great by the small, the divine by the human, that Jesus, the incarnate word of God's eternity, coming into birth and living and dying as a man, fills the whole race with new possibilities and powers, starts resurgent activities, overtops the sin abounding with a grace that much more abounds, and becomes the Adam, so to speak, of a new humanity. Consider now—

5. Some of the scripture evidences of the subject. And here we meet, first of all, as it were at the head of all scripture, the remarkable and rather strangely worded promise, which declares that the seed of the woman shall bruise the serpent's head. The represent-

ation is not that Christ, sometime hereafter to be born of the woman, shall bring under and finally destroy the bad power, though that is true, but that the woman's whole posterity, having Christ included, shall do it. God will of course be always present in the struggle, pushing it on, and turning all the crises of it, by his invisible agency; while outwardly, to human apprehension, it is but a struggle, in one view, of society and man. In this manner, he contrives, by the hiding of himself, in our otherwise poor, dejected humanity, to put us in confidence and keep us at a pitch of courage, quite above our own broken powers.

Here and there, it is true, this interior hidden method is departed from, and he appears to be operating from without, doing something for, or upon, our humanity, and not through it; working some astounding miracle, sending some angel, or appearing by some angelic theophany. In one case he even ordains a supernatural sign that is to be a kind of institution, recurring, like the sun itself, with astronomic regularity; the cloud, I mean, by day and the pillar of fire by night. And yet none of these extraordinary, external things, appear to get much hold of the race, just because they do not get into it. Nothing works like a power that does not work by man. The sacrifice of Abraham and the wrestling of Jacob bring more victory and might into the race, as far as we can see, than the brazen serpent, or the waters drawn out of the rock. When, too, Christ comes, what is he but a man? and though, as such, he has a divine power and plenitude, how careful is he to get his attitude in the race and not above it. He undertakes no outward championship. Seed of the woman, a proper man, he only gets into the common family register as such, and puts the struggle on, as being a struggle of the race itself. Perfect in all divinity even, he is still the Son of Man, claiming the appellation for himself. He dies low. And when he is gone, all that we know is that a gospel is born! In one view there seems to be nothing here but the same humanity there was before, and the same hard fight still going on that before was struggling to bring the serpent under and to bruise his head. But it is a very different fight, as respects the power of it; for there is a Christ now in the race, and the whole seed of man is quickened by the sense of his divine brotherhood.

We shall find, accordingly, that the scriptures are full of images, that conceive the great contest with evil to be a struggle in the bosom of the race itself, and give us the expectation that it will go on, as such, till it has won a complete triumph for the truth. Thus it is that Isaiah uses the word "*increase*," which does not mean to enlarge by additions, but by internal growth; —"And of the *increase* of his government and peace there shall be no end." Thus it is that Daniel represents the kingdom of the Messiah as "a stone cut out without hands," but a most remarkable kind of stone in the fact that it grows from within itself, and becomes a great mountain filling the whole earth. In the same way it is compared, by Christ himself, to a grain of mustard seed, which does not grow by something added on the outside, but by an internal operation, becoming in that manner a tree. He compares it also to leaven hid in a large quantity of meal, there to work till all is leavened; where the working, it will be observed, is not the working only of the original leaven, or that of the atmosphere outside, but such a kind as puts the meal next the leaven working too, and that also on doing the same to what is next to it; and so the propagated working goes on, till the whole body of the bread is leavened.

Here Christ is giving, you will see, his deliberate opinion of the manner in which his kingdom will be extended. The process will be forwarded, he conceives, within the race itself, and will so far be human, that we may rightly say of it—for since by man came the fall of the world, by man came also its restored glory and peace.

Observe, again, how even holy scripture is the scripture also of man, written by man, given to the world by man, bearing, in every book, the particular stamp and style of the particular mind, in whose personal conceptions it was shaped. The subject matter too of the historic and biographic parts is human, showing how men have acted, thought, felt, suffered for the truth, fallen before temptation, triumphed over it. Indeed the value itself of these records consists, to a great extent, in the fact that they give us divine lessons under human incidents, in the molds of human character and life. They show us too, on a larger scale, what is the meaning and way of God's Providence, by the disasters of wrong and the struggles of merit, and also by the overturnings and uprisings of nations.

When we come to the writings of devotion, the Psalms, for example, and other chorals of scripture, these are human sentiments, lifted indeed by holy inspirations, but none the less properly human for that reason—rolling in as such upon us, from the word, even as the tides roll in from the sea.

The proverbs are specially human, being maxims of human wisdom, such as have even gained a proverbial currency, in the judgments of philosophy, and statesmanship, and common life.

The prophets, again—these are all men speaking by men's words and voices. True their voices are voices also of God, but they are none the less human, that God wants to use them as such, or that he sometimes puts them to speaking in the first person for him, saying "I the Lord;" for when he crowds himself thus into men, or men's voices, he only proves how much he may prefer to do as man.

The same is true of the Epistles. They are written by men, to men, in the words of men, under the relationships of teacher and taught, and shepherd and flock. They deal with actual human conduct, in actual human conditions. They speak to human difficulties and human dangers. They show how good men suffer in times of persecution, how they bruise Satan under their feet, how fidelity triumphs; in a word how the great life-struggle of the church goes on.

A corresponding reason doubtless required the gospel

of Christ to be preached by human ministers. It is not commonly expected that theives will be sent to reform thieves, or perjurors to remonstrate with perjury, but sinners are sent to gospel sinners. God certainly could have taken a different method. He could have sent cohorts of angels flying through the air, to publish the good news, even as they began to do, for an hour, when Christ was here. He could have set the stars chiming with the silver music of salvation. He could have made the stones cry it out of the mountain tops, and under the ground, and under the sea. But he wants the great work of the redemption to go on from within the race itself, unfolding by internal growth, intending that his kingdom shall be great and finally universal, only because the powers or principles he has inserted are sufficient of themselves to make it so.

He also constructs a corporate state, called the church, in which, as being corporate, and not subject to death, he deposits the gospel and the sacraments, and all the institutional appointments of religion, thus to be conserved and perpetuated by man.

In the same way too, he makes the church even to be the pillar and ground of the truth itself; for the disciples in it are to be Christ's living epistles, gospels of the life, new incarnations of the word, showing always what is in the text, by what is expressed in their life and walk and character. Were it not for this light continually supplied to the written gospel, from the lives of those who live it, the word of the skies would shortly become an utterly dead language, a kind of Sanscrit jargon, without either salvation or intelligence in it. Living men are its interpretation, living men are its arguments and evidences. It lives by man.

As the disciples are to be new incarnations, in this manner, of Christ, so, in a sense, they are to be vehicles also of the Spirit, demonstrations, revelations, of his otherwise unseen or unobserved agency; and so, many of his most effective operations will be through their gifts, works, prayers, sufferings, personal testimonies, and the pentecostal glow of their assemblies.

Again, last of all, and as it were to include all, it is given to men even to convert the world. Not that they, as being simply men, are able to do any such thing, but that Christ, the Son of Man, being entered into the race, and working as a leaven in the mass of it, will make them a leaven also to one another, and set the ferment on till all is leavened. And so the great world itself, all the empires, known or unknown, all the continents, and islands undiscovered, all most distant ages and times are given as a trust to men, originally to a very few, very humble men. "Ye," said Christ, "are the light of the world." "Go ye into all the world and disciple every creature."

I will not detain you with farther illustrations of the subject in hand, but will simply suggest in conclusion, a few points variously related, in the practical drift of its applications.

We have then a very significant presumption raised, that when any breakage, or damage, occurs in any legitimate institution, or society of the world, God has prepared, or put in somewhere, some kind of self-remedial force to mend it. Thus if any church, or Christian brotherhood, is rent by disagreements, embittered by recriminations, and broken, for the time, as regards a due confidence of the future, the remedy must still be in it, else it is nowhere. Even if God himself undertakes for it, he will accomplish his restoring purpose, in some very important sense, only by man, even by themselves; that is by their strivings after one another, their sorrowings over themselves, their prayers and their longings after the lost love. If there be any remedy for them, it must so far come out of themselves. Not even God will try to bring it from any other quarter.

So if there be a great nation rent by faction, a good government broken down and trampled by rebellion, God has no miraculous fire to flash upon the conspirators and scorch them down. It must be enough that he has given a sword for the punishment of evil doers, that the remedy may come by man, making due use of it. If the people too will know that God is with them, let a spirit be kindled in their manly breast that shall take them to the field, forbidding any word of peace to be spoken, till the laws are vindicated and the foes of order crushed. If God will make a broken world restore itself by man, much more a broken people, and it will as certainly be done as there is quantity enough of manhood in them—enough great sentiment and patriotic fire—to do it.

Again, the immense responsibility thrown upon Christ's followers, in the fact that the salvation of the world is to be in so many ways, by man, ought to be distinctly admitted and practically assumed. If they are to preach the gospel, and light up the gospel by their lives, so to be the gospel, and finally to regain the world to God; if Christ himself lays it on them to be gospelers with him, putting the world in their hands to be lived for, died for, won and saved, then how clear it is that their faith will be no relaxation of responsibility, but the begun fulfillment and seal of it rather. How nearly appalling too is the fact that if God has any good thing to be done, it is to be done somehow by man, and that he has the man, or men, or women, somewhere on whom so great a charge is laid. As he has undertaken to make man good, he will let the good that wants to be done, wait till their goodness gets purpose, and fire, and sacrifice, in a word, reality, enough to do it. And if they make slow progress, if the conversion of the world drags heavily, then so it must; for God will not so far dishonor the great salvation as to push on the propagation of it faster than it has reality enough to propagate itself. If it takes a million of years to recover the world to God, then a million it must have; for it never can be accomplished, either in one, or in a hundred millions, unless it is accomplished by man. O, how preposterous, in this view, is the soft opinion many hold of faith; as if it were the faith of a soldier to expect that his captain will do all the fighting himself, and that he is never to fight under him, or win with him; or as if it were the true believing unto life, to come in, as clinical patients, and lie down upon the gospel to be saved by it! No! the salvation of God is no such washy and thin affair—it has meaning, it has dignity; else it has no mark of God upon it. To really believe is to come into the great life-struggle of Jesus and be with him in it; to be engineering for him, watching for occasions to commend him, watching for souls to receive him, fighting for him in sacrifice, even as heroes fight for their country. The salvation of the world by man—that is the tremendous fact which all true faith takes hold of, and for which it is girded even by the sign of the cross.

There is, furthermore, a great mine of comfort opened here, for such as have settled into heart-sickness over human affairs, and the want of all high movement in them. Some are sick because they hear no thunders, and see no mighty stir in the heavens. If they could see God converting the world by signs, and wonders, and mighty portents, there would seem to be something going on! Nothing could be weaker than such a kind of gospeling. Laying no hold of us by rational evidence, it would only drum us to sleep in the tumults of the senses. And yet they are almost pining to have the world's dull tedium broken, by some such outward stir; never once recollecting that, while commotion is a profitless noise, real motion is silent. Another class are pining, in the same manner, for some new dispensation to break, that shall displace the rotten hopelessness of the old; some second coming of Christ, some purgation by fire, some literal new heavens. They want a Saviour farther off and not one hid in the world's bosom, a Saviour in the clouds of heaven, or in some miraculous new city,—just the Saviour that would take us out of our faith and put us into our senses, and set us running to see, instead of resting in love to know. Still another class, who look for no such mock reliefs, are only the more sick, because seeing no good, they have, beside, no hope of any. There seems to be no good reason why the world should continue, for it comes to nothing, losing always in one year, age, or place, what it gained in another—constitutions, laws, liberties, learning, commerce, religion, all swinging tidally, and as certain to go back in the ebb, as to come in at the flow. Why should such a hopeless, always baffling, laboring vanity be kept on foot? Why, my friends, because it is not hopeless! because the grand, all-regenerating, force is already entered into the world, and is working steadily on through all retrocessions and advances alike. Lift up your heads O ye drooping ones! Christ is in the world! Jesus, Son of God, and word of God's eternity—he is about us, within us, going through all things, moving onward in all. Leaven does not make a noise when it works, and yet it works! And so the gospel works, the progress goes on, a grand, mighty progress, and there is really no retrocession. No river runs to the sea more certainly or steadily, than the great salvation by man runs to conquest and a kingdom. No reason why the world should continue? That is unbelief. Do the men who are lifted up to such grand heights by the progress of society think so? No, there is reason enough to them, why the world should continue; they only steal our gospel and millenium, which, if we reclaim, we shall be as jubilant as they, with only so much better right.

Let us also observe the beautiful delicacy of God in his plan of salvation. He is not willing to make it a salvation *for* man only, as I have said already, but contrives to make it also, as far as possible, a salvation *by* man. As the seed of the woman goes down, so he contrives to get a force into it that will finally bruise and trample its adversary. If he should do every thing simply as acting upon us, it would make us only underlings to eternity, waste timber of creation, that he has only gathered and stored for the dry-rot of a state of impotence, miscalled felicity. No, he wants to raise a character in us, and, to do this, requires a great hiding of power. He must contrive to put us a doing, in all that is to be done, striving to enter the straight gate, working out our salvation with fear and trembling, as only knowing by faith that he is working at all. And then his word of promise at the end will be—"to him that overcometh." The beauty, the delicacy, of his work is that he gets the force of it into our own bosom, and lets it work as if it were a part of ourselves. True it is all by Christ, and yet it is by the Christ within—the law of the Spirit of life in Christ Jesus. And so, instead of making his mercy a mere pity that kills respect, he makes it a power that lifts into character and everlasting manhood. He becomes a second Adam, a kind of better parentage in the race itself, and we rise by a new derivation that nowise shames our feeling, or shatters our confidence. How beautiful and tender the method! and when we conceive, in addition, that we ourselves are to preach, and live, and illustrate, and perpetuate, and spread, this gospel, having it as a gospel to prevail by man, what shall we feel eternally, but that our very sorrow and shame are ennobled by the grace we partake. And when we shall go home to be with Christ, Christ the faithful witness, and prince of the kings of the earth, what shall we do but confess, in loveliest homage—Unto him that loved us and washed us from our sins in his own blood; raising our finale also to sing, in the glorified majesty of our feeling—And hath made us kings and priests unto God.

XIV.

THE BAD CONSCIOUSNESS TAKEN AWAY.

"*Because that the worshipers, once purged, should have had no more conscience of sins.*"—HEB. x, 2.

The reading is not, you observe, "conscience of no more sins,"—as if the sins were stopped, but "no more conscience of sins,"—as if the conscience of sins already past were somehow extirpated, or else the sins taken quite away from it and forever extirpated themselves, as facts, or factors of the life. And the allegation is, that while the old sacrifices of the law had power to accomplish no such thing, it is accomplished by the wonderful, seemingly impossible, efficacy of the gospel sacrifice. Those older sacrifices could not make the comers thereunto perfect—perfect, that is, as pertaining to the conscience—and therefore they must needs be renewed as remembrances of sin every year; but the offering of the body of Jesus, once for all, was sufficient; allowing us forever after to have no more conscience of sins. Now it is this practical wonder, this seeming impossibility accomplished by the cross, to which I invite your attention on the present occasion.

It is what our apostle elsewhere calls—*The mystery of faith in a pure conscience.*

I fell in company, some years ago, with a college acquaintance—not a minister of religion, but a remarkably subtle, closely scientific thinker, and withal a devout Christian—who said to me, in a manner and tone of sensibility I can never forget—My great trial in religion is, to find how a clean bosom, in regard to sin, is ever possible. I can not see how my sin can ever be really gotten away; indeed I fall into such darkness on this point, when I undertake to solve it, that I quite lose my faith in the possibility of a real deliverance, and feel obliged to say with David—"my sin is ever before me." He went on to state his difficulty more fully, but as I have it on hand to make an exposition of the whole subject, the ground of his difficulty will be covered with much other ground beside. How then is it, or how is it to be imagined, that Christ, by his sacrifice, takes away the condemning conscience, or the felt dishonor of transgression? This is the question we are to consider, and, if possible, answer; in doing which I will—

I. Go over, as briefly as may be, certain supposed answers, that do not appear to reach the real point of the question; and—

II. Will endeavor to exhibit and support by sufficient illustrations what appears to be the true scriptural answer.

I. The supposed answers that are not sufficient.

They are various and very unlike among themselves; they still fall short, all of them, at the same point viz., in the fact that they do not touch, or take away at all from the mind, or memory, or conscience, the fact and shame of wrong-doing. Be the remedy this or that, still the man, as a man, is none the less consciously guilty, none the less really dishonored, shamed, damned, before himself. There stands the fact, unmoved and immovable forever, that he is a malefactor soul, none the better for being safe, or forgiven, or justified.

Thus, when it is conceived that Christ has borne our punishment, that, if it were true, might take away our fear of punishment, but fear is one thing, and mortified honor, self-condemning guilt, self-chastising remorse, another and very different thing; and that will be only the more exasperated, that divine innocence itself has been put to suffering on its account.

Neither will it bring any relief to show that the justice of God is satisfied. Be it so; the transgressor is none the better satisfied with himself—his own self-damning justice is as far from being satisfied as before.

Is it then conceived that what has satisfied the justice of God, has also atoned the guilty conscience? Will it then make the guilty conscience less guilty, or say sweeter things of itself, that it sees innocence, purity, goodness divine, put to suffering for it? If any thing could exasperate, even insupportably, the sense of guilt, it should be that.

Is it then brought forward to quell the guilt of the conscience that Christ has evened our account legally by his sacrifice, and that we are even justified of God, for Christ's sake? But if God, in this manner, and by a kind of benevolent fiction, calls us just, do we any the less certainly disapprove and damn ourselves even to eternity? Nothing it would seem can save us from it, but to lose the integrity of our judgments!

Forgiveness taken as a mere release of claim, or a negative letting go of right against transgression, brings, if possible, even less help to the conscience. Christ had forgiven his crucifiers in his dying prayer, but it was the very crime of the cross, nevertheless, that pricked so many hundreds of hearts on the day of pentecost. Christ had forgiven them, but their consciences had not!

But Christ renews the soul itself, it will be said, and makes it just within; when, of course, it will be justified. That does not follow. If Judas at the very point where he confessed—"I have betrayed the innocent blood," could have been instantly transformed into an angel of beauty, his purified sensibility would have been shaken, I think, with a greater horror even of his crime than before.

But the fatherhood of God—the disciple of another and different school will take refuge under that, and say, that here, at least, there is truly no more conscience of sins. Would it not be strange, if a tolerably good father can forgive and forget, and God can not? But who is God, and what most fitly represents him? a mortal father who is able, just because of his weakness, to forgive and forget, or to forgive without forgetting, or to forget without forgiving, or the transgressor's own everlasting immutable conscience, which can neither forgive nor forget? What is this conscience, in fact, but God's throne of judgment in the man? Why, if God, in his fatherhood, were such a kind of being, dealing in laxities and fond accommodations, having no care for his rectoral honor, as the defender of right and order, we certainly are not such to ourselves. A conscience that can say, "no matter, God is rather loose and very easy with his children, therefore I will be to myself as good as good in my sin, and let the matter go,"—I certainly, for one, whatever may be said by others, have no conscience that can go in that loose gait. I love my conscience because it is the one thing in me that goes true and will unalterably, inevitably damn my wrongs, even if God should let them go. Nay, if God be such a God, it would even set me in a shudder, to find how easily I might sigh for a being whom I can more sufficiently respect.

You perceive in this recital, my friends, how great a matter we have undertaken, and how very obstinate, or intractable, our difficulty is. Doubtless a foul vessel may be washed, a fracture mended, a personal injury redressed, a sick body restored to health and soundness, and dressed in a new covering of flesh; nay, there is a clear possibility of raising the dead to life, but to conceive a sinner so wrought in as to obliterate the fact of his sin, leaving no more conscience of it, is a very different matter, and if the possibility were not really shown by the gospel itself, we must certainly give up the question, as one that we can not solve, by any faculty that God has given us. We come then—

II. To the question as it is, and the answer given it by the scriptures of God.

The great question meeting us at this point is, whether it is possible, or how far possible, to change the consciousness of a soul, without any breach of its identity? In this manner, we shall find, the gospel undertakes to remove, and assumes the fact of a removal of, the dishonor and self-condemnation of sin. But we shall conceive the matter more easily and naturally, if we notice, before going into the scripture inquiry, certain analogies discoverable in our human state, which may serve as approaches to the proper truth of the question.

Thus a thoroughly venal, low-principled man, elected President of the United States, will undergo, not unlikely, an inward lifting of sentiment and impulse, corresponding with the immense lift of his position. The great honor put upon him makes him willing to honor himself. He wants to deserve his place and begins to act in character in it. He is the same man, regarding his personal identity, but he is raised, even to himself, in the grade he occupies. His old natural consciousness has a kind of Presidential consciousness superinduced, which holds a higher range of quality. He lives, in fact, Presidentially, and is dignified inwardly by the dignities of his position.

How many thousand soldiers, who before were living in the low, mean vices, lost to character and self-respect, have been raised, in like manner, in our armies, to quite another grade of being. It has given them a wholly different sense of themselves, that their dear, great country has come upon them in so great power. They are consciously ennobled, in the fact that they have borne themselves heroically in the field; and are so become another kind of man even to themselves. They are the same, yet by a vast reach of distance not the same. A certain great something has come into their feeling. They stand more firmly, and bear themselves more erectly; and it gives them an exultant feeling even, that their discouraged and miserably forlorn consciousness is gone—supplanted by the sense of self-respect, and manly honor.

The same, again, is true in a different way, of all the gifted ones in art and speech and poetry, when they are taken by the inspirations of genius. When such a soul, that was down upon the level of uses, torturing itself into production for applause, or even for bread, begins to behold God's signatures upon his works, and worlds, and the magnificent discipline he gives us; discovering in objects ideas, in facts the faces of truth; catching also the fires of a Promethean heat from all subtlest moods and hardest flints of experience;—then it is become, to itself, quite another creature. It is as if the grub-state were gone by, and the winged life had broken loose, to try the freedom of the air. In that finer element he ranges at will, lifted by his etherial seership, to move in altitudes hitherto invisited; consciously another and different being—another, yet still the same.

In these and other like examples, afforded us in the field of our natural life, we are made familiar with the possibility of remarkable liftings in the consciousness of men, such as make them really other to themselves, and set them in a higher range of being; and, by these examples, we are prepared, as it were beforehand, to that more wonderful ascent above ourselves which is accomplished in Christ, when he takes us away from the conscience of sins. He does it—this is the general, or inclusive truth that covers the whole ground of the subject—by so communicating God, or himself as the express image of God, that he changes, in fact, the plane of our existence. Without due note of this, we do not understand Christianity; the very thing it proposes is to bring us up into another level, where the consciousness shall take in other matter, and have a higher range. Thus, when the apostle says—"And hath raised us up together and made us sit together in heavenly places in Christ Jesus," he is speaking of a change purely internal, a conscious lifting to another grade of life, and a higher range of joy. The word *places*, here occurring, belongs to the English only, and it is put in to fill out the plural of the neuter adjective *heavenlies*, used here as a noun. But sitting in the heavenlies, does not mean, of necessity, sitting in other localities. It means sitting in heavenly things, as well; above the world, that is, and the flesh and sin, in the serene, pure element of God's eternal love and glory, there to be folded in harmony, raised in consciousness, filled to the full with all God's heavenlies, even as his angels are; no more to be shamed forever by the little, defiled consciousness that is henceforth over-spread, submerged, and drowned by the sea-full of God's infinite worthiness and righteousness wafted in upon it.

Now it must not be imagined that this one passage of scripture stands by itself in asserting such a sentiment. The whole New Testament is full of it. "If ye then be risen with Christ seek those things which are above where Christ sitteth at the right hand of God,"—"Hath made us kings and priests unto God,"—"A chosen generation—a royal priesthood,"—"Partakers of the divine nature,"—"Sons of God,"—In all such modes of expression, and a hundred others that might be cited, we have the same thought breaking out on our discovery; that Christ is lifting us out of shame and condemnation, into a higher plane and a footing of conscious affiliation with God.

But you will not conceive how very essential this idea of a raising of the consciousness may be, if you do not bring up distinctly the immense fall of our mortal consciousness, in the precipitation of our sin. In their true normal condition, as originally created, human souls are inherently related to God, made permeable and inspirable by him, intended to move in his divine impulse forever. A sponge in the sea is not more truly made to be filled and permeated by the water in which it grows, than a soul to be permeated and possessed by the Infinite Life. It is so made that, over and above the little, tiny consciousness it has of itself, it may have a grand, all-inclusive consciousness of God. In that conciousness it was to be, and be lifted and blessed evermore. The senses it should have of God, always present, were to be its dignity, its base of equilibrium, its everlasting strength, and growth, and majesty, and reigning power in good.

But this higher consciousness, the consciousness of God, is exactly what was lost in trangression, and nothing was left of course but the little, defiled consciousness of ourselves, in which we are all contriving how to get some particles of good, or pleasure, or pride, or passion, that will comfort us. The great, inspirable, and divinely permeable faculty, is closed up. We do not know God any more, we only know ourselves. We have the eyes, and the ears, that were given us, but we are too blind to see, too deaf to hear—"Having the understanding darkened, being alienated from the life of God, through the ignorance that is in us because of the blindness of our heart." The true normal footing or plane of our humanity was thus let down, and it is exactly this which Christ undertakes to restore. And until that restoration is accomplished, the soul occupies a plane of mere self-knowing, and self-loving, and is, in fact, a lower order of being. It lives in the conscience of sins, a guilty, self-denouncing, and miserably shamed life. But as soon as it is opened to God, by the faith of Jesus Christ, and is truly born of God, it begins to be the higher creature God meant it to be—the same yet another. It is no more like the sponge stuck fast on some dry rock, but like the same, filled and vitalized by its own proper element, and spreading itself in its possessorship, so to speak, of the sea!

It is of course to be admitted that the disciple, raised thus in his plane, has the same conscience, and remembers the same sins, and is the very same person that he was before; but the consciousness of God, now restored, makes him so nearly another being to himself, that the old torment of his sin will scarcely so much as ripple the flow of his peace. It takes, in fact, a considerable rock, a little way out from the shore, to do more than dimple or curl the tide-swell coming in; and the sea, at the full, will simply bury it and hide it from the sight, in the depths of its own stillness. Or we may imagine, without much danger of extravagance, that when a soul is really filled with the higher consciousness, moving wholly in the divine movement, so great a lifting of character, and quality, and action, will carry it above the old range so completely, as to let the wrong and shame quite drop away; even as the insect creatures hovering on wings about us, flitting in swift motion, and playing with the air and the light, remember probably no more the cold, slow worms they were, when crawling, but a week ago, in the ground.

You will understand, of course, that if Christ is purging thus men's consciences, by lifting them above themselves, into a higher range of life, the conception will appear and reappear, in many distinct forms, and weave itself, in so many varieties, into the whole texture of Christianity. Notice then three distinct forms, not to speak of others, in which this change of grade or personal consciousness comes into view as a mighty gospel fact.

As the first of these, I name *justification*, or *justification by faith*. The grand last point or final effect of Christian justification is, "no more conscience of sins;" for, having that accomplished, it is inconceivable that God should condemn us when we do not condemn ourselves, and having it not accomplished, but condemning still ourselves, no justification by God will do us any good. But in this matter of justification, the less we make of the old standing alternative the better; what if it should happen that, while we are debating which of two conceptions is the true one, they are neither of them true? And so I think it will sometime be found. According to the scripture, which is very plain, gospel justification turns on no such mere objective matter as the squaring of an account; nor on any such subjective matter as our being made inherently righteous; but it turns on the fact of our being so invested with God, and closeted in his righteous impulse, that he becomes a felt righteousness upon us. Our consciousness is so far changed, in this manner, by the river-flood of God's character upon us, that, as long as our faith keeps the connection good, and permits the river to flow, we are raised above all condemnation and have no more conscience of sins. Inherently speaking we are not righteous; our store is in God not in ourselves; but we have the supply traductively from him, just as we do the supply of light from the sun. But the new divine consciousness in which we live is continually conforming us, more and more deeply, and will settle us, at last, in its own pure habit. In this manner, faith is counted to us for righteousness, because it holds us to God, in whom we have our springs of supply.

See how beautifully and simply Paul sets forth this true Christian idea of justification—"But now the righteousness of God, without the law, is manifested, even the righteousness of God, which is by faith of Jesus Christ, unto all and upon all them that believe." It is not righteousness for us in a book, nor in us by inherent character, but righteousness unto us and upon us, in its own living flow, as long as we believe. It is a higher consciousness which God generates and feeds, and as long as he does it there is no more conscience of sins.

This same truth of a raising of our plane appears in another form, in what is called *the witness of the Spirit.* "The Spirit itself beareth witness with our spirit that we are the children of God; and if children then heirs, heirs of God and joint heirs with Christ." Here the conception is that, as being spirit, we are permeable by the divine Spirit, and that he has a way of working in our working, so as to be consciously known as a better presence in our hearts. And so we have the confidence of children or sons, raised in our before low-bred nature, and dare to count ourselves God's heirs—fellow heirs with Christ our brother. Nothing is said of sins in this connection, but we can see for ourselves that, being thus ennobled by the inflowing Spirit, we shall be too much raised in the confidence of our dignity, to be troubled, or shamed by the past. And this same lifting, or ennobling of our spirit, is put in other forms of assertion; as when Christ, promising the Comforter, says—"At that day ye shall know that I am in my Father, and ye in me, and I in you." To be thus interlocked with the Father and the Son in a firm knowledge of the fact, revealed by the witnessing Spirit, is to have a consciousness opened that is dignity itself and glory begun. The same thing is put more practically, by the apostle, when he says—"Walk in the Spirit and ye shall not fulfill the lusts of the flesh." Keep fast in the higher element, where the senses of God and his joy are lifting the mind into liberty, and the lower and more carnal impulses will be left behind and forgot.

Once more this grand fact of the gospel, the raising of our plane of being, is presented in a still different manner in what is said of *the conscious inhabitation of Christ.* "Christ in you the hope of glory,"—"But ye see me,"—"Abide in me,"—"Until Christ be formed in you." But the great apostle to the Gentiles, himself a Christian man, all through, having that for his sublime distinction, declares himself, on this point, out of his very consciousness—"I am crucified with Christ, nevertheless I live; yet not I, but Christ liveth in me." It is, you perceive, as if his being itself were taken well nigh out of its identity by Christ revealed in it. The old sin—he does not think of it. The old I—why it is gone—"yet not I." He was going to say that he Paul was alive, but he did not like to say so much as that, and so he puts down his negative on it, and says he does not live. But

O, the living, all-quickening Christ—that is boasting enough—"Christ liveth in me; for the life I now live in the flesh, I live by the faith of the Son of God, who loved me and gave himself for me." How great a fact was the lifting of this man's plane, which took him, demonized by bigotry and hate, and made him the hero and strangely Christed propagator of the cross. Then he was Saul, now he is Paul; but the change touches more than a letter—he is raised even in his own feeling to quite another order of being. The conscience of sins—it may be that he has it in a sense; for, being an eternal fact, he must eternally know it; but the Christ-consciousness in him ranges so high above the self-consciousness, that he lives in a summit of exaltation, which the infinitesimal disturbances of his human wrong and shame can not reach.

Here then, my friends, you have opened to view one of the greatest triumphs of Christianity, perhaps the very greatest of all. To bring a clean thing out of an unclean is a much easier matter than to make a good conscience out of an evil or accusing conscience. Here the difficulty appears to be a kind of metaphysical impossibility. Indeed there is no philosopher, who would not say, beforehand, that such a thing is even demonstrably impossible. For if the accusing conscience accuses rightly, then it must either be extirpated, which decomposes the man, or else it must be suborned to give a lying testimony, when of course it will even condemn itself. But our gospel is able to look so great a difficulty in the face, and, what is more, turns it by a method so very simple as to be even sublime. When once you have conceived the possibility of raising a soul into a higher grade and order, where the consciousness shall take in more than the mere self, the body of God's own righteousness, and love, and peace, the problem is solved and that in a way so plain, yet so easily ennobling to our state of shame, that it proves itself by its own self-supporting evidence. This we say instinctively ought to be and must be true.

Only the more strange is it that, when this way of remedy is, and no other can be, sufficient, we so easily fall out of our faith, and begin to put ourselves on methods of purgation that only mock our endeavor. Having the grand possibilities of a good conscience opened to us in Christ, and nothing given us to do but just to receive by faith the manifested righteousness of God, we begin to work, in the lower level of our shame, upon the shameful unclean matter, as if going to purge it ourselves. One will mend himself up in a way of self-correction; which, if he could do, would, alas, not even touch the conscience of his old sins. Another goes to the work of self-cultivation, where he may possibly start some plausible amenities on the top of his bad conscience, even as flowers will sometimes be induced to grow upon a glacier. Another will pacify his bad conscience by his alms and philanthropic sacrifices, when an avalanche on its way could as well be pacified by the same. Others will make up a purgation by their repressive penances and voluntary humiliations, when the very thing their consciences complain of is, that they are too miserably shamed and humiliated already. Multitudes also will expect much from purgatorial fires hereafter, as if being duly chastised could make a good conscience! or as if these supposed fires would not rather burn in the brand of sin than burn it out! Now these poor scanty methods of delusion, unlike as they are to each other, are just as good one as another, because they are all equally worthless. Who could believe that rational beings, having so grand a way open to the new footing of sons of God, and having once conceived that way, could yet subside into these wretched futilities?

Worthier of sympathy but scarcely more worthy of the gospel name, are those hapless souls, who have fallen under their bad conscience to be forever harrowed and tormented by it. They have no faith to believe in a concrete, personal grace, and are only haunted by the nightmare of their moral convictions. They mope along their pathway therefore, looking always shamefully down; as if the sky above were paved with condemnations. If they bear the Christian name, they have yet no real peace, no sweet element of rest and confidence. They seem ever to be saying, "mine iniquities have taken hold upon me so that I am not able to look up." Or sometimes there is a trouble more specific—some one sin, the shame, the inward mortification, or damnation of which, follows them, day and night, and even year by year; a crime unknown to the world, but for which they inwardly blush, or choke with guilty pain, whenever it meets them alone. They seem to be even everlastingly dishonored before themselves. Perhaps they are, and fitly should be; but, my friends, there is a medicine for all such torments. Looking down upon your sins, or your particular sin, you can be, must be, everlastingly shamed; but if you can look away to Christ, take hold of Christ and rise with him, you shall go above your trouble, you shall be strong, and free, and full, and even righteous; established in all glorious confidence, because your very consciousness is lifted and glorified, by what comes into it from God's eternal concourse and friendship.

And here, just here, in fact, we strike the culminating point of wonder and glory in what Christ, by his more perfect offering, has been able and was even required to accomplish, to put us on a footing of complete salvation; viz., a restoration, forever, of the soul's lost honor. We could not take our place among the pure angels of God, and be really united to their blessedness, when we are inwardly self-disgusted, shamed, and even to be eternally stigmatized, by our condemning consciences. Nothing sufficiently restores us, which does not restore the mind's honor. And this, exactly, is our confidence; "that we are to be found unto praise, and honor, and glory, at the appearing of our Lord Jesus Christ." We are even called to "seek for honor, and glory, and immortality." What dishonor, what possible shame, can be our torment, when our very consciousness is robed in the righteousness of God? There is to be no more condemnation, no more conscience of sins; simply because we are so raised in the plane of our sentiment, and life, that we may think of ourselves, without any sense of dishonor upon us. We go in—heirs, sons, princes of God—joining ourselves boldly to all the royalties and sublime honors of the kingdom.

Are there none of us, my friends, that have many times sighed after just this hope, nay, that are sighing for it now? You have lost forever, you say, the chastity of your nature, you are and must forever be a guilty man; how then can you ever think of yourself without mortification? Getting into heaven itself, what can you ever do with so many bad facts upon you, and a bad conscience in you testifying eternally against them? No! no! There is even to be given back the sense of honor that was lost. You shall go in, not to hang your head, but to hold it up in praise and confidence. Now that mighty word is fulfilled according to its utmost meaning—"raised up together to sit in the heavenlies." We are there "together" in the common fold, we "sit" there in a titled security, the "heavenlies" are all ours—the honor, the confidence, the peace, the praise. O my God, what reverence shall every creature have for every other, when thou puttest honor upon all! gathering in before thee, nothing which defileth, or abideth in shame, but only such as Christ hath raised to eternal honor, before both thee and themselves!

XV.

THE BAD MIND MAKES A BAD ELEMENT.

"*Then answered the Jews and said unto him—say we not well, that thou art a Samaritan, and hast a devil?*" —JOHN viii, 48.

It is often remarked as a curious, half ludicrous distinction of insane persons, that they look on others round them as being out of their head. And yet this kind of phenomenon is more or less observable, in all cases of diseased action, whether mental or spiritual; the subject sees his disorder, not in himself, but in the objects and conditions round him.

Under the disease or disaffection called sin, the same is true; as we may see by the answer of these carping hypocrites, when Christ reproves their high pretenses, and sanctimonious lies. "You call yourselves children of Abraham," he says, "when you do none of his works, when your fatherhood is more truly discovered in the father of lies. And as he abode not in the truth, and has no truth in him, so because I tell you the truth ye believe me not." They feel the sharpness of the words, but do not perceive the solemn justice of the argument—throwing it captiously back upon him as in the text; "say we not well, that thou art a Samaritan and hast a devil?" Just as they should if his argument was true; for the men who have a devilish spirit are sure to see their devil objectively in others. There must be a devil on hand somewhere, they are sure, and who will expect them to find it where it is, in themselves? The truth accordingly which I now propose for your consideration is this:

That a bad mind sees bad things, and makes to itself a bad element. In other words, a bad mind projects its own evils into persons and conditions round it; charging the pains of its own inward disorder to the objects that refuse to bless it, and counting, it may be, Christ himself a sting only of annoyance.

It would be far more agreeable to me to assert this truth universally, or so as to include the good; showing how they convert all things to good by their bright and loving spirit, and how the stones even of the field are in league with them to bless them; but this would take me over too large a ground, and therefore I must be content to occupy you, for the time, with a subject not grateful in itself, hoping that you may even find the greater benefit in it. If the errand we are after is not pleasant, if it compels us to go burrowing into the dark, underground, abysses and pains of evil in the soul, let us not recoil from the task, because we find a great deal of our conceit inverted and a great many of our complaints of God and the world turned back upon ourselves.

I do not mean, of course, to say, that we can have nothing to complain of, or that other men can not do us bitter wrongs. Neither do I undertake to say, that we shall not feel them. But he that suffers a wrong rightly, finds a law of compensation going with him, as with God, so that his injury, or injured feeling, is repaid many times over, like that of God, by the consciously sublime repose of his own self-approving spirit. And, this being true, it is only the bad mind in us, after all, that allows us to be really troubled and harassed by wrong. I will only add that what I am going to say may seem to be an over-statement, or exaggeration of the truth, without this qualification, and must therefore ask to have it remembered.

We shall best open the gate of our argument on this subject, if we notice two great facts, or laws of our nature, which are the ground of this tendency in us to refer our own evils to things about us, and in the same way to keep us from a discovery of them as being in ourselves.

First, by a fixed necessity of language, we are obliged, apart from all the blinding effects of our sin, to represent a great part of what transpires in our experience, in a way of objective description. For example, it is the natural way of language to call things "hot," "sweet," "bitter," and the like, when in fact the words really describe nothing but our own inward sensations. So we say that a "subject is dark," not because there is any thing dark in the subject, but that we are dark to it. So again we say that a thing bears a "suspicious look," when we are suspicious of it; or of some spectacle that it "is fearful," when we are fearfully moved by it. We speak in the same way of "taking our chances" and "meeting our dangers," when in fact there is neither chance nor danger in things at all, but only an absolute certainty that this or that will take place. The uncertainty, or ignorance of what is to come is in us, and we call it chance or danger in things. Now the great part of mankind go through life, using every hour these objective terms of language, without ever once suspecting that what they describe as without, is nothing but an experience within themselves. Almost all staple words of language, as related to our inward experience, are of just this kind; it could not, as might easily be shown, have been otherwise. In this manner, we put almost all that we suffer, enjoy, feel, and think, into the objects and doings and characters round us, not understanding that what we figure, as in them, is really transpiring in ourselves—just as we say, how often, that we have "taken a cold," and verily believe that a cold something, we know not what, has seized us; whereas we have simply gotten up a fever—probably by over-indulgence—and then the shiverings and atmospheric chills that follow we take for the causes of the mischief.

But there is another great condition, or law of experience in bad minds, that is operating always and more powerfully in the same direction. A bad mind lives in things and for things, or we might rather say, under things. Condition, pleasure, show, are its god. And then it follows that the worship is only another name for distemper, unreason, hallucination. It is not positively insane, but what is very nearly the same thing, unsane—a nature out of joint, poisoned, racked with pains, a cloudy, wild, ungoverned, misconceiving power. It knows nothing but things, and if things do not bless it, what can it do but fall to cursing them? Being a distempered organ, it sees its distempers only in things and conditions round it. Thus when a diseased ear keeps up a nervous drumming in the brain, all sweetest music will have that drumming in it. So if the taste is bittered by some dyspectic woe, it will find that bitter savor in all most delicate things, and even in the pure waters of the spring. So also, I suppose, if the humors of the eye were jaundiced, the pure light of heaven would be yellowed also. Even the sun is smoky, seen through a smoked glass. Just so we are meeting all sorts of bitter, painful, and bad things, in our life, just because we are bitter, painful, bad, ourselves, and can not see that this is the root of our misery.

Besides it is a fact, under this great law of retributive disorder, that even good things are *really* bad to our feeling, because there is a bad mind in us. They are not given to be our torment, but the subjective badness of the soul makes them so; just as the weakness of the diseased eye makes the light a cause of injury and pain. The light is not bad in itself, but the receiving organ is bad, and so the pure light, image itself of God, shoots in arrows of pain that sting the body. In the same way selfishness and sin make the whole soul a diseased receiving organ; when, of course, every thing received or looked upon is bad, and imparts some kind of pain. The good law is made death unto it, Christ himself a savor of death. Truth is bad to us, holy men are a disturbance, life a burden, death a terror, heaven itself a world of constrained service and unreal or impossible joy.

We come now to the matter of fact itself. Is it only theory of which we have been speaking, or is it fact?

Here we make our appeal first of all to the scripture, where the illustrations are manifold and striking. There was never among men a more inoffensive, winning, and beautiful character than Joseph. But his brethren hated him and could not speak peaceably to him—hated him so intensely that they were willing to put him out of the way, by almost any method, however cruel. They talked with one another about him, painted him as a selfish, proud brother, and set him off in the most odious colors. Having a bad mind towards him, they saw only bad and hateful things in him. But the bad things were all in themselves, not in him. His only crime was his worth, and the beauty of his spirit, and that God, on this account, had advanced him, giving him the precedence his character deserved.

So with Saul; the devil of jealousy creeps into his morbid, selfish heart, and he sees in David, the faithful servant of his throne, a scheming usurper only and traitor, waiting to vault into his place. He is wrought up thus to such a pitch of fear and malice, that, in one of his paroxysms, he hurls a javelin at his head. The evil he sees in David is really in his own wild, ugly passion, but instead of strangling that, he tries to murder him!

Equally mad, exceedingly mad, almost conscientiously mad, as he himself relates, was Saul, the young rabbi of Tarsus, though in a different vein. The fiery young zealot was hot against Jesus, hot against Stephen, hot also against all the disciples of the new religion; but the heat of his passion he afterwards discovered was in the bad fire of his own bad mind, and the miserable bigotry that possessed him.

It is also a fact most remarkable, evincing the same thing, that Jesus Christ, the only spotless and perfect character that ever breathed the air of our planet, was more accused and hated, and charged with worse crimes, than it ever fell to the lot of any mortal to perpetrate. He was not only a Samaritan and had a devil, but he cast out devils by a devil, he broke the Sabbath, he was a mover of sedition, he made himself equal with God, he spoke blasphemy, he was a conspirator against Cæsar, his silence was called obstinacy, his eating and drinking gluttony and drunkenness, his cross the proof of his weakness and a fit mark for jeering, his death his defeat as an impostor and his final expulsion from the world. And yet there was nothing in him to irritate, or anger good men. His life was beauty itself, his spirit breathed the pure benignity even of God. Yes, and for just this reason, he disturbed the bad mind of men only the more bitterly. Troubled, heated, moved with jealousy, convinced of evil, they all rushed upon him as the troubler; becoming, at last, so exasperated against him, as to break out—priests, rabbis, senators, soldiers, populace—crying, all with one voice, crucify him, crucify him. See them gathering round his cross, hear their coarse mockeries and jeers! the poor fools have no thought or suspicion, that they are raging, in this diabolical malice, against exasperating causes that are after all in themselves!

The same truth is continually thrust upon our observation, in the intercourse of life. The passionate, ill-natured man is an example, living always in stormy weather, even though it be the quiet of dew-fall round him—always wronged, always hurt, always complaining of some enemy. He has no conception that this enemy is in his own bosom—in the sourness, the ungoverned irritability, the habitual ill-nature of his own bad spirit and character. I speak not here of some single burst of passion, into which a man of amiable temper may, for once, be betrayed; but I speak, more especially, of the angry characters—always brewing in some tempest of violated feeling. They have a great many enemies, they are unaccountably ill-treated, and can not understand why it is. They have no suspicion that they see and suffer bad things because they are bad, that being ill-natured is about the same thing as having ill-treatment, and that all the enemies they suffer from are snugly closeted in their own devilish temper.

The same is true of fretful persons—men and women that wear away fast and die, because they have worried life completely out. Nothing goes right; husband, or wife, or child, or customer, or sermon. They are pricked and stung at every motion they make, and wonder why it is that others are permitted to float along so peacefully, and they never suffered to have a moment of peace in their lives! And the very simple reason is that life is a field of nettles to them, because their fretful, worrying tempers, are always pricking out, through the tender skin of their uneasiness. Why, if they were set down in Paradise, carrying their bad mind with them, they would fret at the good angels, and the climate, and the colors even of the roses.

The animosities of the world are commonly to be solved in the same way—"Hateful and hating one another." A purely good mind would not hate even the worst of enemies and wrong-doers, but would have a sublime joy in loving him still. Thus we have one kind of enmity that hates differences of thought and sentiment, and is continually rasped by the fact that other men are so generally wrong-headed. Commonly the difficulty is prejudice, or bigotry in ourselves, reigning as a narrow, self-willed principle in the heart. Another misery we suffer, in the pride, and the high airs, and the ambition, and the undeserved successes of others. We wish there was some justice in the world, and that such people had their due! This now is *envy* in the soul, green-eyed, sick, self-tormenting envy. Then, again, we have it as another form of misery, that, having injured some one, we for that reason hate him; and there is no hatred so implacable, so bitter, and so like the pain of hell, as that which a man has to one whom he has injured—not to one who has injured him, but to one whom he has injured himself. And yet he will charge it not to himself, but only to the unaccountable fact, that the object of his malice must be so bad, so unmitigably hateful.

So again in regard to things of condition. The poor hypochondriac is just ready to be stranded in utter poverty and distress, though he holds, it may be, millions of property. We laugh at the strange fatuity he suffers. But every selfish mind is in it, only in some different way, or in some less exaggerated and palpably absurd form. Thus, what care, fear, anxiety, hunger, eagerness, is there in the world; and the secret of it is, that we are all imagining some fault in our condition. We want condition. Our thirsty, weary, discontented soul finds all it wants of blessedness denied, and wonders why it is that God has given us such a miserable desert to live in; as if the desert were in the world and not in ourselves—an immense Sahara wider than Africa knows! Why, if we were in the midst of God's own paradise, carrying our bad mind with us, we should see the desert there. The inward dearth and desolation of a mind separated from God and the all-sufficing rest and fullness of his peace, would raise mutinous questions and harsh accusations of dryness, against the finest, most superlative felicity God has ever been able to invent for his angels themselves.

Let us not omit to notice that the immoralities and crimes of the world are commonly conceived, by those who are in them, to be not of themselves, but to be chargeable on the bad causes round them. What is more continually asserted by thieves and gamblers, than the maxim that the world owes them a living; till, finally, they half teach themselves to feel that the world wrongs them, because it does not pay what it owes, but requires them to take the pay as they may find it. Whereas the bottom fact of all is, that they hate the bad necessity of work. The blasphemer, raging in a storm of imprecations and swearing by all sacred names—he is saying inwardly, even if no one remonstrates with him, how can I help it? an angel would speak some bad words, if he had such a horse as this to manage, or such a neighbor to deal with. The poor victim of drink—was he not disinherited by his father? or broken down by the slanders of enemies? or troubled by loads of debt from misfortunes that overtook him? or married to a wife who was a perpetual thorn to his peace? Was he not driven by the bad world somehow, as he manages to think himself, into this mode of drowning his misery? And so of the traitor hatching his treason—whole states of traitors hatching public treasons. Listen to their grievances—all in others, none in themselves. They have been injured, or insulted, or at any rate they were going to be. They are hot with the sense of injury not yet arrived, and must have their redress! Farewell order! welcome anarchy and blood! What an example of human passion, seeing worlds of wrong and enmity through the smoke of its own guilty jealousies, and the rampant fury of its own domineering habit.

Such is human nature in its bad estate everywhere. No sin sees its own evil; but the world is evil, everything is evil to it. Even truth is evil. Why should the preacher come to us with so many unwelcome messages? as if it were not enough to be dragged through such a world as this, without being disturbed all the way by hard accusations! It may be that we all sin; but the circumstances we live in are all bad, and what do we do, but what the circumstances make us. Let the preacher charge upon the circumstances! When they are not really angry at the truth, how many hearers dislike it. Little conception have they that the badness of the sermon is in themselves—"Say we not well, thou art a Samaritan and hast a devil?"

The subject I have now endeavored to illustrate is itself a purely practical subject, and yet a great many practical things beside are opened by it, that do not seem, at first, to be included. And—

1. It puts in a sad light of evidence what may well enough be called the weak point of Christianity; viz., the fact that the souls to be saved will be always seeing themselves in it, and not seeing it as it is—turning it thus into an element as dry as their dryness, as bitter as their bitterness, as distasteful and oppressive as their own weak thraldom under sin. And so it turns out that Christ is dry, bitter, a hard yoke, any thing but what he is. O, what power would there be in his love, and beauty, and divine greatness, if it were not for this. The grand difficulty in the way of a general conversion

is, that the bad minds of the world so immediately convert the gospel into their own figure. Christ is to them a root out of a dry ground, having no form or comeliness, and no beauty to be desired—they turn away their faces, he is despised and not esteemed. And what does he propose, in their view, but to make them like himself, laying it upon them also to be roots out of a dry ground, even as they are to follow him in self-denial, self-sacrifice, and bearing the cross. "These you propose to us," they say, "for our allotment; and what shall we have after we have sacrificed ourselves in this manner, and given up even our souls to the perdition of righteousness?" Every good and great thing offered is discolored from the bad color of their own bad state. And so the perpetual danger is, that what is given for their life, will be only a savor of death. Even the liberty of Christ appears to be only a way of thraldom—how can they imagine that the only real liberty of mind is the liberty of being in the truth, and the only possession of self the loss of self in God? And so it comes to pass that our gospel—mighty, gracious, captivating enough, we might think, to make an easy conquest of the world—dwindles sadly and gets fatally stifled, because it can not be to men's eyes, what it really is in itself. It can not be the salvation it would, just because a salvation is wanted.

It used to be frequently taught that men have no susceptibility that can be acted on by the gospel, save in a way of revulsion; that they must be only more exasperated by it, the more powerfully they are made to feel it. No, the difficulty commonly is that they project their own bad state into it, so as to almost shut away the feeling of it. As far as they do feel it they are drawn by the beauty of it—sometimes powerfully drawn—but alas! how soon is it discolored by their own turbid state, and the power it was going to have subsides into weakness.

2. We here perceive what is the true value of condition. I do not blame, of course, a proper attention to condition—it is even a duty. But the notion that we are really to make our state as bad or good by the surroundings of life, and not by what is within us, not only violates the scripture counsel, but, quite as palpably, the dictates of good sense—it is in fact the great folly of man. For a bad mind is of necessity its own bad state, and that state will be just as bad as the man is to himself, neither more nor less, come what may. A bad temper, a wrong love, an ungoverned pride, a restive ambition, a fretful, irritable, discontented habit within—why if a man had a den of vipers within, they would not make a state for him more absolutely than these. The surroundings of condition are to the man what the cloak is to the body, and the man who hid the fox under his cloak and hugged him close, till he gnawed into his vitals, might as well have been thinking to be happy because of his cloak, as any bad soul to be happy in sin because of condition. O, that men could be so far disenchanted of this devil that possesses their understanding, as to see how certain it is that their condition, after all, is what they are themselves; that it can be only bad as long as

they are bad, even if all the riches and power and splendor of the world were laid at their feet; and can be only good, if good is the spirit and the inward element of their life. Toil on, O ye slaves, contrive, and strive, and thrust yourselves on to riches and power; and then, at the end, discover that you have only gilded your misery, and built you a condition of more splendid sorrow; embittering bitterness by the mockery you offer to its comfort. Still you will see without, just what you are within, and the curse that is in you will curse every thing round you. The down you sleep on will be hard as your heart is, the silk that robes you will be a vesture of nettles to your ugly tempers, the coach in which you ride will answer to the jolting, night and day, of your bad conscience and your unsteady, gusty passions. If the bad state is in you, then every thing is bad, the internal disorder makes all things an element of disorder—even the sun in the sky will be your enemy.

3. We discover in this subject, what opinion to hold of the meaning and dignity of the state sometimes called misanthropy. Misanthropy is the state of mind that distastes men, the world, and life, and withdraws itself, more or less completely, into a feeling of self-justifying and self-isolating enmity. It is the sentimental state of wickedness, or wicked feeling, and is more common to youth than to persons of a later age. For some reason they are not happy; they begin to sympathize with themselves; they imagine how bad men are, and dislike them because they are selfish, or

proud, or unjust to merit; they disapprove the scheme of life, it is such a miserable affair, an experience so dull and so generally contemptible; they read Lord Byron, steeping their souls in his poetic hate, and specially sympathizing with the truculent sentiment of his Cain, retiring Cain-like, as it were, into the felicity of a self-justifying malice, to look out upon the world and curse it. Now the bottom of their woe, if they could dispossess themselves of a little vanity is that they are bad themselves. If they have such a hatred of men, are they not men themselves? and is it not probable enough that they have some as good title to distaste themselves? Is there not another, in the next house, or chamber, who is hating men, disgusted with men, just as they are? This very foolish state of mind has one legitimate cure, and one that is true reason itself, viz., conviction of sin. As soon as they can pass on just one step farther, and see that what they so much distaste is themselves, and that all the badness of the bad world is in their own bad spirit, they are in a way to come at the true remedy. Accordingly it is in just this manner that the Holy Spirit often leads to Christ. The man begins to be sick and weary, sick in mind and so in body, for a full half of the sicknesses of the body are only distempers of the mind; the world palls and grows distasteful; he sympathizes with himself, in a manner of inward complaint, draws off from that which does not satisfy, and loosens a kind of sentimental animosity towards men and things. But the load grows heavier, chafing through the skin of his conceit into the nerves of conviction; misanthropy changes to self-disgust; the secrets of the heart are opened; the conscience breaks restraint; and finally it stands revealed that sin is in the soul—a bondage, a disease, a shame, a curse. And now the question is who can heal the inward bitterness? Misanthropy, then, and world sickness are the bad state felt, conviction of sin is the bad state understood. That is a conceited misery, this the shame of a self-discovering weakness, guilt, and spiritual disorder.

4. It is clear, in this subject, that we have little reason for troubling ourselves in questions that relate to a place of future misery. Enough to know that the mind is its own place, and will make a place of woe to itself, whithersoever it goes, in a life of sin and separation from God. If the sceptic bolts upon us with the question, where is hell? or the question, whether we suppose that a God of infinite goodness has occupied himself in excavating and fashioning a local state for the torment of bad men? it is enough to answer that a bad mind carries a hell with it, excavates its own place of torment, makes it deep and hot as with fire, and will assuredly be in that place, whatever else may be true. A good mind sits in heavenly places, because it is good. Go where it will it is with God, and God is templed eternally in it; God in his own everlasting beatitude and peace. Exactly what is true of place beyond this, or of place as related to the condition of happy spirits, we do not know, but shall know hereafter. Enough that the bad mind will at least be its

own bad state and element. It has the fire and brimstone in itself, and the suffocating smoke, and the darkness, and the thirst, and the worm that never dies—testifying always, "I myself am Hell." It would turn the golden pavement into burning marl, and the hymns and hallelujahs of the blessed into shrieks of discord.

Finally, it is evident in these illustrations, that the salvation of man is possible, only on the ground of a great and radical change in his inmost temper and spirit. What is wanted for the felicity of man is clearly not a change of place, or condition, but a change in that which makes both place and condition what they are. The bad spirit—this is the woe; and nothing cures the woe, but that which changes the spirit of the mind. Marvel not at this; you have only to take one glance at the world, turn one thought upon yourselves, to see it. Hence it is that Christ has come into the world as the physician of souls—it is that he may impart to them a new life and spirit from himself, and heal the disorders of their bad state, by uniting them to his own person. Think it not strange that he proposes thoughts to you so different from your own. O, ye weary ones, all ye desolate, all ye tossed with tempest and not comforted, all ye world-sick and heavy hearted, hear ye his call—"come unto me and I will give you rest." Why, my friends, what does it mean that we are such a malcontent, miserable race of beings? Did not a good God make us and the world we live in? Why then are we so continually plagued and tormented in it? Why so hungry, so dry, so empty, so bitter, so like the troubled sea and the mire and dirt it casts up in its storms? Has God made some mistake in mixing the ingredients of our state? No, it is we that make all this discord, we that mix in the acid ingredients of misery. The moment you can enter back, out of sin, into this pure element of love in Christ, this world becomes a realm of peace, a paradise of beauty, a feast of satisfying good, an instrument of joyous harmony. Change the inward state and all is changed. Ye shall go out with joy, and be led forth with peace, the mountains and the hills shall break forth before you into singing, and all the trees of the hills shall clap their hands.

XVI.

PRESENT RELATIONS OF CHRIST WITH HIS FOLLOWERS.

"*Ye have heard how I said unto you, I go away and come again unto you.*"—JOHN xiv, 28.

To go away and come again, or to go away in order to come again, would seem, taking the words at their face, to be a rather idle or unmeaning operation; but if we can get far enough into the mind of Christ to apprehend his real meaning, we shall find that he is proposing, in these words, a change of the greatest consequence—a change that is necessary to the working plan of his gospel and even to the complete value of his incarnation itself. In what sense then he is going, and in what sense he will come again, what change of relationship he will inaugurate between himself and his followers, and so *what kind of personal relation he undertakes to hold with them now*, is the subject to which I call your attention this morning, as one of intense practical interest, and even of the tenderest personal concern.

Whoever has reflected much upon the subject of the incarnation has discovered that its value depends on brevity of time, and that no such condition could be permanent, without becoming a limitation upon itself and a real hindrance to its own objects. Remaining permanently on earth in the body, Christ, plainly enough, could never have extended his rule into parts remote, or to persons debarred by distance from the external modes of access and acquaintance. The incarnation, therefore, requires shortly to be inverted. After the immense new revelation, or new salvation, of God has been accomplished, by such a manifested presence and divine life in the flesh, there needs, just as truly, to be a withdrawment from the eyes; otherwise Christ, remaining in the world and permanently fixed in it, could only gather a small circle about him, and become the center of an outward Lama worship, as restricted as the mere sight, or appearing, of the divine man-idol requires it to be.

Therefore he says—"it is expedient for you that I go away," adding the promise—"I will come to you." He means, by this, that the time has now arrived, when there must be a change of administration; when he must needs be taken away from the eyes, and begin to be set in a new spiritual relation, which permits a universal access of men to him, and a universal presence of him with them—so a grand, world-wide kingdom. Saying nothing of the particular objects to be gained by his death, he could not stay here and carry on his work; he had as many friends now as he could speak with, or allow to speak with him; and if he should remain, holding fixed locality, as of a body in space, he could be the head only of a coterie, never of a kingdom. What is wanted now is an unlocalized, invisible, spiritually present, everywhere present, Saviour; such as all may know and receive, being consciously known and received by him.

And this will be his coming again, or his second coming—such a kind of coming as shows him bearing rule in Providence, and riding in the clouds of heaven—rolling on the changes, unfolding the destinies of time, and preparing his universal kingdom. The world, he says, seeth me no more, but ye see me; and having your spiritual eye open for this, it will be as if you saw me coming triumphantly in the clouds. This image is a well-known Eastern figure of princely pomp and majesty; they say of every great monarch, taking ascendancy, that he rides on the clouds of heaven. So, as Christ comes on, bearing sway and ruling invisible, it will be as if he were seen coming on overhead, in the clouds. And especially will this be felt when Jerusalem the Holy City is blotted out, as it were by God's hand of judgment upon it, in the conquest by Titus. By that sign goes out the old, exclusive, Jew-state; and there comes in after it, now to have its place, the Christian, catholic, free state, that is to be gathered under the universal, spiritual headship of Christ. That gathering in, as in power, is to be his coming, or coming again—no bodily appearing, no visible pomp, no manifestation locally as in space; for the very thing that made it expedient for him to go away from the senses, forbids any such outward manifestation. And therefore he adds a caution, telling his disciples expressly, that his coming thus again is not to be a coming with observation. There shall be no calling "Lo, here is Christ, or lo, there," "behold he is in the desert," "behold he is in the secret chambers." The power in which he comes will be morally diffusive and secretly piercing—"as the lightning cometh out of the east and shineth even unto the west, so also shall the coming of the Son of Man be."

In all which Christ, you will perceive, is proposing to do exactly nothing which many of his disciples, specially taken by the faith of his second coming, so fervently preach and so earnestly magnify. They believe that he is to come in a body, and be visible as in body. He will of course be here or there in space, a locally present being, at some particular geographic point—Jerusalem, or London, or Rome, or going about in all places by turns. Hearing now that he is here, or there, we shall think no more of seeing him by faith, and begin to think of seeing him with our eyes. Every ship that sails will be crowded with eager multitudes pressing on to see the visible Christ. Thronging in thus, month by month, a vast seething crowd of pilgrims, curious and devout, poor and rich, houseless all and hungry, trampling each other, many of them sick, not one of them in the enjoyment truly of God's peace, not one of a thousand getting near enough to see him, still fewer to hear him speak—how long will it take under such kind of experience to learn what Christ intended and the solid truth of it, when he said—"it is expedient for you that I go away." Nothing could be more inexpedient, or a profounder affliction, than a locally descended, permanently visible, Saviour. How much better a Saviour present everywhere, and at all times; a Saviour who can say, "Lo, I am with you always," and make the promise good; one whom the heart can know, as being at rest in him, and behold, as by faith; wheeling his chariot on through all the tumults and overturnings of time, till his universal kingdom is complete.

I am well aware that our brethren, who look for Christ's visible coming, will not allow the inconveniences, or almost absurdities, I have here sketched, to be any proper results of their doctrine. "We believe," they will say, "that he will come in a spiritual body, such as he had after his resurrection, not in a coarse, material body. It will be such a body that he can be here, or there, at any given moment, hampered by no conditions of space; even as he came into the room where his disciples were gathered, when the doors were shut." But they only impose upon themselves by such a conception. If their spiritual body is to be visible, it must be as in space and outward appearing; for that is the condition of all visibility. And then we have a flitting Saviour, breaking out here or there, at what time, or on what occasion, no mortal can guess. And the result will be that they are in a worse torment than they would be, if he were established in some known locality. Going after their eyes, they are taken off from all faith, and where their eyes shall find him they know not.

Pardon me then if I suggest the suspicion that they

are more carnal in their expectation than they know. If it is so much better to have a visible Saviour, are they not more weary of faith than they should be, and secretly longing, catching at straws of prophecy, to get away from it? There is nothing, I must frankly say, that would be so nearly a dead loss of Christ to any disciple who knows him in the dear companionship of faith, as to have him come in visible show; either setting up his reign at some geographic point, or reigning aerially, in some flitting and cursitating manner which can not be traced. How beautifully accessible is he now everywhere, present to every heart that loves him; consciously dear, as friend, consoler, guide, and stay, in all conditions; close at hand in every sinking ship in the uttermost parts of the sea; the sweet joy of dungeons under ground, where there is no light to see him in a body; immediately and all-diffusively present, to comfort every sorrow, support every persecution, and even to turn away the tempting thought before it comes. A Saviour in the body and before the eyes can serve no such offices. None can find him, but them that come in his way, or chance to spy him with their eyes.

We have no want then of a locally related, that is of a bodily resident Saviour; we perceive, without difficulty, the expediency of which Christ speaks, that he should go away and not continue the incarnate, or visible state, longer than to serve the particular objects for which he assumed that state. But he gives us to understand, that he is not going to be taken utterly away in the proposed removal, but rather to be as much closer to his disciples as he can be, when all conditions of time and space are cast off. And accordingly the question rises at this point, how is Christ related now to the knowledge and friendship of his people? "Ye have heard how I said unto you I go away and come again unto you." And again—"I will not leave you comfortless, I will come to you." And again—"but ye see me." And again—"Lo, I am with you always." He evidently means to put himself thus in a practically close and dear relation with his people—what is that relation? how set open? how maintained?

Obviously what we want ourselves, is to be somehow with him, and to know that he is with us. We want a social, consciously open state with him, as real as if he were with us bodily, and as diffusive as if he were everywhere; thus to have a personal enjoyment of him, and rest in the felt sympathies of his personal companionship. This, too, exactly is what he means to allow us; not in the external way, but in a way more immediate, and blessed, and evident, and as much more beneficial. If we had him with us in the external way, as his own disciples had, when they journeyed, and talked, and eat, and slept, in his company, we should be living altogether in our eyes, and not in any way of mental realization. And, as a result, we should not be raised and exalted in spiritual force, or character, as we specially need to be. What we want, therefore, is to have a knowledge of him, and presence and society with him, that we can carry with us, and have as the secret joy, and strength, and conscious blessing of our inmost life itself; that we may see him, when we are blind and can see nothing with our eyes; that we may hear him speak, when we are deaf and can hear nothing with our ears; that we may walk with him, when we can not walk at all; sit in heavenly places with him, when we can not sit at all; rise with him when he rises, reign with him when he reigns; never away from him, even when beyond the sea, or passing through the valley of the shadow of death.

Now it is just this relation that he undertakes to fill, when he goes away. Being himself a Comforter, [Paraclete,] for this is the word translated Advocate, he promises "another Comforter;" that is, in some proper sense, another self. Indeed, he really calls the Comforter promised, another self; for he says expressly, in this very connection—"Even the Spirit of truth, whom the world can not receive because it seeth him not; neither knoweth him, but ye know him; for he dwelleth with you and shall be in you;" striking directly into the first person, to say the same thing over again, as relating to himself—"Yet a little while and the world seeth me no more, but ye see me; because I live, ye shall live also. At that day ye shall know that I am in my Father, and ye in me, and I in you." And then, to be still more explicit, he gives the promise, that whosoever of his followers follows faithfully, keeping his commandments, shall have the immediate manifestation always of his presence—"I will manifest myself unto him,"—"If a man love me he will keep my words, and my Father will love him, and we will come unto him and make our abode with him."

The great change of administration thus to be introduced, by the going away and coming again, includes several points that require to be distinctly noted.

1. That Christ now institutes such a relationship between him and his followers, that they can know him when the world can not. Before this, the world had known him just as his disciples had, seeing him with their eyes, hearing his doctrine, observing his miracles, but now he is to be withdrawn, so that only they shall see him—"the world seeth him not." As being rational persons, they may recollect him, they may read other men's recollections of him, but his presence they will not discern, he is not manifest unto them, but only to his followers. He that loveth knoweth God, and he only.

2. It is a point included that the new presence, or social relationship, is to be effected and maintained by the Holy Spirit, the Comforter. And he it is that Christ, in the promise, calls so freely himself. The New Testament writings are not delicate in maintaining any particular formula, or scheme of personality, as regards the distributions of Trinity. They call the Spirit "the Spirit of Christ." They say, "God hath sent the Spirit of his Son into your hearts." They speak of "the supply of the Spirit of Jesus Christ." They speak also of "the law of the Spirit of life in Christ Jesus." They say, "the Lord [Christ] is that Spirit." Christ also is

shown, more than once, fulfilling the official functions of the Spirit; as in Paul's conversion, where the invisible Christ, that is the Spirit, says "I am Jesus of Nazareth whom thou persecutest; or again, when Paul himself describes his conversion by saying, "when it pleased God to reveal his Son in me." No theologic scruples are felt in such free modes of expression, and indeed there never should be; for to every one but the strict tritheist, Christ must, in some sense, be the Spirit, and the Spirit, Christ. And when Christ calls the Comforter he promises, himself, he gives precisely the best and truest representation of the Spirit, in his new office, possible to be given. It is to be as if the disincarnated soul, or person of Christ, were now to go away and return as a universal Spirit invisible; in that form "to abide forever." And the beauty of the conception is, that the Spirit is to be no mere impersonal effluence, or influence, but to be with us in the very feeling and charity of Jesus. All the fullness of Christ is in him; the gentleness, the patience, the tenderness, the self-sacrifice; all that makes Jesus himself such a power of personal mastery in us. He is to be with us in Christ's name as a being with a heart, nay, to be the heart itself that was beating in the Son of Mary. All the charities, and even the blessed humanities of Jesus are to be in him, and, in fact, to be ministered socially, and socially manifested by him; even as Christ expressly declared—"He shall glorify me; for he shall receive of man and show it unto you." This inward showing is, in fact, the virtuality of Christ. He will be to the soul all that

Christ himself would wish to be; for he loves the world with Christ's own love. He will be as forgiving as Christ in his passion, as tenderly burdened as Christ in his agony, as really present to physical suffering, as truly a Comforter to all the shapes of human sorrow. All which Christ outwardly expressed, he will inwardly show.

3. In this coming again of Christ by the Spirit, there is included also the fact that he will be known by the disciple, not only socially, but as the Christ, in such a way as to put us in a personal relationship with him, even as his own disciples were in their outward society with him. "Ye shall know that I am in the Father, and ye in me, and I in you." "But ye know him." "But ye see me." Many persons appear to suppose that the Holy Spirit works in a manner back of all consciousness, and that there is even a kind of extravagance in the disciple who presumes to know him. And so it really is, if the conception is that he knows him by sensation, or by inward phantasy. But what means the apostle when he says—"the Spirit itself beareth witness with our Spirit that we are the children of God"? That bearing witness with imports some kind of inward society, or interchange, in which a divine testimony flows into human impression, or conviction, else it imports nothing. The real Christian fact in regard to this very important subject appears to be, that the Holy Spirit, or Spirit of Christ, though not felt by sensation, or beheld by mental vision, is yet revealed, back of all perception, in the consciousness. We are made originally to be conscious

of God, just as we are of ourselves, and know him by that immediate light. This is our normal state and it is now so far restored. Our finite being was to be complete in the infinite, and apart from that, could only be a poor dead limb, or broken fragment, worthless to itself. And this accordingly is the wonder of a true religious experience begun, that the soul, awakened to the consciousness of God, not knowing how, has a certain mysterious feeling of otherness imparted, which is somehow a new element to it—a pure, inwardly glorious, free element. By and by it gets acquainted with the new and glorious incoming, and dares to say, it is Christ, it is God. A whole side of the nature turning Godward thus, and before closed, is now open, and the man is even more impressively conscious at times of the divine movement in his feeling, than of his own. And this fulfills the promise—"I will manifest myself unto him." A promise which Paul bravely answers, when he says, out of his own conscious experience—"Christ liveth in me,"—"who loved me and gave himself for me."

Here then is the relationship we seek—Christ is so related now, to the soul of them that receive him, that he is present with them in all places, at all times, bearing witness with their spirit, in guidance and holy society; a friend, a consoler, a glorious illuminator, all that he would or could be, if we had him each to himself in outward company. Yes, and he is more than this; for if we simply had him in such outward company, the contrast perceived would be even mortifying and oppressive; but now, as he comes up from within, through our personal consciousness itself, we are raised in dignity, and have him as the sense of a new and nobler self unfolded in us. O, what a footing is this for a mortal creature to occupy, an open relationship with Christ and God, in which it shall receive just all which it wants, being consciously girded with strength for whatever it has to do, patience for suffering, wisdom for guidance. His very nature is penetrated by a higher nature, and, being spirit to Spirit, he moves in the liberty of that superior impulse and advisement. His relationship to Christ is that of the branch to the vine, and the presence that he has with Christ is immediate, vital, and if he will suffer it, perpetual. Its whole gospel in one view it has in the promise—"Lo, I am with you always, even to the end of the world."

But there is a different conception of this whole matter, which I must briefly notice. Many persons appear to assume, that we have, and can have, no relations to Christ, more immediate than those which we have through language and the understanding. The Spirit, they say, works by truth, and only as the truth gets power in our thoughts and choices. Their conception is that we have nothing to do with God, except as we get hold of notions, or notional truths, concerning him—reported facts, for example, and teachings, and doctrinal deductions. Undoubtedly we are to have this notional furniture in the understanding, but it is never to be a fence between us and God, requiring us to know him only at second hand, as we know China by the report of the geographers. We are still to know God, or Christ, by our immediate experience; nay, to know him as we know ourselves, by consciousness. It is useful for us to know ourselves scientifically, intellectually, reflectively; but this kind of artificial self-knowledge is not enough. Some of us, in that way, would scarcely know ourselves at all, and none of us more than partially, intermittently, and in spots. We want to know ourselves all the while, and without study, so as to be all the while possessing and going along with ourselves, and therefore we are gifted with an immediate consciousness of ourselves. But we want, just as much, to know God by this immediate and perpetual knowledge; for apart from God we are nothing, we do not even half exist. Our finite existence becomes complete existence, only as we are complete in Him, and this we can not be, save as he is manifested, or participated, by our consciousness. Thus we might have our advantage in a notional, or scientific conception of the atmosphere, but if we could breathe only by such scientific self-regulation, many of us would stop breathing entirely, and all of us would be gasping for air a great part of the time; what we want is a continual fanning of the breath that shall keep the air at work, feeding our life all the time, without intermission, and without any kind of notional self-regulation. So, too, we want a perpetual inbreathing of God, a witnessing of the divine Spirit with our spirit, else our very nature is abortive and worthless. It is not enough that we have notions, or doctrines, of God, which we may use, or apply, to obtain flavors of good effect through such media—we want the immediate manifestation of God himself. And then, lest we should sink away into the abysses and trances of contemplation, with Plotinus and others who struggle out vaguely into and after the infinite, we have the infinite humanly personated in Christ; so that, instead of wandering off into any abysses at all, we simply let the Son of Man be God in our feeling, and fashion us in the molds of his own humanly divine excellence. Christ we say liveth in us; and therefore by the faith of the Son of God, we live.

But is not this a kind of mysticism, some will ask, better therefore to be avoided than received? I hardly know what is definitely meant by the question; unless perhaps it be that a word is wanted that will serve the uses of a stigma. A great many will begin to suspect some kind of mysticism, just because they are mystified, or misted, and see things only in a fog of obscurity. But if this be mysticism, nothing is plainer than that Christ is the original teacher of it, and his two disciples, John and Paul, specially abundant teachers of it after him. Every man is a mystic in the same way, who believes that Christ is the Life—in such a sense the life that he truly liveth in his followers, and giveth them to live by him. God as the Life, the all-quickener, the all-mover and sustainer, the inward glory and bliss of souls—this may be set down as a thing too high to be any but a mystical notion. And yet all highest things are apt to be most rational, and, at bottom, most credible. What can be more rational, in fact, than to think that

God will give us most certainly what is most wanted—water, and light, and air, and yet more freely, Himself? He will not put us off to know only things about him, truths, notions, items of fact, but will give us to know Himself. And since all souls are dark, living only to grope, without Him—poor, blind pilgrims, straying on the shores of eternity—what will he do, what, in all true reason, must he do, but make himself the true sunrising to them, and the conscious revelation of their inward day.

Our answer then to the question what are Christ's present relations to his followers? is that he is present to them as he is not, and can not be to the world; present as an all-permeating Spirit; present as the all-quickening Life; consciously, socially present; so that no explorations of science, or debates of reason are wanted to find him, no going over the sea to bring him back, or up into heaven to bring him down; because he is already present, always present, in the mouth and in the heart. In this manner he will be revealed in all men, waits to be revealed in all, if only they will suffer it. The word for every loving, trusting heart is, I will come unto it, I will be manifest in it. Lo, I will be with it always.

But the answer at which we thus arrive is a purely spiritual answer, you perceive, one that is real and true only as it is opened to faith, and experimentally proved. But all such spiritualities waver and flicker; we are too much in the senses to hold them constantly and evenly enough to rest in them. Therefore to keep us in the range of this relationship, God has contrived to fasten us in the sense of it, and make it good, by two fixed, partly outward, institutes, that are to stand as forts, or fortresses, in the foreground of it; viz., by the church and by the sacraments.

"Behold the kingdom of God is within you," says the Saviour, meaning that he will be there, and there will have his reign. But he also lays the foundations of a great, perpetual, visible institute, that he names the church, calling it to be the light of the world, even as he, in the body, was the light of the world himself, and because he is now, in the Spirit, to be entered into and fill the body of the church with light. His apostle calls it too "the pillar and ground of the truth," because it is to be that corporate body that never dies, receiving the written word as a deposit and trust for all ages to come, and becoming itself a living epistle, answering faithfully to it, and shedding, from its own luminous property, a perpetual light of interpretation upon it. Of this body, called the church, he is to be the Head himself, and all the members joined together in him, are to be so related to Him as to make a virtually real, and perpetually diffusive, incarnation of him in the world. While, therefore, it was expedient for him to go away as the Son of Man, or of Mary, it was yet to be found, as he comes again by revelation to the consciousness of his disciples, that he is again taking body, in fact, for all time, in them; so to be manifested organically, and, as it were, instituted in their undying and corporate membership—"Head over all things to the church which is his body, the fullness of him that filleth all in all." The members are to know him personally, each in his own immediate life, and then they are to know him again even the more firmly, that they are consciously instituted and framed into body by his life. It is to be as if their divine consciousness itself were certified, and sealed, and made visible, by its own organizing power—that power which ages and times can not weaken, which outlives the kingdoms and their persecutions, and defies the gates of hell. "From whence the whole body, fitly joined together and compacted by that which every joint supplieth, according to the effectual working in the measure of every part, maketh increase of the body unto the edifying of itself in love." What solidity is there now in such a relation to Christ! Spiritual as the relation is, it is yet even more intellectually fixed, and carries better evidence, than Christ in the body was ever able to give his followers.

But the spiritualities of the relation Christ maintains with his disciples were to be settled and fortified by still another institute; I mean the sacraments, and especially the sacrament of the Holy Supper. The very object of the supper appears to be the settlement, and practical, or experimental, certification of that revelation to consciousness, of which we have been speaking. "This is my body, take and eat." "This is my blood, drink ye all of it." And this, to establish, as by institute, the fact that Christ here present, is to be communicated and received, as by nutrition, or as life. And this is what is meant by discerning his body, and the showing forth of his death; for there is to be an accepting, in the partaker, of his here represented embodiment, and a confession of trust in his death, to which he will, by these instituted symbols and pledges, be inwardly discovered, as certainly and as often as the rite is duly observed. When, therefore, he says, "this do in remembrance of me," we are not to take his words in the lightest, shallowest, possible meaning, as if he were only giving us a mnemonic to refresh our memories, but in the deepest and most sacredly inward sense; viz., that he is giving it to us here, to receive the dearest hospitality, the communion of his own divine Life. All that famous discourse of his about the bread and the blood, in the 6th chapter of John, is but the fit opening of his meaning. "I am the bread of life—the living bread that came down from heaven—if any man eat of this bread he shall live forever. My flesh is meat indeed, and my blood is drink indeed. Except ye eat the flesh of the Son of Man and drink his blood, ye have no life in you."

And this exactly is the great institute of the supper. Christ engages to be present in it, by a most real presence, without a miracle of transubstantiation; so that when we come to offer him up ourselves, and open our inmost receptivities to the appropriation of his presence, it is no vague, volunteer, possibly presumptuous, thing that we do, as if venturing on some almost aerial flight, in the way of coming unto God, but we have the grace by institution, firmly pledged, and given, as it were, by routine. Here is Christ to be communicated. Here are we to commune. There is no miracle, but what is a great deal better, viz., life; community of life with Christ and God. What we get in the conscious revelation of his Spirit, we here receive by an outward and perpetually instituted dispensation. And we have this communion also with each other as with Christ; because he is the common life, which is endeavoring always a common growth in the members.

O, that we might receive this supper to-day, my brethren, according to its true meaning, and eat and drink worthily. Take it as no mere commemorative ceremony over Christ dead, but as the appointed vehicle of Christ living, and in you to live. Come not here to be sad and sit mourning for your Master's body, like the women weeping for Tammuz. Consider, above all, this, that Christ, once dead, is here alive, that he may here dispense himself to you. Blessed is the heart that shall be fully opened to him. Be that true, as it may be, of you all; that you may go forth loving one another as you love your Master, and shining without, by the light he gives you within. Neither forget how that open, dear, relation of spirit with him, of which we have been speaking, is here sanctioned publicly for you, and sanctified before you, even as by an institute of God. As he has gone away, so believe, henceforth and always, that he has come again. Count this coming in the Spirit to be with you, dearer than even outward society with him would be, such as his disciples had at the first; and expect to be always with him in this manner, in the closest, most immediate, knowledge; even as he said himself—BUT YE SEE ME.

XVII.

THE WRATH OF THE LAMB.

"*And said to the mountains and rocks, Fall on us and hide us from the face of him that sitteth on the throne, and from the wrath of the Lamb. For the great day of his wrath is come; and who shall be able to stand?*"—REV. vi, 16–17.

The lamb is the most simply innocent of all animals. Historically also it had become a name for sacrifice. For this twofold reason, Christ is set forth as the Lamb. Under this name, as fulfilling the conception of gentleness and sacrifice in God, we give him ready welcome. We magnify him as the Lamb, and expect to magnify him even eternally, in ascriptions offered to that dear name. Even such as are most remote from the life of religion are commonly satisfied with conceptions of God under this gentle, patient figure; making up, not seldom, schemes of divine character and order, that have only the innocuous way of the lamb—just as thousands of the devotees of liberty will magnify liberty, as being the whole substance of government; counting it really the same thing as a release from being governed. Yet liberty is but justice secured; and, in just the same manner, the Lamb is but the complemental gentleness of God's judicial vigor.

All which appears to be represented by a most paradoxical, jarring, combination of words, that predicates wrath of the very lambhood of Christ. To speak simply of the wrath of God is bad enough to some; it is even a real offense. They recoil from such expressions as unworthy, and as indicating, either a degree of irreverence in those who use them, or else low ideas of God, such as may not be revolted by the ascription of a temper so unregulated and so essentially coarse. It is commonly no sufficient answer to such, that the scriptures of God speak of his wrath in this way without compunction; for the scriptures, they will suspect, are not as far refined themselves, in the moral tastes and proprieties, as they might be. But here we have "the wrath of the Lamb;"—which not only violates a first principle of rhetoric, forbidding the conjunction of symbols that have no agreement of kind or quality, but also shocks our cherished conceptions of Christ, as the suffering victim, or the all-merciful and beneficent friend, in either way, the Saviour of sinners. Who will ever speak of a lamb's wrath? Who, much more, of the wrath of the Lamb of God? And yet the scripture does it without any sense of impropriety, or moral incongruity—what shall we make of such a fact?

Simply this, I answer, that while our particular age is at the point of apogee from all the more robust and vigorous conceptions of God in his relation to evil; while it makes nothing of God as a person or governing will; less, if possible, of sin as a wrong-doing by subject wills; we are still to believe in christianity, and not in the new religion of nature; in Christ, and not in the literary gentlemen. It does not, in my view, require a very great degree of nerve to do this. Only we must have the right to believe in the real Christ, and not that theologic Christ which has so long been praised, as it were into weakness, by the showing that separates him from all God's decisive energies and fires of combustion, and puts him over against them, to be only a pacifier of them by his suffering goodness. Our Christ must be the real king—Messiah—and no mere victim; he must govern, have his indignations, take the regal way in his salvation. His goodness must have fire and fibre enough to make it divine.

We take the principle, in brief, without scruple, *that if we can settle what is to be understood by the wrath of God, we shall not only find the wrath in God, but as much more intensely revealed, in the incarnate life and ministry of Christ, as the love is, or the patience, or any other character of God.* Since he is the Lamb, in other words, the most emphatic and appalling of all epithets will have its place, viz.,—the wrath of the Lamb.

We want very much, in English, a word that we have not, to express more definitely the true force of the original scripture word [οργη] occurring in this relation. We have a considerable family of words that we can employ for this purpose; such as *wrath*, *anger*, *indignation*, *fury*, *vengeance*, *judgment*, *justice*, and the like, but they are all more or less defective. *Indignation* is the most unexceptionable, but it is too prosy and weak to carry such a meaning with due effect. *Wrath* is the term most commonly used in our translation, and it is really the best, if only we can hold it closely enough to the idea of a moral, in distinction from a merely animal passion; else, failing in this, it will connect associations of unregulated temper that are painful, and as far as possible from being sacred. It requires in this view, like the safety-lamps of the miners, a gauze of definition round it, to save it from blazing into an explosion too fierce to serve the purposes of light.

We understand then by wrath, as applied to God and to Christ, a certain principled heat of resentment towards evil doing and evil doers, such as arms the good to inflictions of pain, or just retribution, upon them. It is not the heat of revenge, girding up itself in fiery passion, to repay the personal injuries it has suffered; but it is that holy heat which kindles about order, and law, and truth, and right; going in, as it were, spontaneously, to redress their wrongs and chastise the injuries they have suffered. It is that, in every moral nature, which prepares it to be an essentially beneficent avenger, a holy knight-errant champion for the right, and true, and good. It can be let in to nerve a resentment, or to bitter a grudge, and commonly is, in souls given up to resentments and grudges; but it was ordained specially to be such an equipment of moral natures, that goodness would be an armed state, capable not only of beneficence, but of inflicting pain where pain is wanted, in the fit vindication of order and right.

How it works, we may see, almost every hour, in

some example greater, or less, in its magnitude. Only to see a large boy in the street harassing and persecuting a small one, stirs the natural wrath-principle in us, in such a manner that, if we do not actually lay hands upon him ourselves, we could easily be much satisfied if a considerable chastisement should overtake him. So, if an officer of the law arrests a woman in the street, haling her away to justice, you will see a multitude, excited by her outcries, rushing quickly together, wanting to know what a strong man can be doing in that fashion with a woman, and about half ready to interfere, before they have learned whether it is a case of oppression or not. We had an illustration, a few days ago, of this wrath-principle in human bosoms, on a much grander scale—the whole New England people, or rather the whole nation itself, waiting, as it were, by the gallows of a Webster, and giving their spontaneous sanction to his death, by their emphatic and hearty Amen. Under the solemn wrath-principle of which I am here speaking, every healthy and robust soul took the penalty with appetite, and with a certain good revenge, stood stiff and firm by the impartial and righteous sentence of the law. So if this great and awful rebellion against which we are now in arms, should finally collapse and go down, and the friends of Union, so long and bitterly oppressed by their tyrants, should rise upon them and drag them to summary justice, compelling them to expiate, by their death, the most terrible and bloodiest, and really most impious, crime ever committed on earth, save the crucifixion of Jesus itself, who of us would blame, or in the least regret, the judicial severity of the retribution? Why, the unspeakable desolations, the latitudes and longitudes of the woe, would even take on a smile, in our thought, and we should find ourselves thanking God, even before we knew it, that he has put a wrath-principle in human bosoms for the avenging of so great a crime. Nay, we should be quite willing to imagine this wrath-principle residing also in the very ground itself, and crying unto God, from every blood-sodden field and region, even as the blood of Abel did, in Cain's one, solitary, merely initial, comparatively insignificant, murder.

In all these and similar examples that could be cited without number, there is, you perceive, a function of wrath, or an instinctively vindicatory function, that pertains to all moral natures, and arms them to be the supporters of justice and the avengers of wrong. They have this high moral instinct, or function, not as a vice to be extirpated or stifled, but as an integral part of their inmost original nature. It is constituent, consubstantial, and is to be eternal.

Having distinguished, in this manner, what is to be understood by wrath, as predicated, whether of God or of the Lamb, we are ready to proceed with the main subject of inquiry. Is it then a fact that Christ, as the incarnate Word of God, embodies and reveals the wrath-principle of God, even as he does the patience or love-principle, and as much more intensely? On this point we have many distinct evidences. And—

1. It is very obvious, at the outset, that Christ can not be a true manifestation of God, when he comes in half the character of God, to act upon, or qualify, or pacify, the other half. He must be God manifest in the flesh, and not one side of God. If only God's affectional nature is represented in him, then he is but a half manifestation. And if we assign him, in that character, a special value, then we say, by implication, what amounts to the worst irreverence, that God is a being to be most desired when he is only half presented, and when his other half is either kept back, or somehow smoothed to a condition of silence. I take issue with all such conceptions of Christ. He is God manifested truly, God as he is, God in all his attributes combined, else he is nothing, or at least no fair exhibition. If the purposes of God, the justice of God, the indignations of God, are not in Him; if any thing is shut away, or let down, or covered over, then he is not in God's proportions, and does not incarnate his character.

2. It will be noted that Christ can be the manifested wrath of God, without being any the less tender in his feeling, or gentle in his patience. If God may fitly comprehend these opposite poles of character, so also may Christ; and if the fires of God's retributive indignations are no contradiction to the fact that he is love, no more is there any such contradiction to be apprehended, when these indignations are displayed in Christ. Indeed we have occasions in the history of Jesus, when he actually displays the judicial and the tender, most affectingly, together and in the very same scene. "And

when he had looked about on them with anger," says Mark, "being grieved for the hardness of their hearts." Here we have the wrath, [οργη] in a connection of feeling so tender and loving, that he is even grieved. His indignations have quickened his more tender sensibilities, and these, in turn, have fired his indignations. And we have exactly the same conjunction over again, when we find him even weeping over Jerusalem, and, at the same moment, denouncing against it, in stern retribution, the day of its final visitation. "If thou hadst known the things that belong to thy peace! but now they are hid from thine eyes!" How tenderly, and yet how firmly spoken is the wrath. And then, while the tears of his compassion are scarcely dried away upon his face, he goes directly into the temple and drives out, in a terrible outburst of indignant zeal, the whole crowd of hucksters and traders that have made even that sacred place, to his pure feeling, no better than a den of thieves. His tears did not extinguish his wrath, and his wrath did not stifle the tenderness that issued in tears.

Indeed these two poles of sensibility, wrath and tender love, are not only compatible; I must go farther and say, that the tenderest, purest souls will, for just that reason, be hottest in the wrath-principle, where any bitter wrong, or shameful crime, is committed. They take fire and burn, because they feel. Furthermore you will observe that the man whose dull-hearted phlegm keeps prudent silence, utters no condemnation, burns with no indignant fire, when some wicked cruelty or oppression is perpetrated, is, in almost every case, deficient in the finer, nobler, and more tender sympathies. His cold, apathetic, politic, sour nature is just about as defective in the gentle sensibilities, as it is in the fiery and strong impulses.

3. It is another and distinct consideration that God, without the wrath-principle; never was, and Christ never can be, a complete character. This element belongs inherently to every moral nature. God is no God without it, man is no man without it. Take it away from God and he is simply Brama, a mere Fate, or Infinite Thing—no Governor of the world, but an ideal, in the neuter gender, of the True and the Good; a Beauty that lies in sweet lassitude on the world, for literary souls to make a religion of, for themselves. Take it away from man, and he is only paste, or, at best, an animal; for though animals have the capacity of brute passion, or infuriated excitement, yet that moral passion or vindicatory instinct, of which we are now speaking, they as little share as they do the instinct of language, or that of scientific inquiry. They have no moral ideas, and of course have no moral armature of wrath to set them on the side of moral ideas, and steel them, as in principled resentment, to be avengers of the same. Now it is this principled wrath, in one view, that gives staminal force and majesty to character. It is in this principle of the moral nature that it becomes a regal nature. In these indignations against wrong, it champions the right and judges the world. Without this, or apart from this, submission to wrong is pusillanimity, forgive-

ness to enemies a flimsy and feeble habit, love a merely clinging devotement. All such tender passivities become great, only as they consciously consent to bathe, what fiery judgment has a right to burn. There is no dignity in them, till the grand vindicatory instinct, the governmental wrath-principle, is found united with them. This also it is, in our humanity, that is always volunteering government, and is, in that manner, the capacity of society—all movements of redress, all institutes of penalty, all executed pains of justice, being issued, as it were naturally, from this. It is, in fact, a kind of electric battery moral that God has put in the body of society, to shock, or stun, or kill, the violators of order and right. No wrong-doer can so much as touch it, without being struck and paralyzed by it. And it is in virtue of this same regal or judicial instinct, that God's moral nature, including his lovely and gentle sympathies, becomes everlastingly electric, in its wrath against misdoing and wrong. He governs with a will, he towers in personal majesty, he is great in his authority, because the regal attribute is in him. Which if we suppose to be true in no sense of Christ, if we take him to be a gentle way of goodness only, separated wholly from this flaming kind of vigor—soft only, and submissive, and patient—we put him in a grade almost unmoral, and show him making feeble suit to the world, in the merely plaintive airs of suffering. The character is weak, unkingly, unchristly, and it can not be more, till the wrath, is added to the patience, of the Lamb.

4. It is a conceded principle of justice, that wrong-doers are to suffer just according to what they deserve. It was unavoidable, therefore, that if Christ brought in new mercies and gifts of grace, the liabilities of justice must be correspondently increased—not diminished, as many try to imagine. As the score of justice, too, is augmented, the judicial wrath must be, and be also as much more forcibly manifested—just as we shall find it to be, in fact, in the new assertion made of God, by Christ's personal life and doctrine. First he asserts the principle—"For unto whomsoever much is given, of him shall much be required." Next he asserts the new liability that has actually accrued under it—"If I had not done among them the works that none other man did, they had not had sin, but now they have both seen and hated both me and my Father." Then again he makes specific denouncement both of the principle and the liability, declaring to the cities that reject his ministry, that they are bringing a doom of judgment on them, worse than God ever put upon the worst and wickedest of the past ages—"Woe unto thee, Chorazin, woe unto thee, Bethsaida; it shall be more tolerable for Tyre and Sidon at the day of judgment than for you." "And thou, Capernaum, it shall be more tolerable for the land of Sodom, in the day of judgment, than for thee." His apostles, too, only represent him fitly, when they say—"treasurest up unto thyself wrath, against the day of wrath and revelation of the righteous judgment of God;" or again—"Of how much sorer punishment suppose ye shall he be thought worthy, who hath trod-

den under foot the Son of God, and hath counted the blood of the covenant wherewith he was sanctified an unholy thing, and hath done despite unto the Spirit of grace." The wrath-principle and justice, you will thus perceive, have the same place under christianity that they had before. The divine government is not made new, but is only new revealed. God is not less just, nor more merciful, but more fitly and proportionately expressed.

5. One of the things most needed in the recovery of men to God, is this very thing; a more decisive manifestation of the wrath-principle and justice of God. Intimidation is the first means of grace. No bad mind is arrested by love and beauty, till such time as it is balked in evil and put on ways of thoughtfulness. And nothing will be so effectual for this, as a distinct apprehension of the wrath to come. Then, when it is brought to a condition of thoughtfulness by the apprehension of damage and loss, the vehemence of God and his judgments starts a correspondent moral vehemence in its own self-condemnations; when of course it is ready to be melted by the compassions and won by the beauty of the cross—that is born of God. Now it is no longer swayed by interest and fear, but having come into God's occupancy and become spirit, as being permeated by God's impulse, it ranges in liberty with God himself. The precise thing not wanted, in this view, is to get justice out of the way. To know that the avenging wrath-principle of God's moral nature is forever hushed, would be fatal. The weak point of sin is that

it can tremble—does inwardly tremble even in its boldest moods. Too low in its moral conceptions to be taken by goodness and love it for its own sake, it can be seized and shaken by the rough hand of wrath. Hence the wrath is wanted, and at this point the attack of salvation begins. It could not be a salvation by rose-water, or by any means less stringent than God's roughest enforcements.

6. We can see for ourselves that the more impressive revelation of wrath, which appears to be wanted, is actually made in the person of Christ. I will not stop here to speak of the driving out of the money-changers from the temple, which has been the scandal of so many, just because of the imagined over vehemence of the wrath, and which his disciples took as being the zeal that was to eat him up; I will not stay upon the fiery denunciations and imprecations of woe by which he scorched the oppressions and the sanctimonious hypocrisies of the priests and the Pharisees; I will not recur again to the terrible judgments he denounced upon so many guilty cities, and among them even upon Jerusalem itself; but pass directly to the fact that no other preacher ever had appealed as strenuously as he to the sense of fear, or employed with as little restraint the artillery of God's penalties. The terrible and abundantly unwelcome, or unpopular, doctrine of future punishment is specially his. Previously, the sanctions of religion had been temporal, and the future state itself had been only dimly revealed; save that in two or three single passages of the prophets it had finally

obtained a more distinct recognition and pronounced its more fearful awards. But Christ, when he came, opened up formally and distinctly the great world of the future, and pressed home the claims of duty and repentance by the tremendous sanctions of eternity. He uses, without scruple, in his language, the most appalling terms, which, though they are certainly figures of speech, are yet such figures as show that he is in no mood of delicacy, but is keyed up in the wrath-principle, as intensely and heartily as he is in the love-principle—speaking to men as offended majesty should, when it goes to rebels in arms. He denounces what he calls "everlasting punishment," "destruction," "death," "fire," "the worm that never dies," "the gnashing of teeth," "thirst," "outer darkness," "torment." I can not stop to settle the precise meaning of these figures. I only ask you to note, first, that they are new, almost every one of them, never heard of before, even under what is called the hard and pitiless rigors of the Old Testament; and, secondly, that they are from Christ, the all-merciful Saviour, and tenderly suffering friend of the world. We call him the Lamb, for God's mercy was never before revealed, by a sacrifice of simple, unoffending innocence. And just so these are the wrath of the Lamb; which never before shook human bosoms by such words of doom and sanctions of eternal majesty.

Once more Christ is appointed, and publicly undertakes, to maintain the wrath-principle officially, as the judge of the world—even as he maintains the love-principle officially, as the Saviour of the world. He consents, that is, when every attempt to do better by men, than they have deserved, has failed to win them, to fall back on the merely retributive regimen of his kingdom, and do by them as they deserve. He even declares that authority is given him to execute judgment, *because* he is the Son of Man; for as he has come into the flesh to unfold God's human sympathy and tenderness, so, to maintain what is only fit proportion, he must needs be clothed in the rigors of judicial majesty. He, then, is to be the judge, as he himself openly declares, and before his judgment-seat all mankind, including all his rejectors, shall be gathered. He will separate them to their fit award. He will say, "ye did it not to me." He will speak the "depart." Whoever has joined himself wholly to evil, put himself to the uses of evil, that is, of the devil and his angels, he will consign to the devil and his angels, according to their real affinities and according to what they deserve. And this is the wrath, and this the day of wrath; "for the great day of his wrath is come, and who shall be able to stand?"

But it will be objected, I suppose, by some that in the view now presented, the hope of a possible salvation is quite taken away. You can not, any more, deserve God's favor, how then can you be saved, unless God's justice be somehow satisfied in your behalf? You could not, I answer, if God were obliged to execute justice, having no option concerning it. But exactly contrary to this, the wrath-principle in him is only that judicial impulse that backs him in the infliction of justice, whenever justice requires to be inflicted. And it does not require to be inflicted always; it never ought to be, when there is any thing better that is possible. The law of right, or righteousness, is absolute and eternal. Not so the vindicatory principle of justice. Since penal justice is only a matter of means to ends in government, backed by the wrath-impulse, the means and occasions are to be regulated by counsel, and the wrath moderated by counsel. It is with God, in these matters, as it is with us. We are never bound to do by men as they deserve, simply because the wrath-impulse moves us to this, if only we are able to do what is better for them, and involves no injury to others. We do not want our justice satisfied before we can forgive. No more does God. As certainly as we may, at any time, do by our enemy and for him, better than he deserves, however pungently we may feel the wrong he has done us, so also may God. Something may be necessary on his part to save an appearance of laxity, when he forgives—some kind of honor paid to the instituted order of justice, that will keep it in as high respect as the exact execution of it. Christ will see to that. I can not here describe the provision he has made; enough that when he remits the penalties of justice, in his moral distributions, he shows most convincingly still, that he adheres to justice in his feeling as firmly as ever. It does not follow, when I forgive my enemy, that I condemn any the less heartily, or hotly, the wrongs he has done me. The very heat, too, of my rebukes, and of my decisive measures of redress, may be the means, in part, by which he is subdued, and the redress of justice made unnecessary.

Put it down, then, first of all, at the close of this great subject, that the New Testament gives us no new God, or better God, or less just God, than we had before. He is the I Am of all ages; the I Am that was, and is, and is to come; the same that was declared from the beginning—"The Lord God, gracious and merciful, forgiving iniquity, transgressions, and sin, and that will by no means clear the guilty."

At the same time, let no one be concerned to find how God's justice has been satisfied, or please himself in the discovery how Christ has made up the needed satisfaction, by the pains and penalties of his cross. For if Christ has satisfied God's justice, then who is going to satisfy the justice of Christ? If the offered Lamb has propitiated, or appeased, the wrath of God against transgressors, then a question of some point remains, viz., who is going to propitiate the wrath of the Lamb? Furthermore, if the lighter penalty of justice has been taken off, on the original score of retribution, who is going to lift the more tremendous liabilities of justice incurred by those who have trodden under foot the blood of the Son of God, and cast away forever all the glorious mercies and helps of the cross? O, it grieves me to think of the poor, speculated inventions we have wearied ourselves to set up on this summit, and most central point, of gospel truth! Wood, hay, stubble—God grant that when it is burned we may not perish in the fire ourselves.

How plain is it, also, in such a view of God and the inevitable wrath-principle of his nature, that the charity, so called, of our modern philanthropism, is an effeminate and false charity. It reprobates all condemning judgments and all inflictions of penalty. It does not really believe in government, or sin as an act of responsible liberty. Sin is only misdirection, and the misdirecting power is circumstance. Are we not all what our conditions make us to be? Why, then, do we lay severe judgments, or even torments of penalty, on the head of transgression? Just contrary to this, we have seen that no man even is a proper man, whose moral nature is not put in armor by the wrath-principle. Much less is God true God, when no such central fire burns in his bosom, to make him the moral avenger of the world. Neither let any one argue that God, as he is good, must desire the happiness of all, and that, being omnipotent also, what he desires he will certainly bring to pass. What if it should also be true, that there is a wrath-impulse in his nature, burning to have every wrong chastised by the pain it deserves; is not the argument as good to show that the chastisement will certainly be inflicted? The argument, in fact, holds neither way, least of all in showing that God will make every creature happy; for we know, as a plain matter of fact, that he does not. There may seem to be a considerable show of reason in the vaunted liberality of this new philanthropism; still it is only that weak light of moonshine which the higher light of day dispels. The eternal King is King indeed, and no such dispenser only of the confections and other sweet delectations of favor, as this feeble gospel of philanthropy requires him to be. O, the wrath of the Lamb!—there is the rugged majesty of meaning that transgression wants to meet! Smooth and soft things only will not do. As certainly as God is God, and Christ his prophet, he will not come bringing pardons only, suing and suing to the guilty, but over against all obstinacy he will kindle his fires of justice, and by these he will reign—even where by love he can not.

We are brought out thus, at the close, just where John began, when he came to make prophetic announcement of the new dispensation. He looks, you may see, for no merely soft salvation, but for a great and appalling salvation rather. "Now the axe will be laid," he says, "unto the root of the trees. He that cometh after me is mightier than I, his fan is in his hand, he will thoroughly purge his floor, the chaff he will burn with unquenchable fire." The doctrines of religion will now be more spiritual and the tests more severe. God will not be changed, but will only be more perfectly shown. Responsibilities will not be diminished, but increased with the increase of light. If Christ bends low at his cross, no such fearful words of warning and severity as his were ever before spoken. The Old Testament is a dew-fall in comparison with the simply judicial, spiritual, unbending, and impartial wrath of the New. And this exactly is the impression, we can see, of Christ himself—putting forth his most ominous warning in the tender shape even of a blessing—"Blessed is he whosoever is not offended in me." He speaks also of a taking away, and a still farther taking away, in his parable of the talents, where he seems to be looking distinctly on the fact that, as life progresses, every soul is descending more and more closely down to justice; losing out the conditions and prospects, one after another, of being treated better than it deserves; to be finally suited in the only alternative left—treated in strict justice as it deserves. In his tenderest accents of mercy, there is always blended, as it were, some reverberative note of judgment; as if there was a voice behind saying, behold, therefore, the goodness—and severity of God! It does not signify as much when he unmasks his judgment throne, and shows the gathering in, and tells the issues to be made, as it does that his very love is so visibly tempered with dread, in the sense of what his rejectors are doing. O, how far away the conceit of that clumsy speculation which shows him smoothing down the rugged front of justice. No such conception of his gospel mission has he, as we can easily see for ourselves. Christianity to him, my friends, is not the same thing that it has been to many of you. Doubtless it is a great salvation to him; and you may also think it such yourselves; but if you take it simply as a penal satisfaction for your sins, placing its value wholly in that, so great an abuse will scarcely suffer it to have been, or in fact ever to be, any real salvation to you at all. You presume upon the cross. You take it for granted that Christ is going to do by you better than you deserve, whereas that depends in part on you. If you can not be turned away from your sin, then he is preparing to do by you exactly as you deserve. Christ understands christianity—hear him therefore say, with a manner of dread how deep, in words that toll in a warning as deep for you—Whosoever shall fall on this stone shall be broken, but on whomsoever it shall fall, it will grind him to powder.

XVIII.

CHRISTIAN FORGIVENESS.

"*Forgiving one another, even as God for Christ's sake hath forgiven you.*"—EPH. iv, 32.

Under these words, "*even as*," and the relation or comparison they introduce, a very serious and high truth is presented; viz., that our human or Christian forgivenesses are to correspond with the forgiveness of sins by Christ himself; to be cast in the same molds of quality and bestowed under similar conditions. And that we may not fail of receiving such an impression, the principle or idea is made to recur many times over, and in such ways that we can not miss of it, or throw a doubt upon it. Thus we read again—"forgiving one another, if any man have a quarrel against any; even as Christ forgave you so also do ye." Again, in the gospels, it is given us in Christ's own words—"forgive, and ye shall be forgiven"—"for if ye forgive men their trespasses, your heavenly Father will also forgive you; but if ye forgive not men their trespasses, neither will your heavenly Father forgive your trespasses." He will not even allow us to pray for forgiveness, save as we ourselves forgive—"Forgive us our trespasses, even as we forgive those who trespass against us." All this on the ground that there is such an analogy between the forgiveness of Christ to us, and ours to our brethren and our fellow-men, as makes them virtually alike in spirit and kind, though not equal of course in degree. The quality of the virtue, the greatness of feeling, and height of meaning, will be so far correspondent, at least, that the smaller will represent the larger, and, according to its measure, reveal the same properties.

I state the point thus distinctly, because, in the matter of forgiveness among men, a kind of lapse, or sinking of grade, appears to have somehow occurred; so that, holding still the duty of forgiveness, we have it in a form so cheap and low, as to signify little when it is practiced. "O, yes," says the brother, finally worn out by much expostulation, on account of the grudge he is holding against another who has greatly injured him, "I will forgive him, but I hope never to see him again." Christ does not say that to the man whom he forgives, and I suppose it would commonly be regarded among brethren, as a rather scant mode of forgiveness—such a mode of it as scarely fulfills the idea. Another degree of it, which would probably pass, says—"Yes, let him come to me and ask to be forgiven, and it will be time for me to answer him." Probably a quotation is made, in this connection, of the scripture text which says—"If thy brother repent forgive him." And most certainly he should be thus forgiven, when the repentance appears to be an actual and present fact; but suppose that no such repentance has yet appeared. Is it then enough to say, "let him come and ask to be forgiven?" Many think so, and the argument appears to be conclusive, when they demand—"How can I be expected to forgive, where there is no repentance, and the wrong is just as stubbornly adhered to as ever? What but a mockery is it for me to forgive, when there is no forgiveness wanted, and my adversary has not even come into the right?"

Well then, suppose that Christ had stopped just there. Nobody is asking to be forgiven, all are in their sins and mean to be there. They love their sins. They have asked no release or forgiveness. They are not repentant in the least degree? What then is there for him to do? Is he not absolved from any such matter as the preparing and publishing of forgiveness, by the simple fact that nobody wants it, or asks for it?" "If they were penitent," he might say, "it would lay a heavy charge upon me. But they are not, and what is forgiveness thrust upon souls that do not even so much as care for it?"

Why, my friends, it is just here that Christ and his gospel begin—just here, in fact, that his forgiveness begins; viz., in for-giving, giving himself for, and to, the blinded and dead heart of unrepentant men, to make them penitent, and regain them to God. The real gist of his forgiveness antedates their penitence; it is what he does, shows, suffers, in a way of gaining his enemy—bringing him off and away, that is, from his wrongs, to seek, and, in a true sorrow, find, the forgiveness that has been searching beforehand so tenderly after him.

If we are to understand this matter accurately, as it

stands in the New Testament, we need to observe that two very distinct and, in some respects, dissimilar Greek words are employed here, to denote the virtue under consideration; both of which are translated by the single, very beautiful, but strangely dishonored English word, forgiveness. One signifies merely a letting go, a release of charges, an exemption from punishment, the merely negative good of not being held in condemnation; a word accurately translated here and there by the word "remission." The other signifies the very positive and operative matter of sacrifice and suffering to gain the heart of an adversary; that which not merely lets go, but prepares men to be let go. Literally this word means "to bestow grace." Thus in the text, where it is translated forgive, we may read—"dealing grace, one towards another, even as God for Christ's sake, hath dealt grace towards you." There is also this remarkable contrast between the two words, translating both by forgiveness, that one fixes on the very last point, or final effect of forgiveness, viz., the release, the letting go of charges, the absolution which says, "go in peace;" and the other finds its main idea in the first things of forgiveness, the love, the going after, the giving-for, by which the soul is taken hold of sooner than it asks to be; that which did not wait for penitence to come, that it might let penitence go, but which undertook to bring on penitence, prepare it, melt the heart into it, and so to execute the letting go of the soul, by making the sins let go of it.

Now both of these words are names, we have said, of

the same grace; viz., the grace of forgiveness; only one names it from a last incident or effect, and the other from the initiative movement of love and operative goodness, in which it took its spring—just as one might name the dawn, as a mere effect, or call it the sunrising, as denoting the cause or spring of the returning light; where of course the names are coincident, though inherently different from each other. In the present case, there is an immense difference between the two words employed, as regards the dignity and the real amount of their meaning—all the moral greatness, or high beneficence, appears to lie in the grace-dealing of love and sacrifice that prepares the remission; and yet when the lower, feebler word is used, as it is in a majority of cases, all that is in the other word is supposed to pass into its meaning, and keep along with it. Nothing is further off from Christ and his apostles, than to suppose, in any case, that the forgiveness they speak of is nothing but the simple letting go of charges against the penitent. They have it understood always that the grand reality of the forgiveness preached is that which went before, in the putting by of so much injured feeling, the going after them that want no forgiveness, the giving for, and suffering for, by which they may be drawn to God;—just that which is described historically and transactionally, when the apostle says, "Who gave himself a ransom for all," "who gave himself for me." For it is precisely this which goes into the higher word "grace-dealing" and composes the reality of its meaning. This *is* the grace, that Christ gives himself for us, and so works in us, by his sacrifice, that we are transformed, reconciled, covered in with God's feeling, in one word, forgiven.

Do not understand me to say that the higher Greek word is made up of the verb *to give*, with the preposition *for*, like our English word. It is not; it signifies literally and simply "*dealing grace*," or "doing grace upon;" which is represented by the genius of our tongue, in the word "for-giving;" and, what is remarkable, the Latin and all the principal modern tongues, [as in *con-dono*, *par-don*, *ver-geben*,] make up their word signifying remission in the same way, by compounding their verb *to give* with a preposition answering to *for;* giving it, as it were by vote, and declaring it as their inward sense or conviction, that the true forgiving of wrong and evil is that which has its beauty and greatness and the spring of its operative power, in a giving-for the sinners and the sins to be forgiven.

And lest this might seem to be scarcely better than a suggestion of the fancy, or a curiosity of speech, let us glance a moment at the practical, or practically Christian, import of forgiveness when it is received. What is it practically to us, or in us? What does it do for us? What internal changes of position, or experience, does it bring? Answering these questions, we shall find that forgiveness, when ascribed to Christ, has suffered a lapse or fall in our understanding, much like that which it has suffered when applied to men. For the word is taken by multitudes, including even teachers of theology, as if it had no reach of meaning above the lower and more negative of the two words just referred to. Thus we say that Christ first prepares a ground of forgiveness, by suffering before God (penally or not penally) in a manner to even the account of our sin; and then, having magnified the justice of God, he is able to let go, remit, release the charge of, in that sense, forgive, our sin. Well, suppose the absolution is passed and we are let go, declared to be let go, as I let go verbally my enemy when I forgive him. What does this signify, that God has let go, taken off all charges against, his enemy? Just nothing but a most barren mockery, unless he has somehow got into the man's bosom and *executed* his pardon, by making the sins let go of him. And precisely here is the stress, the struggle, the wonder and glory of the forgiveness; that Christ, going before, has gotten him away from his sin; and, in all this previous grace-dealing, the reality of the letting go, otherwise nothing but empty words, is accomplished. Why, the man to be redeemed had a hell of retributive causes tearing in his disordered nature, and the mere letting him go only lets him have that hell to himself! No, the grand effort of forgiveness begins farther back, in what is undertaken for the sinner to win upon him, change him, get him loose from sin, loose from retribution, and then the letting go is only the ending off, or completion declared. And so the real forgiveness is that Jesus came, to be for his adversary and execute the great release in him. Long ages ago, before the foundation of the world, his mind of love began to grapple with the wrong and bitter woe of his adversary. He was not saying, "let him come to me, in his day, and ask it if he will, and then I will forgive him;" as little was it in him to say, "let him be a better man and by-gones shall be by-gones." But he was the Lamb slain already. He was contriving how to get beforehand in his forgiveness, postponing his just indignations, laying himself into the case of his adversaries to gain them back, planning a descent into the flesh and a suffering life—giving himself for, in a word forgiving, in all profoundest reality of feeling, ages before they arrive, and of course before they come to ask forgiveness. And when they come along in their day, and say for their scanty testimony in receiving such a grace, "Christ has let us go, Christ has remitted our sins," he will himself have a deeper solution, in the consciousness of having long ago given himself for them, and had the enjoyment of their forgiven state. Neither will he ever think of it as any fit summation of his work in the world, to say that he has first prepared a ground of forgiveness, and then that having made forgiveness safe in that manner, he is able to release or let go, or in that sense forgive sins. No, but he will understand that he was lifted up to draw men away from their sins, and be the release in them; that, by showing how God suffers in feeling for sinners, he has gotten a power in their feeling; in a word, that, by giving himself for his adversaries, in such burdens of sympathy, and fear, and care, and against such tempests of murderous and bloody wrong, he has slid himself into the secret place of their sins and made them all let go—in that manner executed the release; so that now he can say, with real truth in the words, "thy sins are forgiven thee."

We go back now from this excursion, to the subject-matter at which we began; viz., the duty of forgiveness between brethren, or fellow-men. And we carry back this very important principle or discovery; that the reality of forgiveness, or the grace of a forgiving spirit in us, lies not so much in our ability to let go, or to be persuaded to let go, the remembrance of injuries, as in what we are able to do, what volunteer sacrifices to make, what painstaking to undergo, that we may get our adversary softened, to want, or gently accept, our forgiveness. If it is in us to forgive, in any real and properly Christian sense of the term, it will not be that we can somehow be gotten down to it, by the expostulations of brethren, nor that we only do not expressly claim a right to stay in our grudge, or the hurt feeling raised by the wrongs of our adversary, till he comes to us in a better mind. Perhaps he ought to come, or to have come long ago, but that is nothing as regards our justification. If we know how to forgive, we shall be like Christ our Master, we shall be giving ourselves for our adversary, circumventing him by our prayers, contriving ways to reach his tenderness and turn the bad will he is in, taking pains, even to the extent of great loss and suffering, that we may get him into the right again; thus to accept our remission, and be joined to us openly for Christ our Master's sake.

But this, it may be objected, carries the obligation too high—Christ was a peculiar being, in a very peculiar office, and it can not be expected of us to follow him and be like him, in what belonged rather to his official work, than to the merely inherent principle of personal excellence in his character. Now it may be very true that we are not called to work out the same problems of divine government, but we are required to have, in our degree, exactly the same modes of character, and all that he did was the simple coming out of his character. He had no good ways, or qualities, that were more than good, no merits of character that were superlative and above all the known standards of merit. On the contrary one of the great and blessed objects of his mission was to consist, in the true unfolding of God's feelings, graces, perfections, so as to draw us into the same, or impregnate our fallen life with the same. No matter what relations he may have filled, or solved, in the great mystery of government, still every thing he undertook and bore was for forgiveness' sake, and he had precisely the same reasons of feeling for withholding himself that we have, when we withhold from our adversaries. He had his personal indignations against the wrong of transgressors, he had his disgusts towards their character, he had feelings wounded by the sense of their wrongs, and if he could have let a little pride play among his passions, he would have had his bitter, invincible grudges against them; so that when he thought of them he would have said, "I want no more to do with them. Perhaps I will consider them, if they come to me in a better mind, but until they do, I shall let them take the wages of their sin, giving myself no farther trouble." The only reason why he did not do this was that he was too perfect in excellence to do it. He must dispense forgiveness. He must go before, and give himself for, and watch, and wait, and suffer, and sue, at the gate of his adversaries. And why not we? Because, says the objection, Christ was peculiar, and could do things out of his peculiarity that are too high for us. No! no! his great peculiarity was that he could be right. "Faithful and just," says an apostle, "to forgive us our sins." He could not be faithful to his trust as Creator and Lord, could not be consciously just or righteous, (for that is what the term here means,) if he did not prepare and offer the forgiveness of sins. If there be some kind of rectoral, or public, justice that required to be maintained by some fit compensation, or compensative expression, that is another matter, but there wanted nothing in him better than that most solid justice, which is everlasting, immutable, righteousness, to make him a forgiver of sin. And in all that you distinguish of a nobler and diviner life, in his bearing of his enemies and their sins, he is simply showing what belongs, in righteousness, to every moral nature from the Uncreated Lord down to the humblest created intelligence. Forgiveness, this same Christly forgiveness, belongs to all; to you, to me, to every lowest mortal that bears God's image.

Do we, then, undertake to say, that there is no salvation, out of this same Christly forgiveness—has no man a right to expect salvation, whose soul hangs fire at the point of such forgiveness? must he forgive, in this Christly manner, going before and giving himself for, his adversary, if he is to be forgiven? What then does the Saviour himself say to this? When he has taught you to pray—"forgive us our debts *as we* forgive our debtors," and has added, "but if ye forgive not men their trespasses, neither will your Heavenly Father forgive your trespasses," what does it mean, or to what does it bring you? Can you turn off the bad conclusion, by contriving a sort of forgiveness that is lower, such barely as can manage to choke down a grudge, or not choke down an adversary, when he comes to ask a reconciliation? And was that Christ's meaning? was he saying "forgive in your own sense, or else I will not forgive in mine?" O, these niggard forgivenesses! He would even make you repent of them! He wants you to be with him in his own! He wants such a feeling struggling in your bosom, that you can not bear to have an adversary, can not rest from your prayers and sacrifices and the life-long suit of your concern, till you have gained him away from his wrong, and brought him into peace. This in fact *is* salvation; to be with Christ, in all the travail of his forgivenesses.

Besides, there is another answer to this question of salvation. As we just now said that Christ was simply fulfilling the right in his blessed ways of forgiveness, so we may conceive that he is simply fulfilling the eternal love. For what is right coincides with love, and love with what is right. Now Christ is in this kind of forgiveness—unable to stand for the relenting of his adversaries, going before them, and giving himself for them—just because it is in the nature of love to do so. For it is a vicarious principle and must insert itself into whatever sorrow, sin, suffering, danger, it looks upon; and, for this most affecting reason, can not rest till it has either gotten its adversary to its bosom, or discovered the impossibility that he ever should be. Are we then to look for salvation, when we are out of this love? What do we most readily believe and most commonly hold, but that our salvation lies in loving God and having his love upon us. The being in heaven's love is, we all agree, the bond of heaven's perfectness, the very life and constituent beatitude of heaven itself. And what will this love do in us but just what it does in Christ? If it keeps down all grudges and hard judgments in him, if it makes forgiveness his dearest opportunity, if it puts him into the case of his adversary, bearing his wrongs, and contriving only how to prepare him to forgiveness—if, I say, the love so works in him, what will it do and how will it work in you? Let it not be disguised from you, that there are many kinds of mock love, and but one that is true, even that which works so sublimely in the self-sacrificing ways of Jesus our Master. Thus there is a theologic love, a state that is tested by merely defined contrasts of feeling, apart from any effects in the practical sacrifices of the life. There is also a sentimental love, taken with God's beauty. And again there is a philanthropic love, which is caught with great expectations for man, coming out of its own prodigious, better than Christian, reforms. Now the test of all these mock species of love is that there is no forgiveness in them. You may be in this, or that, or all of them, and they will not help you to bear one enemy, or put you into any tender ways of seeking after an adversary. Could there be any more damning evidence against your love, whether it be the defined evangelical, or the sentimental, or the philanthropic, than that there is no Christly forgiveness in it? That being true, how is any salvation to come out of it? No, my friends, this is the love—the only true—"Hereby perceive we the love of God, because he laid down his life for us; and we ought to lay down our lives for the brethren."

Taking now this high view of the Christian spirit as related to Christ, it would not surprise me, if there should be a feeling of special revulsion, or repulsion, rising up in some of your hearts, to thrust away even farther than ever the claims of religion. "I could not be a Christian after this kind," you will say, "and I never can be. If I must forgive all the wrongs I meet, after this manner, I must give up any right to be a proper man. Such a volunteering of forgiveness before it is sought, and even when smarting under the bitter wrongs of an enemy, is too spiritless and weak in the look of it—I could not endure being held down to any such forgiving way." All this, my friends, may be very true, regarding only the present key of your feeling and life—I presume it is. But it may be equally true, at the same time, that your judgment is a false one, and that this very impossible looking forgiveness, when you are once really in it, by the grace of God, will be such an element of dignity, and rest, and strength, and conscious superiority to all wrong-doers and wrongs, that you will even seem to be raised by it in the relative grade of your nature itself. Why, my friends, instead of being humbled, and tamed, and put in mortification, by this entering into forgiveness with Christ, you will ascend rather into greatness and conscious sovereignty with him, and will then, for the first time, begin to conceive what it is to be free and a king! No, the forgiveness you so much distaste is probably not the forgiveness I describe, but the low, false kind of your old associations; that niggard, misnamed forgiveness that cheapens the grace by putting all sacrifice out of question, and makes it distasteful by reducing it to so low a figure, that pride can be just goaded into it. Sticking fast in its bitternesses, resentments, and grudges, and contriving how little and late to forgive, it is only dogged into some verbal letting go, which is the more certainly cross to self-respect, that there is no genuine meaning in it, and nothing genuine but the fit mortification. Not so is it, but far otherwise, with the really Christly forgiveness. Here the soul has a really great feeling to begin with, and the moment it undertakes for its adversary, it goes above him. No matter what his power and the dignity of his station, the humblest peasant puts him under, when he begins to pray for him, and contrive and labor for his sake. No matter what, or how great, the wrong you have suffered, the way to make it greater is to hug it fast in grudges and blistering resentments. Pride, passion, hate, will make a great wrong out of a very small one; but in the true forgiveness, you ascend to a range of feeling so high, so immovably serene, that the greatest wrong looks small under you, and quite as truly the greatest wrong-doer. O, there is no greatness possible to man, none that lifts him so nearly out of the world, and above it, as the true Christly forgiveness. This was the greatness of Christ himself. Did any being ever tread the world in such majesty as he? And his wrongs were bitter enough, and his adversaries high enough, and, what is quite as conspicuous, he keeps the true sense always of their wrongs, and hates the hateful in their sins, and feels a fit disgust for what is disgusting in their character, holding all his judgments level and true, as if he were going to proceed entirely by them; yet giving himself, as it were out of majesty, for the wrongs he condemns and the enemies he is obliged to pity. Do you call this an humble, mortifying key to live in? Must you shrink from this? Why, my friends, the moment you are born into this high consciousness you will feel that your heads strike heaven rather.

Brethren in Christ, let me also turn the lessons of this subject specially towards you; for it was specially Christian brethren, even those of Ephesus, that the apostle was addressing when he exhorted—"forgiving one another, even as God for Christ's sake hath forgiven you."

You have seen what this forgiveness means, what a volunteering there is in it, how the true Christian works in it, long before the forgiveness is wanted, works in sacrifice and patience, even as all love must. What I want therefore to know, my brethren, is whether you find this forgiveness in you? Can you give yourself for your brother, or do you hold off in the stiff pretense, that he must come to you first and right himself? Can you be the Christian towards him, or can you more easily hug your injury, as a wound bleeding internally, and hold yourself aloof? Let me tell you then how very bad the sign is, when a Christian is slow to forgive. It does not show, it is true, that he is a vicious, or viciously depraved, man, as other kinds of fault, or deviation would, but it shows a great amount of unsanctified nature in him—none can tell or guess how much. For it is our proud, wild nature, just that in kind, though not in degree, that is observed to burn so inextinguishably, in the bloody resentments of savages, which makes it so hard for us to forgive. Therefore, if any one finds it more easy to stay in the savage feeling, than to go after his adversary in the Christian, the indication is fearfully bad. Nay, it is even a very unpleasant and doubtful sign, when one has an adversary long to forgive; for when a true Christian goes after his adversary, in such temper as he ought, tender, assiduous, proving himself in his love, by the most faithful sacrifices, he is not like to stay by his enmity long. As the heat of a warm day will make even a willful man take off his overcoat, so the silent melting of forgiveness at the heart will compel it, even before it is aware, to let the grudges go. Still a really good man may have enemies, all his life-long, even as Christ had, and the real blame may be chargeable not against him, but against them, and it would be too much to make their obstinacy a certain proof against his fidelity. Enough that he follows his Master, and allows them no reason for their obstinacy, by the stint of his own affectionate and self-sacrificing endeavors. Commonly the wrong-doer of two parties will be the most unforgiving, and, for just that reason, the wrong sufferer will be readiest and most forward in forgiveness.

Sometimes the alienated, or aggrieved parties, will both of them be Christian brethren; and how very sad a sight is it, and how much to be pitied when two brethren fall into an enmity! How frightfully fallen is their look when you look at them! How much worse their internal look to themselves! When they go to pray in secret, how are they choked in their prayers! How very likely are they also, to be even choked off soon from prayer itself. How certain are they in this manner, even against much endeavor, to go down in their piety. The warm heart they once had, or seemed to have—where is it? If they beamed in rich feeling once on every body, and it was a blessing to meet them and be warmed in the glow of their faces, the blessing and the glow are soon gone, and we may almost say the faces too; for there is scarcely any but a negative meaning left in them. O, ye pitiable and sad pair of disciples, that are paired in your enmity! How easily and beautifully paired might you be in your forgiveness! Go apart and think of this! go apart and pray over it! Nay, come together and pray over it! Pray especially, as you most need, that God will forgive you, even as you forgive each other—thus or—never.

Sometimes it will happen that a whole brotherhood of disciples will be scored and scorched by disaffections, jealousies, wounded feelings that are akin to enmity, in the same manner. There is much talk and a general talking down of course, and as a family quarrel brings down family respect, so it is when brethren are set to the work of diminishing each other's worth and character. Believe them and they are all no better than they should be. If they once loved each other, and were firmly locked together in their common cause, so much the worse now, for the dishonor falls on their tendernesses and prayers, and all the good things that seemed to be in their love. The Holy Dove flies their assemblies, or only hovers doubtfully over them, unable to light where there is no peace. When they come to pray together, it is only locally together, and not in spirit that they pray. There is a dreary chill in their assemblies. Neither the prayers appear to go up, nor the preaching to come down. There is no savoring element for the word, and of course there is as little due sense of savor from it. It is neither fire, nor hammer, but a chill made audible rather, like the ripping, rifting noises of some ice-clad lake or river in a silent, freezing night. The power is all gone, fatally benumbed. The power of the word, the power of the living epistle, that of the prayers—every sort is gone, and there is no fire of heaven left.

What then shall they do? Some of them perhaps will finally begin to say, let us take the counsel of Lot and Abraham—go to the right, and go to the left. Yes, but there is a difference; these friends, Abraham and Lot, parted because they were agreed, not because they were at variance; parted to save their agreement and not to comfort their repugnances. Have then Christian brethren, under Christ's own gospel, nothing better left, than to take themselves out of sight of each other?—going apart just to get rid of forgiveness; going to carry the rankling with them, live in the bitterness, die in the grudges of their untamable passion? What is our gospel but a reconciling power even for sin itself, and what is it good for—cross, and love, and patience, and all—if it can not reconcile? No, there is a better way; Christ lays it on them, by his own dear passion where he gave himself for them, by his bloody sweat, by his pierced hands, and by his open side, to go about the matter of forgiving one another even as he went about forgiving them. O, it is a short method, and how beautiful, and one that never failed. When they are ready to go before all relentings, and above all grudges, and be weary, and sick, and sad, and sorrowful, and so to give themselves for their adversaries, weeping on their necks in tender and true confession, they will not be adversaries long, but they will be turning all together to the cross, and joining in the prayer—forgive us our trespasses, as we forgive those who trespass against us.

They had much to say before of forgiveness, they were all ready to forgive, but they could not find how much, or when, or how, because they took forgiveness in too light a key. Now they take it in Christ's meaning, and how shortly are their troubles ended. They can not forgive enough, or soon enough, or with half as much love as they would. The bitterness, and wrath, and anger, and clamor, and evil speaking, are put away, with all malice. They are kind one to another, tender-hearted, forgiving one another, EVEN AS GOD, FOR CHRIST'S SAKE, HAS FORGIVEN THEM.

XIX.

CHRIST BEARING THE SINS OF TRANSGRESSORS.

"*So Christ was once offered to bear the sins of many.*"—HEB. ix, 28.

Christ bearing our sins ought to be the tenderest and most soul-subduing of all facts conceivable. And yet it may even be made quite revolting, by the over literal, and legally hard, face put upon it. Perhaps I ought to say that it too often is, and that what is given to be the new creating power of God in our lives, is made, in this manner, to be an offense that even balks our repentances. What I propose then, at the present time, is to answer, in a very practical way, the very practical question—

In what sense, or manner, it is, that Christ bears the sins of the world?

To make the answer clear, I begin by specifying some things which are not to be understood by it.

Thus we are not to understand that the sins of the world are put upon him, or transferred to him, so as to be his. That is impossible. Guilt is a matter so strictly and eternally personal, that nobody can be in it, but the transgressor himself to whom it belongs. Apart from him it is nothing. Strike him out of existence and it no longer exists. The bad conscience, the blame, the damning self-conviction, is as incommunicably his, even as his brain, or his will. Indeed, the creatorship of the world can as well be transferred, as the doership of a sin. The *meum* and *tuum* of property can be transferred, but the *meum* and *tuum* of sin is even absolute. If I owe a debt, another man can make himself a debtor in my place, but if I am a felon, no other man can be the felon for me.

It follows, in the same view, that Christ does not bear our sins in the sense that he bears our punishment. Everlasting justice forbids any such commutation of places in punishment. What is this justice? An indignation against wrong that wants pain out of somebody, caring only that the quantum be made up? Or is it, rather, an indignation against the wrong-doer himself, and no other? No matter if another *consents* to bear that indignation, and suffer all the deserved pains of the wrong-doer, when that second person comes to offer himself, God's justice will forthwith object in the question—"Are you guilty of this man's sin? Doubtless you may be his friend, but the only thing you can do for him is to be innocence in him, and you can as well do that as to be guilty instead of him. But as long as you are innocence yourself, what kind of transaction is it that you undertake, when you come to be punished in innocence? What opinion have you of my justice, when you expect me to release the pains deserved, if only I can get enough that are not deserved? Did I ever threaten to punish the guilty man, or somebody else, when my law should be broken? You ask more than is possible, when you ask me to smooth over even the everlasting distinctions of principle, and be satisfied with the punishment of innocence. I can only be revolted by the thought, and should be everlastingly by the deed."

Again, it is not conceivable that Christ bears our sin, in the sense that the abhorrence of God to our sin is laid upon him, and expressed through, and by means of, his sufferings. How can God lay abhorrence upon what is not abhorrent? Is he going to abhor goodness, truth, beauty itself? And if Jesus, being all this, comes in as a volunteer into the place of transgressors, challenging upon himself the abhorrence due to them, will God falsify and mock all his own approving judgments and moral affinities, by acting an abhorrence which he must renounce every one of his perfections to feel? Perhaps it will be imagined that he only puts great pains on Christ, which we ourselves are to look upon as tokens of abhorrence to us. That would be very ingenious in us, but how are we going to take up such a thought? In the first place, God did not inflict those pains, but we ourselves. Are we then going to put Christ to death and take it up as a religious discovery, having a gospel in it, that God's abhorrence to us is so far expressed by our very abominable deed of murder, that it need not be any more, by our punishment? We can easily enough imagine God's abhorrence, in such a case, to the sin perpetrated, and the murderers by whom it is perpetrated, but the difficulty is to get either Christ or his suffering into the same line; for the last thing any human soul can think of will be, that God's abhorrence touches him any how, or looks out any where from his pains.

We come now, having dismissed these rather common misconceptions, to the positive matter of the question, or the positive answer to be given. And here let me indicate, beforehand, a certain point of fact that will probably distinguish any true answer; viz., that Christ, in bearing the sins of transgressors, simply fulfills principles of duty, or holiness, that are common to all moral beings, and does it as being obliged by those principles. If there is any fundamental truth in morals, it is that there is no superlative *kind* of merit or excellence; that as far as kind is concerned, the same kind is for all, and there is no other. Thus, if Christ has it incumbent on him, as a point of beneficence, or love, to bear the sins of transgressors, it will be incumbent on every moral being in the universe, ourselves included, to bear sins; only not perhaps in the same degree, or with the same effect. If he is to be a sacrifice for sin, it will be laid upon us to be, every man, a sacrifice and an offering in like manner, only not to accomplish all the same results. We are not then to look for some artificial, theologically contrived, never before heard of, kind of good, in the bearing of sins, but simply to look after what lies in the first principles of religious love and devotion, as related to the conduct of all. Having this intent in view I shall make out—

I. A general or inclusive answer to the question, and then, secondly, a threefold, particular answer, the points of which are included under it. The general is this—that Christ bears the sins of the world in a certain representative sense, analogous to that in which the priests and the sacrifices of the former altar-service, bore the sins of the people worshiping. The phrase, "he shall bear his sin," or "bear his iniquity," means, it is true, when applied to the guilty person, that he shall be punished for his sin. But when it is applied, as it is many times, to the priests and sacrifices at the altar, we are not to conceive that the priests, or the altar victims, have the guilt actually put upon them—nothing could be more absurd—but we are to take the words in an accommodated, ritually formal sense, where the same thing is true representatively; the design being to let the people feel or believe, that their sins are being taken away, *as if* put over upon the priests, or upon the head of the victims. Not to multiply instances, we have the phrase "to bear sins" used in both senses in a single passage, (Numb. xviii, 22, 23)—"Neither must the children of Israel henceforth come near the tabernacle of the congregation, lest they bear sin [that is, their own sin] and die. But the Levites shall do the service of the tabernacle of the congregation, and *they* shall bear their iniquity." No one will be so absurd as to imagine, that the iniquity of the people is here declared to be literally put on the priesthood. They are only to bear it representatively, coming so far in place of the people before God, as to conduct their sacrifice for them, and, as God accepts the sacrifice, put them in the state, formally at least, of reconciliation. In a similarly representative sense, the prophet Ezekiel lies upon his left side three hundred and ninety days, "bearing," as he says, "the iniquity of the house of Israel," and upon his right side forty days "bearing the iniquity of the house of Judah;" where it is simply meant that the iniquity was made visible representatively in that sign. So when "all the iniquities of the children of Israel, and all their transgressions in all their sins," were put, as we read, upon the head of their scape-goat, and he was driven out into the desert, they knew not where, there was neither any sin upon the goat, nor any punishment. The reality of the whole matter stood in what was representatively signified; viz., the removal and clearance of their sin.

And here is the ready solution of all those expressions in the New Testament, which are brought over from the priesthood and sacrifices of the Old Testament, and used, with so great power, to represent the relation of Christ to the sins of the world. Thus he is declared to be "made sin for us," just as the Levites were, in bearing the iniquities of the congregation. Thus also it is declared that he "was once offered to bear the sins of many." The meaning is that he comes representatively in our place, undertaking, or taking on himself, the case of our sin, even as the priests at the altar did. Such forms of speech come to be natural, as it were, to the Jewish mind, under the uses of their ritual, and pass into new applications of a different shade. Thus Paul speaks of Christ "being made a curse for us." Regarding Christ as having come into our state of corporate evil, under the curse, and borne the bitterness of it, and at so great expense delivered us from it, he takes up the representative figure of the altar-service, and shows him, in that manner, bearing the curse for us. He does not mean that Christ was literally and legally substituted, in the matter of our punishment, but that he was substituted, as the priests were, in bearing the sins of the people, and with a like result. Thus also Peter says, in the fervor of his obligation to Christ—"Who his own self bare our sins, in his own body on the tree;" as if our very sins were personally chastised, or punished, in the pains of his cross; and yet he does not say it, but turns the sentence, in what follows, in a way to show that he means no such thing—"that we being dead to sin, might live unto righteousness; by whose stripes ye were healed." After all he is only showing, at what expense, Christ takes us away from our sin, and makes us "live unto righteousness." And though he speaks of "stripes," a penal word, he does not say "by whose stripes God's justice was satisfied," but, "by whose stripes ye were healed."

Christ then bears our sin, we answer inclusively and generally, in the sense that he has come representatively into our place and got such power in us by his sacrifice, as to take it wholly away.

Pause here now a moment at the threshhold, and raise the question, whether we, as human beings, can have any thing in common with him, in such a sacrifice?

Of course we can not do the same things; for we have not the same grade of character and power over human sentiment, nor the same undertaking for the world upon us. We are sinners ourselves, wanting, for outfit in duty, just that taking away of sin and renewing in good, which are to be the fruit of his sacrifice. It is not to be expected, therefore, that we shall come into any such answering for sin, as to have the representative figures of the altar applied to us; unless it be in ways more restricted and partial. We shall only follow him, as our very much abused faculty, and humbler key of being, allow us to follow.

Still it is remarkable how many of the scripture terms of sacrifice and priestly intervention are applied to Christian disciples, and how constantly they are called to maintain precisely the way of the cross. Nothing, in fact, is farther off from the New Testament, than to conceive that Christ is in a superlative *kind* of virtue, inappropriate, or impossible, to mortals.

Thus we are called to be sacrifices and priests of sacrifice. "I beseech you therefore, brethren, by the mercies of God, [that is, in Jesus Christ,] that you present your bodies a living sacrifice, [in the same manner,] holy, acceptable to God, which is your reasonable service," [the dictate of your moral nature as it was of his.] The phrase "acceptable to God," you will also observe, is a sacrificial phrase, bearing an allusion to God's acceptance of the sin offerings. And, in this sense, it occurs again —"Ye also, as lively stones, are built up a spiritual house, an holy priesthood, to offer up spiritual sacrifices, acceptable to God by Jesus Christ." The disciples are taken often as being thus a priesthood, all, with their Master—"Kings and priests unto God," "entering into the holiest with boldness;" entering in thither also to act the part of intercessors—to anoint and raise up the sick, as James represents; to obtain forgiveness of sins for the brethren that have committed sin; to convert sinning brethren from the error of their ways, in such a sense as to be in fact their human saviours—"saving their souls from death and hiding the multitude of their sins." And this word *hiding* it should also be observed is a word of sacrificial atonement; for to atone is literally to *cover*, that is, to hide; put away, forever, make as naught. Not that we are to do these things in our own right, and by our own power, as Christ did, but, as in the language just now cited, "by Jesus Christ." The conception is that our life is to be so far in the analogy of his, and moved by his inspirations, that the same words, priest, sacrifice, intercession, saving of souls, converting sinners, hiding, or covering sins, will be fitly applied to us—that is, in senses modified by our human capacities and conditions.

Having sketched this general outline of what is to be understood by the bearing of sins, we now proceed—

II. To fill up the outline by a more particular statement of the subject matter included under it. Christ, we have seen, bears the sins of the world representatively, in a figure, much as the priesthood, or the scapegoat, bore them, only procuring an absolution for them as much more real and spiritual, as the heavenly things themselves are more quickening and substantial in him, than their shadows in the forms of the altar. This for the general statement; which includes, we shall find, when we look into the subject matter of his life more closely, three particular modes, or distinctly and rationally conceived methods, of bearing sin by him, in his mission as a Redeemer.

1. He bears the sin of the world, by that assumption which his love must needs make of it. Love puts every being, from the eternal God downward, into the case of all sufferers, wrong-doers, and enemies, to assume their evils, and be concerned for them. Being love, it assumes their loss, danger, present suffering, suffering to be; all their want, sorrow, shame, and disorder; and goes into their case to restore and save. As a father, who has a dear son straying from honor and virtue, assumes that son to be an inevitable burden on his love, and bears him, sin and all, as a heavy load upon his feeling, striving after him in many tears, and prayers, and weary contrivings, and it may be under great personal abuse, that he may regain him to a better life, just so God assumes in Christ all transgressors and enemies, and all their sin, and all their coming woes, and bears them on his paternal feeling, through great waves of living conflict and dying passion—"For God so loved the world that he gave his only begotten son, that whosoever believeth in him should not perish but have everlasting life." The assumption is such that we may even look upon it and speak of it, as a kind of substitu-

tion. Hence the strongly substitutional language employed concerning it. But there is no room for mistaking the meaning of such language. The precise nature of the assumption, or substitution, is given when the evangelist says of Christ's healing works—"That it might be fulfilled that was spoken by Esaias the prophet, himself took our infirmities, and bare our sicknesses." It does not mean that Christ literally took into his body, and bore, himself, all the fevers, pains, lamenesses, blindnesses, leprosies he healed, but simply that he took them upon his sympathy, bore them as a burden upon his compassionate love. In that sense, exactly, he assumed and bore the sins of the world; not that he became the sinner and suffered the due punishment himself, but that he took them on his love, and put himself by mighty throes of feeling, and sacrifice, and mortal passion, to the working out of their deliverance. And these were the throes in which we find him often struggling; declaring now that his soul is troubled, heaving now, in prostrate weakness, and bloody sweat, on the ground. In these throes he died, saying, "It is finished"—viz., the bearing of sins that he had undertaken to bear. The sins were never his, the deserved pains never touched him as being deserved, but they were upon his feeling in so heavy a burden as to make him sigh, "my soul is exceeding sorrowful." And just because the world in sin took hold of his feeling in this manner, was he able, in turn, to get hold of the feeling of the world, and become its true deliverer and Saviour. In this fact lay bosomed the everlasting gospel.

Let me not be understood now, in transferring this analogy, to say, or suggest, that Christ came into such a life of sympathy and death of passion, just to give us an example which we are to copy. Nothing could be more impotent, or farther from the truth. Giving and copying examples is too tame a matter to be conceived as making out a gospel. No, Christ took our sin upon him in this manner and bore it as the burden of his mission, just because it was in his love to do it; and that same love, in any being, of any world, in us just struggling up out of our lowness and bondage, will put us, in our human grade, and according to the measure of our love, on making the same kind of assumption. We shall take the child of sin, or sorrow, our friend, our enemy, any one, every one we see to be in evil, on our feeling, and make him a charge upon our sacrifices and prayers. Paul knew exactly what this meant when he said—"Bear ye one another's burdens and so fulfill the law of Christ;"—that is, the eternal love-law, or standard of obligation, that he himself fulfilled. Paul had the meaning too, the very Gethsemane of it, in his own heart, when he cried, under his burden—"I have great heaviness, and continual sorrow in my heart. For I could wish that myself were accursed from Christ for my brethren, my kinsmen, according to the flesh." And the same we find recurring, in one form or another, in all the apostles, all the brethren. When they hear the Master lay it on them to minister—"Even as the Son of Man came, not to be ministered unto, but to minister and to give his life a ransom for many"—they take the sense of it; for, having his love in them, they are not afraid to find a cross of sacrifice in the love, just the cross that he called them to bear as followers. Thus also it is that he institutes a communion for them, and calls them to show forth his death; by which he means, not that they are to simply remember his death, or make mention of it, but that they are to show the love that can bear sins with him, and be a sacrifice even up to that stern limit.

O, what a calling is this, my brethren, the bearing of sins, with Christ. Of course you have not the same things to do that he had, or the same capacity to do them; you have not even the same things to do, one as another; but if his love has really been quickened in you, the fact will be known by the burdens that have come upon your heart; covetousness, world-greediness, self-indulgence, prejudices, resentments, feelings wounded by injury—none of these will hold you; but there will be a most dear love going forth in you, not to your friends only, but even more consciously to your enemies, and God's enemies. There will be times when you seem to be well nigh crushed, by the concern you feel and the burdens you bear. Is it so with you? Is it here that you sometimes find even your joy—the same which Christ himself had and bequeathed to you? Have you found, as every mother, for example, has, and every Christian may, that love-pains are the deepest attainable joys; tragic exaltations of a consciously great feeling that, in bearing enemies and sins, challenges eternal affinity with Christ and with God?

2. It is another and equally true conception of the

bearing of sins by Christ, that he is incarnated into the state of sin, including all the corporate woes of penalty, or natural retribution, under it—woes that infest the world, the body, and the social and political departments of human affairs. These disorders and mischiefs comprehend what is called, in scripture, "the curse;" for the curse is just that state of retributive disorder, and disjunction, that follows, under natural laws, the outbreak of sin The virus of disease, possibly of all disease, is generated under and by these laws. Natural causes are beneficent henceforth, only in the qualified sense, that they are attacking sin with due mixtures of pain, as well as with favors undeserved. Dreadful superstitions cloud the general understanding. Truth is obscured. Passion is made coarse and violent. Envies, ambitions, grudges, hatreds, are loosened, and bloody wrongs are instigated everywhere by them. Oppressions, persecutions, rebellions, wars, roll across the nations, and turn the world's history into a kind of Alcedama. This now is the curse, the corporate woe of the world, and when Christ comes down into the world to be incarnate in it, and do his work of love, he enters himself into its corporate evils, and takes them just as they are; even as a man, plunging into the sea, would take the waves and the monsters coursing in it as they are. All which is described by an apostle, when he says, that Christ "was made a curse for us." Nor, when he adds, "for it is written, cursed is every one that hangeth on a tree," does he mean to say that Christ is made a curse for us only in the sense that he is crucified, or at the particular point of his crucifixion; he merely drops in this allusion, touching that particular point, taken as a good type of all that he does and suffers in the world; for he meets the corporate woe and retribution of the world at every step. His body, as being born of the flesh, has the mortal maladies and temptations of the curse working subtly in it. When there is no room at the inn but only in the manger, that is the corporate mischief and curse of society, where the great rule down the humble, and respect goes only by appearances. The jealousy of Herod is the curse, before which he flies into Egypt. The bigotry of the priests was the curse. The slowness of his friends, the denial by one, the betrayal by another, the flight of all, was the curse. The chief priests and the rabbis, and the council, and Pilate, and Herod, all combined against him, only represent the corporate wrath, and wrong, and curse, of the world. Incarnated thus into the curse, he had the living contact of it at every breath. The waves of God's retribution dashed against him all the way, as he waded through on his course. Innocent he was, but had none of the rights, or proper fortunes of innocence. Not that any thing befell him as punishment, and yet he was scorching, every hour, under the great world's corporate evils; those which God's retributions had kindled for the chastisement of its sin. And why is he here, for what is he bearing thus the sin of the world? Not that he may suffer, not that he may idly brave so much of suffering—of what possible use were this?—no, but he is here because he has an errand that brought him, or required him to come. His object is to gain the human heart; and, to do it, he must open the heart of God; and to do that, he must not come flying over the world, but must be incarnated into it, put upon the same human footing in his human life, that we are—all this to make God's feeling intelligible, or what is the same, to open God's sympathies to us, and open our sympathies to God; thus to beget us anew in God's likeness. If he had come to be an exceptional man, whom the waves of the world's corporate evils could not touch, or if he had come as a man of brass, not to feel their touch, he were in fact nothing to us. But now that we have him struggling in the waves with us, touched with all our infirmities, and bearing, in deep sympathy, all our human evils, O, how tenderly do we cling to him and what strength do we get from his power and patience in our hearts!

Now, my friends, it would seem, at first view, to be very wide of all possibility, that we should be called to any such bearing of sin as this. Are we going to be incarnated like our divine Master? Even so! Dropping only the form of the word, the coming into flesh, it is no inconsiderable part of our dignity and God-likeness in sacrifice, that we are able to go directly down into the corporate evils of men, for their good!—into some house, for example, or village, or city, where a dreadful pestilence rages, to minister to their sick ones and comfort their dying; into the disgusts of low and filthy society, where vice rages, rescuing the victims and their children; into works of reformation, or maintenances of truth, that are unpopular, just because society has lost the truth. Christ bids you make a feast and call the lame, the halt, and the blind, passing, for the time, into their range of sympathy—what is that but a kind of incarnation, like that which brought him down out of heaven's orders of glory, into the lame and halting sorrows of our human apostasy. When, too, you go out, in God's love, into scenes of dissipation, or of splendid profligacy, it is an almost literal incarnation—a going into the flesh to be tempted as Christ was. Perhaps you are just now in the question, whether you shall forsake the refinements and comforts of a Christian home, and go down as a missionary, for all your future life, into the level of a barbarous and idolatrous people, where your motives will not, for many long years, be even so much as conceived, where your sympathies will be repelled, your operations looked on with jealousy, your beginnings crushed by violence, and many a sad long night of tears and groanings, witness your Gethsemane? Will you go, or will you not? What is it, in fact, but the question, whether you can be incarnated with your Master, under a little different version of the word? Almost half our duties come to us in this shape, raising the question, whether we can take the corporate evils of some condition that is unpopular, distasteful, unappreciative, hostile, or without dignity? In these things it is one of our greatest privileges to follow, and know that we follow, our Master—are we ready?

3. Christ bears the sin of the world, in the sense that he bears, consentingly, the direct attacks of wrong, or

sin, upon his person; doing it, of course, in but a few instances, such as may have been included in his comparatively short life, but showing, in those few instances, how all the human wrongs are related to his feeling, or would be if he suffered them all. And here again it is that he gets an amazing power, as a redeemer, over the sins of the world. He did not come into the world to suffer these wrongs as an end, or to brave them by an ostentation of patience, as possibly some may understand, when they hear him commanding one who is smitten on one cheek to turn the other. He is not counseling, in such words, a defiant, but only a total non-resistance. Coming into the world thus as the incarnate Word of God, God manifest in the flesh, he bears the wrong-doing of sin, not defiantly, but as feeling after the sin; letting it see what wrong it has in its own nature to do, when the Son of God comes to it ministering love and forgiveness. And what a spectacle is this to look upon! the Eternal King coming in love to win transgression back—mocked in his doctrine, hated for his miracles, insulted, struck, spit upon, crucified! And the more strangely impressive is the spectacle, that the sufferer is dumb, makes no protestation of his rights, parries no accusation, answers none. Pilate himself is "afraid" before such dignity. All that he will answer is, that he is come into the world "to bear witness to the truth." He does not say that he is here to bear the worst they can do upon him, nor that he is here to suffer at all as an end, but that his end is everlasting truth. That accordingly which so visibly shook the courage of

Pilate, at the trial, fell with as heavy a shock, on all sin, everywhere, afterwards. When the sin found such a being, even the incarnate Word of the Father, taking its blows, in such patience, and dying under the blows, how dreadful the recoil of feeling it suffered! How wild, and weak, and low, was it made to appear in its own sight. Thus it was that, in his bearing of sin upon his cross, Christ broke it down forever. Or, if it better please, thus it was that sin broke itself across the silence of Jesus, and the wood, and the nails, of his cross. And thus it was that the just now angry multitudes, "all the people that came together to see that sight, beholding the things that were done, smote their breasts and returned." All sin was broken, as it were, in that sight; it was the sight of Lucifer falling from heaven, even as he had testified in vision before.

And this kind also is for us, my brethren. Here we also are to take the cross and follow, as our Master bade us. Many persons appear to suppose, that we are required to submit ourselves to wrong as a kind of tax, or tariff, levied upon us, without any particular end. They take it as a mere blind appointment, and think it must be so accepted. Far from that as possible! On the contrary it is to be evil or wrong encountered in a work of sacrifice, encountered by one who is after the ends of love, even as Christ was. That death of his was great in power, not because he bore it, but because he was in the work of God's love, and bore it on his way, unable to be diverted from his end by that or any other death. In just that manner and degree, it was in his heart to bear sin. So if wrongs are done to you, and the same love is in you, the sin will have a great discovery to make in your patience, of its own cruelty and weakness. If you do but suffer well, nobody can long triumph over you, or live before you unforgiven. Do you then remember, that a great part of your Christian power and privilege is here, in the bearing of sin with your Master. Perhaps you talk down your enemies, perhaps you mix hot resentments with your words, perhaps you break the silence of Christ first, and then break every thing else in his example. Come back then if it be so, and read, and settle into your memory, and transcribe on your heart, that one sentence of the apostle concerning charity—"Beareth all things, believeth all things, hopeth all things, endureth all things." There you have the power of Jesus himself, and it is for you!

Having reached this point I see no reason why the subject should be farther protracted. There is nothing, in fact, to add, even for persuasion's sake. The gospel, as we have here seen it, is complete in itself, asking, and in fact, permitting, no help from its advocate.

XX.

THE PUTTING ON OF CHRIST.

"*But put ye on the Lord Jesus Christ.*"—ROM. xiii, 14.

The highest distinction of man, taken as an animal among animals, lies not in his two-handedness, or his erect figure, but in his necessity and right of dress. The inferior animals have no option concerning their outward figure and appearing. Their dress, or covering, is a part of their organization, growing on them, or out of them, as their bones are grown within. Be it feathers, or fur, or hair, or wool; be it in this color or that, brilliant as the rainbow, or shaggy, or grizzled, or rusty and dull, they have no liberty to change it, even if they could desire the change, for one that is glossier and more to their taste. But man, as a creature gifted with a larger option, begins, at the very outset, to show his superior dignity in the necessary option of dress. It is given him for his really high prerogative, to dress himself, and come into just what form of appearing will best satisfy the tastes into which he has grown; or, what is very nearly the same thing, will best represent the quality of his feeling and character. With this kind of liberty comes, of course, an immense peril; for there is a peril that belongs to every kind of liberty. As dress and equipage may create a difference of appearing, that very nearly amounts to a difference of order and kind, the race of ambition, as soon as ambition is born, will here begin. And now the tremendous option of dress, given as a point of dignity, becomes, under sin, a mighty instigator in the fearful race of money, society, and fashion.

You already understand from this course of remark, that I am going to speak of dress as the outward analogon, or figure of character, and of character as the grand "putting on" of the soul. It would be instructive here to notice the immense reacting power of dress on character, showing how we not only choose our own figure in it, but our figure in turn chooses us; requiring us to feel and act, or helping us to feel and act, according to the appearing we are in. But I hasten to speak of the analogy referred to. Dress relates to the form or figure of the body, character to the form or figure of the soul—it is, in fact, the dress of the soul. The option we have, in one, typifies the grander option we have in the other. The right we have in one, above the mere animals, to choose the color, type and figure of the outward man, foreshadows the nobler right we also have to cast the mold, fashion or despoil the beauty, of the inward man. There is also an immense reaction in character; what we have become already, in the cast of life, going far to shape our doings and possible becomings hereafter.

On the ground of this analogy it is that the scriptures

so frequently make use of dress, to signify what lies in character, and represent character, in one way or another, as being the dress of the soul. Thus they speak of "the wedding-garment," "the garment of praise," that "of cursing," that "of pride;" "the robe of righteousness," and "of judgment," and "the white robe," and "the best robe" given to the returning prodigal, and "the robe that has been washed," and "judgment put on as a robe;" of "white raiment," and "white apparel," of "glorious apparel," of "filthiness," or "righteousness that are filthy rags," of "filthiness in the skirts;" and more inclusively and generally still, of being "clothed with salvation," "with strength and power," "with humility," "with majesty," "with shame," "with fine linen clean and white, which is the righteousness of saints;" "I put on righteousness," says Job, "and it clothed me." And, in the same way, it is that Paul, conceiving Christ to be the soul's new dress, or what is no wise different, its new character, says "Put ye on the Lord Jesus Christ."

All the figures of dress or clothing are used up, in this manner, by the scriptures, to represent the forms of disgrace and filthiness, or of beauty and glory, into which the inner man of the soul may be fashioned—wearing heaven's livery or that of sin. As character is the soul's dress, and dress analogical to character, whatever has power to produce a character when received, is represented as a dress to be put on.

Passing thus into the great problem of life as a moral

and spiritual affair, we are surprised to find that inward character and outward covering are so closely related, as to be taken, by a kind of natural instinct, one for the other, and the loss of one for the loss of the other. What do the first human pair imagine when they fall into sin, and make the loss of character, but that they have lost their covering? It does not appear to be merely a stroke of art in the description given, but a most natural turn of fact, that the shamed consciousness within is taken, by their unpracticed simplicity, as a shock that has come upon their modesty.

No sooner is the deed done, than the culprits, all covered in before by the sense of God's beauty on their feeling—for exactly that was their original righteousness and not any beauty of their own culture—begin to be troubled by the discovery of their nakedness! The real difficulty is that the pure investiture of God upon their consciousness has been stripped away, thrown off by their sin. Nothing is changed without, as they foolishly think—stitching their scant leaves, vain hope! to hide a loss that is within. And probably the same is true of the immense dressing art and trade of the world; it is put agoing and continued, as regards the fearfully deep zeal of it, by just that shame of the mind which keeps it company in evil, and makes it always emulous of some better figure. Were this inward shame taken away, and the soul inwrapped, as at the first, by the sense of God's beauty upon it, the secret phrenzy at least would soon be over. The maiden would forget her torment in the sense of a holier beauty within, the hidden man of the heart, the ornament of a meek and quiet spirit; and the man of the world would be striving no more after the outward shows and trappings that are needed to cover the lost honors of the mind.

In the same way it is, just according to the manner of the fig-leaf history, that such an immense patching art, in the matter of character, is kept in practice in all ages of the world. It is the general admission of souls, that they are not in a true figure of respect before themselves; but instead of returning to God, and the complete investure in which he will cover them, they imagine, or get up, small shows of excellence, which they contrive to think are as good, for the matter of character, as they need. These small shows we have a name for, calling them *pretexts*, shows of covering that, after all, do not cover—patches, fig-leaves. In one view the absurd figures continually put forward as pretexts, in this way, are abundantly ludicrous; in another they carry a look most sad, as well as profoundly serious. Politeness—this is one of the fig-leaves; taken for a complete character by many, and carefully maintained, as the standard excellence of life. Honor is another and scantier, assuming still to be even a superlative kind of character; more imposing and airy than it could be under the restrictions of virtue. Bravery, again, is a fig-leaf pretext, put on to cover the loss of courage; for evil in the soul is of a coward nature, and can only keep itself up, without heart, by sallies and wild dashes of bravery from the will. These and many others of the same class are pretexts of character outside of religion, but immensely significant, as revelations of the shamed consciousness of sin. Passing into the more immediate field of religion, the pretexts there invented and put forward, as covers to the soul's nakedness, are scarcely to be numbered or named—such as sacrifices offered the world over to idols, self-tortures of the body to cover the sin of the soul, penances, austerities of solitude, vows of abstinence and poverty, exactness in rites and traditions, orthodoxy, alms-givings, honesty in trade, the doing others no harm, resignations and fatalizing submissions to God, works of reform and philanthropy, patience without feeling, liberality without character. This fig-leaf stitching is, in fact, the great business of the world; in which we may see, more convincingly than by any thing else, the certainty that men are goaded everywhere by the secret, inexpugnable feeling of nakedness or a want of character. It is a most sad picture to look upon. Then how piercing and fearful is the revelation, when the Holy Spirit strips away all the illusions they practice, and they are made to see that their righteousnesses are rags and not garments, and that they are wretched, and miserable, and poor, and blind, and naked. O, this nakedness of the soul! how dismal a figure it is even to itself! Jesus pities it, and comes to it saying, in what gentleness of promise—"buy of me gold tried in the fire, that thou mayest be rich, and white raiment that thou mayest be clothed, that the shame of thy nakedness may not appear."

Nor let any one imagine that these deep wants of spiritual nakedness we speak of are to be satisfied, by any uprightness in the moral life. The shame is religious, not moral—it belongs entirely to the religious nature, divested as it is of what was to be everlastingly upon it, the conscious infolding of God. The law moral is a law of this world, sanctioned by this world's custom. It was not this out which the first man fell; for custom had not yet arrived. No, it was the original inspiration, that enveloped and, as it were, covered in his life; the holy investiture that he had inductively from God, by community of being with him—this it was that he had put off, and the loss of which was the dreadful shame of his uncovering. Impossible, therefore, it is for any one to reinvest himself with the covering he needs. He can not dew himself in the dews of his lost morning, can not cover in himself in the righteousness that was God's infolding of character upon him. What he had by community of being he can never reproduce by his personal will. He must have it again, as he had it at the first; only by that same righteousness of God revealed to faith, in Christ his Son. Here again the robe is offered back, and he may have good use of his liberty in putting it on; he only can not make a thread of it himself; the warp and woof must be wholly divine—the incovering beauty of God's own feeling and Spirit, that enveloped our first father, and, in Christ, are offered to us all.

We pass, then, here to another point in advance, viz.,

to the fact that Christ our Lord comes into the world to restore the investiture we have lost; or rather to be himself, for us and upon us, all that our sin has cast away. The original word of scripture, represented in our English version by the word *atone*, or *make atonement*, literally means to *cover*. In this manner, Jesus the Lord comes to cover our sin; covering, first, our liabilities in the sins that are past, by the forbearance of God, and the honor he confers on God's instituted justice, by community with us in the penal scathing and curse of our transgression; and, secondly and principally, in the sense that he undertook to be the divine character upon us—yea, the divine glory. For he does not merely teach us something, as many fancy, which we are to take up notionally and copy, item by item, in ourselves, but he undertakes to copy himself into us, and be the righteousness of God upon us. Had we been taught, in the best manner possible, what things in character to add, what things to change, or qualify, or put away, or put on, what could we have done, in the weaving of so many and such infinite subtleties and shadings of quality, but inevitably miss of all the really divine proportions; producing only a grotesque and half absurd caricature? But when Jesus comes to us bearing all these finest, holiest proportions of beauty in himself, we have nothing to do but to believe in him, or receive him in his person, and he copies himself into us, by the wondrous power of his feeling and sacrifice upon us. Then, as every shade is from him, nothing is overdone, distorted, missed, or omitted. The glory of the Father, all the Father's character, is upon him, and he is able to say—"the glory which thou gavest me I have given them."

Furthermore, there is this wonderful art, so to speak, in the incarnate human appearing of Jesus, that he humanizes God to us, or brings out into the human molds of feeling, conduct and expression, the infinite perfection, otherwise inappropriable and very nearly inconceivable. Since we are finite, God must needs take the finite in all revelation. He can never draw himself close enough to get hold of our feeling, or sympathy, and be revealed to our heart, till he takes the finite of humanity. In the man-wise form only can we put him on. Otherwise his very perfections, elaborated by our human thought, would be only impassive, distant, autocratic, it may be, and even repulsive; as they often are, even in the teachings now of Christian theology. That he has any particular feeling for men, or this, or that man, that his great spirit can be overcast and burdened with concern for us under sin, that he is complete in all the passive virtues he puts it upon us to practice—how could we think it, or be at all sure of it? But here he is, in Jesus Christ, moving up out of a childhood, into a great manhood, filling all the human relations with offices and ministries in human shapes of good; helping the sick with kind words, and healing them by the touch, so to speak, of his sympathies, careful of the poor, patient with enemies, burdened for them in feeling even to the pitch of agony, simple, and true, and faithful unto death. And so we have God's infinite perfections in our own finite molds, and are ready to have them even upon ourselves. God is now no more some blank idol of reason, some fate, or infinite abyss, or some frigid, thin immensity of pantheistic unconsciousness; his vast superhuman proportions no longer baffle us, or spread themselves in phantoms of glory, which we can as little think as partake. But they are given us in the traits of Jesus, who being Son of God, has come to be the Son of Man among us, living out, in his human way, and so helping us to conceive, that excellence of God, in which we require to be invested. The ineffable character is made human, set forth in the human proportions, and we have it as a glorious, full suit, prepared in the exactest fit of our humanity, yet still divine. The virtues, graces, glories, sympathies infinite, are so brought forth and embodied in the incarnate whole of his life, that we can have them all upon us at once, when we could not even sketch the pattern, by simply embracing, in trust, his human person.

In this manner, for this, in brief, is the gospel, we are to be new charactered, by the putting on of Christ; not by some imitation or copying of Christ that we practice, item by item, in a way of self-culture—the Christian idea is not that—but that Christ is to be a complete wardrobe for us himself, and that by simply receiving his person, we are to have the holy texture of his life upon us, and live in the infolding of his character. And this is the meaning of that "righteousness of faith" which is variously spoken of in the scriptures. It is that Christ is everything for us and upon us, and that we are to see our whole supply—righteousness, beauty, peace, liberty in good, graces, and stores of character, putatively ours in him; reckoned to be ours by faith, always derivable by faith from him; for this exactly is the difference between a Christian and a merely humanly virtuous person, that one draws on Christ for everything, and the other on himself—on his will, his works, his self-criticism, shaping all his amendments himself. Or, reversing the order of comparison, one manufactures a suit for himself, in patches of character gotten together and laid upon the ground of his sin, and the other takes a whole robe of life, graciously fitted and freely tendered, in the humanly divine excellence of Christ his Saviour—who is thus made unto him wisdom, righteousness, sanctification and redemption.

But we are to put him on—"put ye on the Lord Jesus Christ." And here is the difficulty—you can not see, it may be, how it is done. The very conception is unintelligible, or mystical, and you can not guess, it may be, what it means. What then does it mean to put on Christ?

It does not mean, of course, that you are only to make an experiment of putting on the garb of a new life, and see how you will like it. No man puts on Christ for any thing short of eternity. The act must be a finality, even at the beginning. He must be accepted as the Alpha and Omega. Whoever contemplates even the possibility of being without him, or of ever being without him again, does not put him on.

Neither do you put him on, when you undertake to copy some one or more of the virtues, or characters, in him—the gentleness, for example, the love, the dignity—without being willing to accept the sacrifice in him, to bear the world's contempt with him, to be singular, to be hated, to go through your Gethsemane, and groan with him under the burdens of love. There can be no choosing out here of shreds and patches from his divine beauty; you must take the whole suit, else you can not put him on. The garment is seamless, and can not be divided.

Neither do you put him on, when you undertake only to realize some previous conceptions of character that are your own. The dress is to be not from you, but from him—the whole Christ, just as he is, taken upon you to shape you in the molds of his own divine life and spirit.

But we must be more positive. First, then, there must be a full and hearty renunciation of your past life. As the apostle words it in another place, you must put off the old man in order to put on the new. You can not have the new character to put on over the old. The filthy garments, all the rags, must be thrown off, thrown completely away. Christ will be no mere overall to the old affections and lusts.

How, then, for the next thing, do we put him on? By faith, I answer, only by faith. For in that the soul comes to him, shivering in the cold shame of its sin, and gives itself over to him, to be loved, protected, covered in, by his gracious life and passion. It sees such beauty upon him that it dares trust him, and says—"be thou my all, the washing away of my sin, the covering of my vileness, my character and life. O Lord, my hope is in thee!" And this is faith; it is coming to Jesus in all his manlike sympathies, characters, molds of life, and receiving him, by a total act of trust, to be upon you, as the Lord your righteousness. Your iniquities are thus to be forgiven, your sin to be covered. Righteousness from him, and not from your own will and works, is to be upon you thus, by the infolding of a divine power; even the righteousness that is of God by faith, unto all and upon all them that believe.

Take another conception, which may be more intelligible to some, viz., that you will put on Christ by obedience to him; for whoever obeys Christ willingly trusts him, and whoever trusts him obeys him. Hence the promise—"If a man love me, he will keep my words, and my father will love him, and we will come unto him and make our abode with him." And then it follows that whoever has the abode with him, consciously, of the Father and the Son, will be all folded in by the thought of it, and will live as being in the sacred investiture of the divine character and power. If then, you can not understand faith, you can understand obedience, and if you go into that, as the final, total, giving over of your life, I will answer for it, that there will be a faith in your obedience, and that Christ will be with you, manifested in you, truly put on, as the consciously divine attire of your life.

I have only to add on this point, that you are to be always putting on Christ afterwards, as you begin to put him on at the first. All the success of your Christian life will consist in the closeness of your walk with Christ, and the completeness of your trust in him. You are not so much to fashion yourself by him, as to let him fashion you by himself—to be upon you, as he is with you, and cover you with all the graces of his inimitable love and beauty; and this you will do most perfectly, when you trust him most implicitly, and keep his words most faithfully.

It only remains, now, to bring our subject to its fit conclusion, by speaking of the consequences of this putting on of Christ. And I name, first of all, that which the apostle suggests, in a kind of cadence that immediately follows and finishes out the text. "But put ye on," he says, "the Lord Jesus Christ, and make not provision for the flesh, to fulfill the lusts thereof." Where he conceives, it will be seen, that one substitutes, or takes place of, the other—that when Christ is really put on, the world falls off, and the lusts of property, and fame, and power, and appetite, subside or fall away. The effect runs both ways, under the great law of action and reaction—as the old man is put off that the new may be put on, so the new put on still further displaces the old. This, too, we know by the attestations of experience. He that has the sense of Christ upon him, has himself ennobled. He is raised in the pitch of his feeling every way; having such a consciousness awakened of his inward relation to God, that money, and pleasure, and all the petty lustings of the lower life are sunk out of sight and forgot. Sometimes you will see that an appetite which has become a madness, like the appetite for drink, and has shaken down all the man's resolutions, and floored him at every point of struggle, utterly dies and is felt no more, from the moment when he has put on Christ. He wants no more a sensation, when the sentiment of his soul is full. It is as if he were in Christ's own appetites, instead of those which have so long domineered over his diseased nature. And so it will be universally. If there be any over-mastering temptation which baffles you, and keeps turning you off in your endeavors, and boasting itself against you, here is your deliverance—raise no fight with it in your own will, as you always have done when you have failed, but simply turn yourself to Christ alone: put on Christ, let your soul be so covered in by the power of his grace upon you, that you feel yourself raised and caparisoned for glory in him, and all the little and low lustings of this world will be silent—felt no more.

There is also this most admirable effect in the putting on of Christ, that being thus enveloped in his life and feeling, a power will move inward from him, that will search out all most subtle, inbred evils in you, even those which are hidden from your consciousness, and will finally assimilate you in them, and in all beside, to what he himself was. This, in fact, is the wonderful power of dress, that, while no person who has spent his life in the rags of poverty, and the coarseness of low-bred manners, can possibly fashion himself to ways of elegance, by superintending his every particular look, motion, gesture, and tone, the simple insphering of his life in new associations and new proprieties of dress, may and often does suffice, in a very few years, to re-compose and assimilate his whole manner as a man. And so it is that Christ will be able, when put on, to fashion us into a character of innumerable graces, all consolidated, in a harmonious whole of beauty like his own.

Here, too, is the true idea of Christian sanctification. It is that we may so put on Christ, and be so infolded in him, as to be consciously raised above all bad impulse into good, above all guiltiness into a conscience void of offense, above all detentions of bondage into perfect liberty, above all fear into perfect assurance, and so continue as long as we falter not in the faith, by which Christ is thus brought in upon the soul, to be its impulse and the appetizing force of its life. But whether this can be fitly called a perfect sanctification is more doubtful. That it leaves the soul in a temptable state all must and do in fact agree, and if the faith, at any time, gives way, the subject will immediately lapse into some kind of sin. Nay, if he were sanctified far down, in all the deepest, most underground cells of feeling he was ever conscious of, there would yet be treasons hid still deeper in the soul, and he would fall at once, the moment he let go his faith. The truth appears to be that, in such a state of perfect liberty and good impulse as we have described, the character still is not wholly inherent, but only in part;—a kind of supervening, or superinduced character; a garment of grace put on, the grace of which has not yet struck through into the inmost nature of him who is covered by it. Christ is perfect on him, and he is in Christ, but he is not perfected in himself. The transformation of the man has not yet come up to the type of his Christly investiture. He is like a soldier in the fiery panoply and dress of war. When he has it on him, and hears the trumpet sounding bravely, he is bold enough to face all danger in the fight; but there still are vestiges of a naturally coward feeling, it may be, in the center and core of his personality, such that if you strip him of the warlike trappings, and send him out to fight a silent engagement in that common figure, he will not unlikely turn and flee for his life. It is one thing in this way to have on a pure garment, clean and white, and so to act purely, and quite another to be clean and white all through, in the inmost substance, and deepest impulse, and subtlest windings, of the soul's own habit. This requires time, and it may be a long time. Even if he were to be in Christ so perfectly as not to commit one conscious sin for many years, which is possible, there would still be in him, after all this long investiture by Christ, old vestiges of disease, and disorder, and bad passion, not yet sanctified away.

But it is much, how very much, that all these can

be thus kept under, so as never again to break out and reign, as long as Christ is faithfully put on by a believing, consecrated life. Potentially speaking, all sanctification is here; for the superinduced character may be kept up bright, and clean, full, and free to the last; when, of course, it will complete itself in the all-renovated, absolutely perfect, through and through character of the glorified.

Observe again the consciousness of strength, and the exalted confidence of feeling, that must gird any soul that has truly put on Christ. It will be with him, in his faith, as it was with the prodigal, when the Father said, "bring forth the best robe and put it on him, and put a ring on his finger and shoes on his feet." From that moment he felt strong in the family. The shame fell off as the robe went on, and the confidence of a son come back upon him. So it is that every Christian is strong who has really put on Christ. He is clothed with strength and honor, as with salvation. He lives in the garment of praise. All misgivings flee, all mutinous passions fall under. Do you sometimes try, my brethren, to be strong by your will, strong by your works, strong by what you can raise of excitement, or high resolve, that is only weakness, and a great part of all weakness comes in that way. Nothing is more natural for a Christian losing ground, than to put forth all the force he has, in a strain of hard endeavor, lashing up and thrusting on himself; but in that, he is believing, probably, just as much less as he is goading himself more. Let him go back to faith, see that he lets go mere self-endeavor, to put on Christ, and he will have all strength and victory.

Here, too, be it understood, is the source of that strange power of impression, which is felt in the life and society of all earnest Christians. Everybody feels that there is a something about them not human. And the reason is that they have put on Christ. The serious, loving, gentle, sacrificing and firm spirit of Jesus, is revealed within, or upon them, and they signify to men's feeling just what he signified. They fulfill that gracious name that was formerly in so great favor in the Church—they are all Christophers, Christ-bearers. They will even put so much meaning into their "good morning," or their bow of courtesy, as to carry a Christly impression in the heart of a stranger. This, my brethren, is the true power. Would that the multitude in our day, who can think to be powerful only as they strive and cry, and go dinning through the world in a perpetual ado of hard endeavor, could just learn how much it means, to put on Christ.

It only remains to add, what has been coming into view in the whole progress of our subject, that the only true salvation-title is Christ put on, and found upon the soul as its heavenly investiture. A great many persons are at work, in these times, to fashion a character for themselves, and demanding it of them who preach the gospel, that they preach conduct, tell men how to be good and right, correct their faults, make them good husbands, wives, children, citizens—cease, in a word, from the mystic matter of faith and divine experience, and put the world on doing something more solid and satisfactory. This kind of cant has gone so far, too, that many professed preachers of the gospel itself are in it. The Master owns them not, so far, at least. He wants, not simply a better conduct, but a solid, new man—so, new husbands, wives, children, citizens; new kindness, truthfulness, honor, honesty, beauty. This new man to be put on, as having put off the old, is a very different matter from the old man in a better style of behavior. It is that which after God, is created in righteousness and true holiness—a man after God, even as Christ was, when he came in God's love to take us on his soul, that we may take him on our soul, and be covered in by the new investiture of his life; that sighing we may sigh with him, dying die with him, rising rise with him, carrying up all our once low affections to sit with him where he sitteth, at the right hand of God. All which he figures in the parable of the great king's wedding-feast; where the guests are called by sending round to each, for his card of invitation, a *caftan*, or splendid wedding-robe. Putting on this robe the guests are to come in, and, by this found upon them, are to be admitted and have their places assigned. But it happens, at the great eternal feast, as the Saviour represents, that the King comes in and finds one there that has no robe on him but his own. It may be a very fine, wonderfully elaborate robe; he may even have thought to shine there in it more than if it were the king's providing. But the king says—"Friend, how camest thou in hither not having on the wedding-garment? And he was speechless. The king said—"bind him hand and foot, and take him away." Inasmuch as holy character in created beings is and must eternally be derivative, finite from infinite, who shall be able to stand by self-originative goodness, who that will not put on Christ! Putting on his robe of self-criticism, self-endeavor, self-righteousness, will not answer. All such fine attire is only rags at the best. The true wedding-garment is Jesus himself, and there is no other.

Here then, brethren and friends, I speak now to you all without distinction, here is the fearfully precise point on which our eternity hinges—the putting on of Christ. Observe, we are to put on no great name or standard, no sectarian badge or livery, no lawn, or saintly drab, or veil, or stole, or girdle—none of these are the real new man to be put on. No! Christ! we must put on Christ himself, *and none but him.* We must be in-Christed, found in him, covered in the seamless, indivisible robe of his blessed life and passion. Far be it also from us, when we put on Christ, to think of turning ourselves about, in the search after some other, finer, pretext that we may put on over him, to make him attractive, pleasing, acceptable. No, we are to put him on just as he is, wear him outside, walk in him, bear his reproach, glory in his beauty, call it good to die with him, so to be found in him not having our own righteousness, but the righteousness that is of God by faith. Cover us in it, O thou Christ of God, and let our shame be hid eternally in thee.

XXI.

HEAVEN OPENED.

"*And he saith unto him— Verily, verily, I say unto you, Hereafter ye shall see heaven open, and the angels of God ascending and descending on the Son of Man.*"—JOHN i, 31.

With a singular felicity and power of statement, Mr. Coleridge gives it for his doctrine of scripture inspiration—"In the Bible there is more that *finds* me, than I have experienced in all other books put together; the words of the Bible find me at greater depths of my being; and whatever finds me brings with it an irresistible evidence of its having proceeded from the Holy Spirit." God only can be so far privy, that is, to the soul, as to make it answer thus, all through, in its deepest and most hidden parts, to his words. Whatever may be thought of his doctrine, as a complete and sufficient solution of the question, it is certainly good, and even powerfully good, as far as it goes. And it has a beautiful coincidence, which he probably had never observed, with the very simple and truly natural sentiment of Christ's interview with Nathanael.

Fig-trees make a very dense covering of leaves and sometimes drop their boughs very low. Nathanael had lately retired into the cabin of thick foliage thus provided by some tree of his garden, and closeted there with God, was opening his heart, in regard to some particular difficulty, or enemy, or question of duty, or promise of a Messiah to come, in a manner only the more guileless, that he felt himself to be so entirely removed from human observation. Shortly after, probably on that same day, being notified by Philip, he comes to see Jesus, who is even thought to be the great Messiah himself. Jesus saw Nathanael coming to him and saith of him—"Behold an Israelite indeed in whom is no guile!" Nathanael saith unto him—"Whence knowest thou me?" Jesus answered and said unto him—"Before Philip called thee, when thou wast under the fig-tree, I saw thee." Nathanael saith unto him—"Rabbi, thou art the Son of God, thou art the king of Israel." Jesus answered and said unto him—"Because I saw thee under the fig-tree believest thou? thou shalt see greater things than these." And he saith unto him—"Verily, verily I say unto you, Hereafter ye shall see heaven open, and the angels of God ascending and descending on the Son of Man."

The two main points of the dialogue are, first, that Nathanael was so impressed by the *finding* of Christ, or the privity of Christ's knowledge of him, under the fig-tree, that he at once declared his belief in him as the Messiah; and secondly, that Christ immediately proclaims a deeper finding, and a more convincing privity of knowledge, that shall, in due time, be shown or proved, by the opening, within his own bosom, of a supernatural, sense and the discovery to him thus of supernatural beings, the passing and repassing, the flow and reflow of their blessed society. According to the description given, it will be as if that isthmus barrier between the two great oceans of the world were cloven down, for the oscillating tides to begin their coming and returning flow; when also the ships of the nations, wafted convergently thither, shall be sailing freely through, burdened with the fruits and golden riches of all climes and shores.

Now this opening of heaven, which is to be our subject, is presented by the Saviour in terms that may seem to be a little enigmatical. We shall conceive his meaning perhaps more sufficiently, if we note three principal views of the heavenly state that occur in the scripture. First, there is the local objective view, that conceives it as a place somewhere in the upper worlds of heaven or the sky. Secondly, there is the terrestrial objective view, where the New Jerusalem descending from God out of heaven and refitting our world itself to be the abode of God with men, makes it a province, in that manner, of the other. Thirdly, the subjective view, which has nothing to do with place or locality, but conceives the heavenly state simply as a state of spiritual beholding and social commerce opened in the soul itself. There is no necessary contradiction or disagreement between the three conceptions stated; they are all true, though probably in different senses, and may be taken as complementary, in fact, to each other. The first is more impressive and popular and more commonly used; the second, as being more geographical, is more closely connected with our mundane prospects and affairs; the third is more entirely moral and rational, being simply the condition of character. All are to be used with entire freedom, and without any attempt to maintain one against the others; the presumption being that a state so transcendent will be only feebly conceived, when they are all brought in, to intensify and qualify, or complement, each other.

In the conversation with Nathanael, the Saviour appears to be speaking in the subjective way, as of a heaven to be opened in the soul itself. In his terms of description, he refers, apparently, to Jacob's dream, where that patriarch beholds, not without, but in the chamber of his own brain, in a dream of the night when the senses are fast locked in sleep, a ladder set up and the angels of God coursing up and down upon it; only what transpired subjectively in his brain he naturally associated with the place, conceiving also that the sky above was somehow specially set open there, saying—"how dreadful is this place," and calling it "the gate of heaven." So the Saviour says, "ascending and descending," putting the ascending first; as if the metropolis or point or departure, in the commerce begun, were to be from within the soul itself. There lives the Son of Man, reigning in his heavenly kingdom at the soul's own center, and from him go up couriers and ministers of glory, descending also back upon him there. The precise point made, in this manner, with Nathanael is, that as he was discovered under the fig-tree, so he shall be discovered, as regards the immense upper world of the soul, existing unsuspected in him hitherto, but now set open. These two propositions cover the ground of the subject stated, and these I shall endeavor to substantiate.

I. That there is a supernatural sense, now slumbering or closed up in souls, by which they might perceive, or cognize, supernatural beings and things, even as they cognize material beings and things by the natural sense. And

II. That Christ undertakes to open this supernatural sense, and make it the organ or inlet of universal society.

I. There is a supernatural sense now closed up, or existing under a state of suppression.

We encounter a difficulty here, in attempting to prove the existence of faculties and powers that are shut in, or suppressed in their action. And yet even our natural faculties are very nearly in that condition at the first—no man knowing, or conceiving, what is in him, till it is brought forth. We also know that all finest qualities and highest powers are stifled, for the time, or even permanently, by wrongs and vices. What we here suppose to be true is, that in the original and properly normal state, souls were open to God, and a full, free commerce with his upright society. Being made in God's image, they were to be children with God their Father, living in society with him, having him to know, enjoy, and love, and having all their desires freely met and satisfied by the open ministry of his friendship. He was, and, with all his glorious company, was eternally to be, revealed in them, as in a heaven of present bliss, and immediately conscious communion of life.

But this original and properly normal state was necessarily broken up and brought to a full end, by their fall into sin. They now become afraid of him and hide themselves instinctively from him. No longer can he be revealed to their immediate knowledge, because the personal affinities through which he was to be revealed are closed up in them. They fall off thus into their senses, and become occupied with the objects of the senses; having the understanding darkened, being alienated from the life of God, through the ignorance that is in them. So they live as under heavy storm-clouds in the night; the lightning flashes in sharp gleams across the clouds, or glares in red anger fits from within their body, but there is no opening through, to let in the light of the stars. Heaven is gone out to them in the same manner; God is hid, and they know not where they can find Him; spirit and spiritual being and spiritual society with his great family is so far a lost possibility, that, if they think it, they can not give it reality. There is something too in guilt, or the state of guiltiness, that amounts to a virtual shutting up, or suppression, of all affinities with supernatural being. It freezes in perception. It condenses all the Godward and pure aspirations and gathers them in, by the dreadful recoil it makes on the soul's own center. It pronounces a damnation too upon itself, and by its own remorseful severities makes the sentence good. Falling away thus from God, and closing itself up as regards all supernatural relations and perceptions, it becomes self-centered, isolated, a worm in the ground, having its belongings there and not in the element of day.

Is there now any such supernatural sense existing under suppression in the soul, as the statement I have made supposes? The question is a very great, and is getting to be the almost only, question for our day.

To go over the evidence briefly, there is obviously nothing impossible in the fact of such a sense. There may as well be a power to cognize immaterial, supernatural being, as material.

Neither is it any thing, that our philosophers recognize no such higher ranges of faculty. No faculty is ever recognized, save as it comes into consciousness by use. That which is shut up, therefore, can be nothing to philosophy. When the lantern of a light-house has no light burning within, it will be an opaque body at the top, as it is in the base below—even the transparency will be opaque.

But we can affirm, I think, with confidence, for one distinct argument, that there ought to be just this upper world of supernatural insight in souls. As they are related to God, there ought to be a power of immediate knowledge, in which he is revealed—they require, in fact, to be as truly conscious of God as of themselves; for God is the complement of their being, and without him they only half exist. Again, as they are related to eternal society with all good beings, they ought also to have powers of discerning that may apprehend them. In this manner, as they are not made to be mere plodders, however intelligent, or scientific in distinguishing the laws and causes of things, but to have their summits and supreme destinies of life, in their commerce with God, and the supernatural society of his realm, their fit equipment requires, obviously enough, a higher sense opening towards the supernatural. How can the understanding, operating on the subject matter of sense, discover, or attain, by mere inference, to what is not in the premises of sense, but in a totally different range? Whoever then adheres to immortality and religion, and denies the credibility of what is supernatural, confesses, at once, that he wants the commerce of God's universal society, and cuts off the possibility of finding it.

Again, there not only ought to be aspirations in the soul, and powers of sensing for the supernatural, but we can see, by many signs, more or less definite, that there are. Sometimes a groping will signify as much as an open discovery, and what has the race been doing, in all the past ages and everywhere, but groping after gods, and demons, and populating even the earth and the sky with mythologic creations. It is as if some divine phrenzy were in them, goading them on after what they so mightily want. Little, indeed, do they discover of what is real and true; they only go a marveling, as the phrenologists would say, carried off from the mere plane of reason, by they know not what. They grope with their eyes shut, and their groping signifies more than their discoveries. I think also that we can find, every one of us, in ourselves, dim yearnings, imaginations coasting round unknown realms, guesses asking after the commerce of good and great beings, that put us in profound sympathy with them. Nothing will account for what we find thus in ourselves and the world, but the fact of supernatural longings and perceptions, existing in us under suppression. Indeed, I think we should very nearly suffocate, all of us, including even the infidel deniers, shut down close under nature and her causes. After all, we do think higher things, and there is more comfort in it than perhaps we know.

We are able, again, to conceive certain things about this supernatural sense, taking in supernatural things and beings, which makes it seem less extravagant. To say that we can sense, or could, other ranges of being, and have them in the open heaven of the soul, appears to be violent, or extravagant. Just as violent is it still to say, that we do take in the world of matter by the natural senses, and have it in us, even from the sky downward. We do not go to things in our perception of them, neither do they come locally to us; the latitudes, and longitudes, and altitudes, are still there; we do not spread ourselves in presence upon them; and yet we somehow have them in us, and subjectively possess them. Besides, in the relation of spirits and beings supernatural, we know not by what presences and revelations they may come within the precincts of knowledge; as little by what fences they are kept asunder. Place in this matter may be nothing, congenialities every thing. It does not surprise us that the bad should somehow come upon the bad; as little should it that the good have a way of social presence with the good. Perhaps, too, it will relieve the aspect of extravagance here, if I say, that faith is nothing but the opening of the supernatural sense of the soul on the supernatural being to be apprehended. It opens, in other words, the heaven of the mind, and God, and Christ, and the good supernatural society press in to fill it. Faith is the evidence, in this manner, even as the scriptures declare, of things not seen, and the substance, or substantiation, of things hoped for. There is even a kind of faith in the sensing of sight, turning mere images, in the eye, to things, and making them real. That there is a higher sense, realizing beings supernatural, is a fact every way correspondent.

Furthermore it is a fact well attested, in all ages, and proved by manifold experience, that minds do consciously approximate God and the heavenly society, accordingly as they are turned away from evil and set open to good. They feel a certain nearness to beings and words supernatural, that amounts to society begun. And then how very often, as their affinities are more completely fined and set open, do they, in their last hours, hail the Saviour present, and good angels revealed, and departed friends whom they salute by name, waiting to receive them. Doubtless all such things will be set down as the illusions of their wandering faculty, but what if they should happen to be true —even the truest truths ever beheld by them, and most profoundly wanted by us all?

I will only add that the scriptures constantly assume,

and in many ways assert, the fact of a supernatural sense in souls, that is shut up and requires to be opened. Christ declares this truth again and again, as, for instance, when he says, "For this people's heart is waxed gross, and their ears are dull of hearing, and their eyes have they closed, lest at any time they should see with their eyes, and hear with their ears, and understand with their heart." He does not say this of the natural senses and judgments, but of the higher perceptions of the heart, or the religious and spiritual man. The same thing also is very deliberately and carefully put by the apostle, when he says—"But the natural man receiveth not the things of the Spirit of God, neither can he know them, because they are spiritually discerned. But he that is spiritual judgeth all things." There is, in other words, a natural man and a spiritual, a lower range of perception and a higher; and by this latter only, set open to the light, can the spiritual and supernatural things of God be discerned and judged. And this is the supernatural sense of which I have been speaking, the upper range of faculty that belongs to religion, prepared for a seeing of the invisible. By this it was that Christ expected to be in the soul's inward beholding, as when he said—"but ye see me." By this it was that a whole heaven of being and society is conceived to reveal itself to souls, when they are converted and set open to God—"But ye are come unto mount Zion, the city of the living God, the heavenly Jerusalem, and to an innumerable company of angels, and to the general assembly and church of the first-born which are written in heaven, and to God the Judge of all, and to the spirits of just men made perfect." And so glorious and clear was their inward beholding, at times, that one disciple seemed to be caught up into some "third heaven" by it, though the heaven, as he well understood, was within. Another also declared, as in vision, "I see heaven opened," and though he "looked steadfastly up" at the time, it was only that altitude is the natural language, or line of direction, in such inward exaltations. So intensely perceptive, according to the scripture view, may a human soul become, when awakened inwardly, and drawn out in its higher apprehensions, after those invisible, supernatural, associations for which it is created.

Assuming now the fact of a supernatural sense in souls, that it is shut up by sin, we are next to consider—

II. How Christ, as he declares to Nathanael, will open this suppressed faculty, and make it the organ, or inlet, of universal society.

And here it will be remembered, that angelic visitations had been coursing back and forth upon the world and through it, in all ages, both before Christ's coming, and at his coming, and after. Moses had gone up into the mount and brought down tables lettered, as it were, in heaven. Fires had been kindled, from above, in sacrifices offered on rocks, and altars of turf. Two holy men had been visibly translated. And yet heaven still appears to be somehow shut. The angels—not ascending and descending but descending and ascending—are thought of only as having gone away, to some invisible nowhere whence they came. The great public miracles only help the chosen people to believe in a kind of Jew-God reigning under limitations, and holding their little patch of territory for his field. Instead of catching the hint from so many wonders, and so many bright visitants, of a world above the world, waiting to receive them in eternal society, it even makes them angry to hear, that God will include, in one circle of being, all that come to him on earth. A holy few found real access to the king, led in, to his seat, by the teachings of their prophets and the more secret teachings of the Spirit. But it is a most singular fact that no one of these, no dying saint most enlightened by holy experience, speaks, in these former ages, of going to heaven, or even of there being a heavenly world where righteous souls are gathered; unless it be that one or two expressions of the prophets are to be taken in that sense. Many critics therefore have denied, that there is any revelation of immortality, or a second life, before Christ's coming. And we know that, when he came, it was even an open question, whether any such being as "angel or spirit" really exists?

If now any one should ask what this means—how the world above seems to be already opened if it ever can be, and yet is shut?—the answer is, that all this apparitional machinery goes on without, before men's eyes, while the heaven of the soul is shut; and that so many angels therefore, coming and going, are looked upon only as ghosts of the fancy, or at least mere outsiders and strangers. They do not stay to be citizens, they are seen only as *in transitu;* they flit across the stage and are gone—gone, as many will think, to the same blind nowhere that receives all phantasms.

Here then is the deeper work Christ undertakes to do; viz., to open the heaven of the soul itself, or what is nowise different, to waken in it that higher sense, by which it may discern the supernatural being and society of God's realm. How he does it we shall hardly be at a loss to find.

First, he comes into the world himself, not apparitionally, like an irruption of angels, but he comes up, so to speak, out of humanity, emerging into his visibly divine glory, through a glorious and perfect manhood. And so it comes to pass that, while they accomplish nothing by their character, and have, in fact, no character beyond what is implied in their message, he is bringing on his wonderful, visibly divine manhood, and becoming, by force of his mere supernatural character alone, the greatest miracle of time—with the advantage that, being self-evident, even as the sun, all other miracle is upheld by it. At first he appears to be only a man among men, the Son of Mary, growing up in the mold and mortal weakness of a man; but his life unfolds silently and imperceptibly, till the magnificent proportions of his Godhood begin to appear in his manhood, and the tremendous fact is revealed, that a being from above the world is living in it! Supernatural event and character are built in solidly thus, into the world's history, to be an integral part of it. Mere nature is no longer all, and never can be again. The very world has another world interfused and working jointly with it.

He comes too in no light figure, but in the heavy tread of one that bears eternal government upon his shoulder—comes to reconcile the world, to justify, and gather, and pacify, and save, the world; "For it pleased the Father that in him should all fullness dwell, and having made peace by the blood of his cross, by him to reconcile all unto himself, whether they be things in earth or things in heaven." Everlasting order hangs tremulous in expectation round his cross, and eternity rings out from it, tolling in the world. As the veil of the temple is rent, so the way into the holiest opens. As the dead are shaken out their graves when he dies, so the souls shut up in death are loosened from the senses, to behold the new-sprung day. The middle wall is now broken down, the dividing isthmus cut through, and things in heaven, and things in earth, are set in a common headship in his person. Heaven is become an open door which no man shutteth, an abundant and free entrance is ministered, that we may enter with boldness into the holiest.

It is a great point also, as regards the impression effected, that every thing taught by him, in his doctrine, holds the footing of immortality and eternity, looking towards a higher and relatively supernatural state. Nothing is allowed to stop short, within the boundaries of time, as in the old religion. The very law of God is carried forward into spiritual applications; the temporal and outward sanctions are taken away, and the inmost principle of duty under it is enforced by the tremendous allotments of a future, everlasting state. Outward sacrifices and remissions will not answer. There must be a sacrifice that purges even the conscience itself. There must be a righteousness found, that exceeds the righteousness of the Scribes and Pharisees—even the righteousness of God. Every thing in the doctrine out-reaches nature and time, piercing even to the dividing asunder, and stirring all the inmost senses, sentiments, and fears of the religious nature. Not that any mere standards, or sanctions, can force open the shut heaven of souls; but that, by these things, grinding hard upon the supernatural sense, it is made to feel a reverberative movement of the powers of the world to come, and look in, through the rifts that are opened in the stony casement that surrounds it.

Let us not imagine now that, by any or all these things, the supernatural sense, or heaven of the soul, is really opened. These are preparations, all, including even the cross itself—powers that move on our consent, but without that consent accomplish no result. Nothing done will ever accomplish that result with many; they will go to their graves denying that any such upper world of faculty is in them. But with some it will be otherwise; they will respond, they will believe, and their faith will be the opening of heaven. In that faith the Son of Man will be revealed, and the angels of God ascending and descending upon him. But this faith, in still another view, is love, and here we have the grand finality. Christ and his cross are a movement on the world's love, and love itself is the higher sense, or apprehending power of the soul. Love is perceptive; whatever is loved is most really known, or discovered. He that loveth knoweth God, and, in that manner, he that loveth universal society knoweth universal society. Worlds above the world are present to the sense of love. All the immense longings of souls after universal society are consummated and crowned, when they are issued in love. And this is the opening of the soul, this the state and character which are its heaven—the kingdom of God within.

And what a finding of the soul will it be! what a sublime privity of knowledge will it reveal! when Christ, as in the promise made to Nathanael, shall have made it conscious eternally, in this manner, of the paradise hid in its own higher faculty, so long shut up and suppressed.

Some very important consequences follow, in the train of the subject thus presented, and with these I conclude.

1. The real merit of the issue made up between Christ and the naturalizing critics of his gospels is here distinctly shown. Professing much respect to his character, they are offended by the supernatural matters reported in his life, and set themselves at work to produce a new Christianity, without either miracle or mystery, or more than natural fact in it—and, of course, without even Christ himself, who is the greatest miracle of all. Christ, on the other hand, undertakes to give them, over and above the supernatural facts they reject,

supernatural evidences; viz., to set open a higher range of faculty in them related to himself and all supernatural beings, and so to *find* them at the point of deeper sentiments and apprehensions in their nature, than they are themselves aware of. They do not even imagine, that they have any thing included in their nature, above the mere basement story so much investigated and magnified by the philosophers; viz., reason, memory, imagination, affectional capacities and the like, including, perhaps, a merely moral, in distinction from a religious, conscience; practically ignoring, because they are shut, the sublime upper ranges of their spiritual nature—their transcendent affinities prepared for immense supernatural relations, their capacities to apprehend what is above the test of mere intellectual judgments, divine being, viz., and concourse and the flow and reflow of God's universal society. The heaven of their nature being shut, and the supernatural sense practically undiscovered, they proceed to bring the great questions of the gospels down for trial before the basement court of their criticism; where it results, that having made their souls small enough for their doctrine, they have no great difficulty in making their doctrine small enough for their souls.

They are men of high talent, if any talent is high in the lower ranges only of the nature, they are some of them scholars specially advanced in their culture, but talent and scholarship are, alas, how pitiably shriveled in their figure, when they undertake to handle the questions of religion, without so much as a conception of the inherently supernatural relations and discerning powers of the religious mind. Why, the humble, guileless Nathanaels, who never had a speculation in their lives, but have the heaven of their faith set open, and have found the Son of Man deep set in the heart's own center, have a better competence in the supernatural than Hennel, or Parker, or Strauss, or Renan, or than all these brilliant gospel extirpators together. No, gentlemen, Christ did not come to be approved before the tribunal of your mere logic, or lore, or critical acumen, but before a nobler and more competent, which, though it be in you, is yet hidden from you. Having a nature boundlessly related to the supernatural, flowering never, save in the knowledge and concourse of supernatural society, you put your critical extinguishers on it and stifle it, and then you can even triumph in the discovery that all you most sublimely want is incredible—scientifically impossible! Hardly could you make yourselves a more fit mark for Christian pity; for, with all your fine stores of learning, you are in fact the least knowing men of your day. Would that Christ might only find you, in that glorious opening of the nature of which he speaks; what a revelation would it be—and, first of all, because it would be a revelation so wonderful of yourselves!

You assume that you can settle questions of being, or not being—supernatural being, or not being—by logic, and criticism, and the processes of the head, even as you do questions of thought, or idea. Can you then reason a rock, as being or not being, in that manner? No, you will answer; subjects of being can not, in the first instance, be thought or reasoned, they can only be cognized, or perceived, by the senses. And so it is of all supernatural being, God, angels, worlds above the world, universal society; they are known only as they are cognized, by the supernatural sensing of the spiritual man; or, what is nowise different, by faith. And when it is done, they are had in as complete evidence even as the solids of matter. I do not undertake to say what particular facts of the gospel will, or will not be proved in this manner, but only that nothing will be rejected, because it is supernatural. The soul will be going after things supernatural and the commerce of the supernatural society, because it is practically open to their concourse. Here then is Christ, on one side, contriving how to open this immense upper world of the soul, and you, on your side, protesting that there is not, and must not be, any such upper world in you. He would make the soul a sky-full of glorious and blessed concourse, and you set yourselves to it, as a problem worthy of your industry, to make it a cavern! His work may be a hard one, but yours will be much harder. The emptiness of your cavern will ring back answers, stronger to most men, after all, than your arguments. For heaven is as much a necessity to men as bread, and souls can no more live without the supernatural, than the senses without matters of sense. In the same way—

2. We have given back to us, here, the most solid, only sufficient, proof of our immortality. How often do we stagger at this point, even the best of us. All mere

rational arguments, here, fall quite short of the mark. They never established any body. And yet every man ought to know his immortality, even as he knows that he is alive. He is made, to have an immediate, self-asserting consciousness of immortality, and would never have a doubt of it, if he had not shut up and darkened the divine side of the soul. And for just the same reason, Christ, when he opens the soul, opens immortality also. What was so dimly revealed, under the old religion, stands out visible everywhere under the new. There is no room here for a Sadducee to live. The metropolis of the world is here in Christ's person, and the visitants of all unknown spheres crowd about him, ascending and descending upon him. And they are all certified to our faith, by his supernatural character. We grow familiar thus with spirit, realize it, and know it in ourselves. Immortality! why the dead Christ proves it. And again the resurrection proves it; for what could such a being do but rise? It would even be a greater wonder if he did not. Away to their native abyss fly all our doubts—life and immortality are brought to light through the gospel! It only remains—

3. To note precisely, as we can at no other point of view, the meaning of salvation, or the saving of souls. Christ does not undertake to save them as they are—only half existing in the plane of nature. Do we call it saving the hand, that we save it in all but the fingers? Is it saving an eye, that we save it in all but the sight? Do we save a tree, when we save the stump and the roots, and not the leafy crown of shade and flower?

No more is it saving a soul to save the economic under-work only of opinion, judgment, memory, and the like. These are not the soul, and if we take them to be, we only come as near saying, as possible, that the soul is gone already. And it is in just this condition that Christ finds us—O, that he might also find us in the deeper sense of his promise! He comes to the soul as having a whole heaven hid in its possibilities, which heaven is shut up, which possibilities are even ignored and hid. He finds it made little, a fire almost gone out. Related constitutionally to a vast supernatural society, and to ranges of life and knowledge, as much broader than all causes and laws of the world, as eternity is broader than time, he undertakes to open it again upon its true field, relieve the pinch of its compression, give it enlargement, and make it truly live. Whatever man of opinion, taking on the airs of science, tells him that his gospel is incredible because it is supernatural, will get no answer, but that his soul is very nearly gone out already, and is wanting simply salvation. And just here it is that the soul gets such an immense lifting of pitch, and outspreading of dimensions, when it comes to Christ. The coming unto Christ is, in another view, Christ coming unto it and being revealed in it. Even as the apostle says—"When it pleased God to reveal his Son in me." And what a revelation was it to him! —as great proportionally to all who receive it. It is as if they had gotten a new soul, with a heaven-full of society gathered round the Son of Man there revealed. Therefore it is called "the new man;" not because it is new, for it is older even than the old man put away, being the original, normal, man of Paradise, hitherto stifled and suppressed; still it is new, all things are new. The change is so great as to be sometimes even bewildering. It is as if some wondrous, unknown light had broken in; the whole sky is luminous. The soul is in day; for the day has dawned and the day-star is risen. God, eternity, immortality, universal love and society—into these broad ranges it has come, and in these it is free, having them all for its element and its conversation in them, as in heaven. The unknowing state, the old, blank ignorance that was, because of the blindness of the heart, is gone; and a wondrous knowledge opens because the heart can see. Before it was a doubter possibly, mighty in opinion, wise in the wisdom of this world, pleased with its own questions and reasons, now it has come up where the light is, and the old questions and reasons do not mean any thing—the judgments of moles, in matters of astronomy, are as good. O, what strength, and majesty, and general height of being, are felt in the new life begun! And this is salvation! great because it saves, not some small part of the soul, but because it saves and glorifies the sublime whole; restoring its integrity and proportion, and setting it complete in God's own order, as in everlasting life. Who could wish it to do less? who could ask it do more?

NOTICES OF NATURE AND SUPERNATURAL CONTINUED.

The *Mercersburg Review* says:—"We welcome this book with all our heart, as a most valuable accession to the theological literature of the age. Dr. Bushnell has contrived to throw into it the full vivacity and freshness of his own nature. It is rich throughout with thoughts that breathe and words that glow and burn. The book is one which deserves to live, and that may be expected to take its place, we think, among the enduring works of the age."

SERMONS FOR THE NEW LIFE.

BY HORACE BUSHNELL, D.D.

1 vol. 12mo. 456 pages. $2 00.

Contents.—I.—Every Man's Life a Plan of God. II.—The Spirit in Man. III.—Dignity of Human Nature shown from its Ruins. IV.—The Hunger of the Soul. V.—The Reason of Faith. VI.—Regeneration. VII.—The Personal Love and Lead of Christ. VIII.—Light on the Cloud. IX.—The Capacity of Religion Extirpated by Disuse. X.—Unconscious Influence. XI.—Obligation a Privilege. XII.—Happiness and Joy. XIII.—The True Problem of Christian Experience. XIV.—The Lost Purity Restored. XV.—Living to God in Small Things. XVI.—The Power of an Endless Life. XVII.—Respectable Sin. XVIII.—The Power of God in Self-Sacrifice. XIX. Duty not Measured by Our Own Ability. XX.—He that Knows God will Confess Him. XXI.—The Efficiency of the Passive Virtues. XXII.—Spiritual Dislodgments. XXIII.—Christ as Separate from the World.

The *Methodist Quarterly* for July says:—"Our American pulpit has lately furnished no volume presenting so deep a reach of thought in the speaker, or presupposing so high a moral and intellectual appreciation on the part of the congregation. * * Dr. Bushnell has a deep insight, and a searching power of tracing the relations of great truths to each other. The overmastering trait of his productions is cool, stern, slow, moving *intellect;* yet intellect gently interpenetrated and made malleable by moral feeling—imagination, too, there is, but none for its own sake."

The *Princeton Review* says:—"These discourses, although they apparently differ a good deal in character, bear the clear impress of Dr. Bushnell's genius."

The *North American Review* says:—"In original forms of thought, that highest order of originality, which comes more from nice elaboration than from wayward spontaneity, it is surpassingly rich. Another generation will peruse it as a book that has life in it—the double life of its author and of vital truth."

The *Monthly Religious Magazine* says:—"Nor are these sermons written on the same level with any of the author's preceding productions. They betoken a deeper experience. They speak from a richer knowledge. They are the expression of a faith wrought patiently out by a harder discipline."

CHRISTIAN NURTURE.

By Horace Bushnell, D.D. 1 vol. 12mo. Price $2 00.

Part I.—The Doctrine.—I.—What Christian Nurture is. II.—The Ostrich Nurture. III.—The Organic Unity of the Family. IV.—Infant Baptism, how Developed. V.—Apostolic Authority of Infant Baptism. VI.—Church Membership of Children. VII.—The Out-populating Power of the Christian Stock.

Part II.—The Mode.—I.—When and where the Nurture begins. II.—Parental qualifications. III.—Physical Nurture, to be a means of Grace. IV.—The Treatment that discourages Piety. V.—Family Government. VI.—Plays and Pastimes, Holidays and Sundays. VII.—The Christian Teaching of Children. VIII.—Family Prayers.

"It takes up the difficult problems of Christian education one by one in a clear, practical manner, with good sense, scriptural knowledge, and devotional feeling."—*Boston Journal.*

"As we have read chapter after chapter of this volume with unmingled delight, we have mentally resolved upon making each the theme of an editorial article embodying the substance of its teachings. But it is impossible to condense Dr. Bushnell's thoughts into fewer words than he himself employs, or to exhaust a subject in briefer compass than he allots to it. And most assuredly it would be impossible to substitute words for his, which would as clearly and nicely express the meaning. We would most earnestly recommend the book to parents, for the profit of themselves and their children."—*N. Y. Independent.*

"We cannot but welcome these earnest and powerful presentations of the influence of the parent over the faith, and character, and whole being of the child, which are fitted to quicken the conscience of every father and mother, and make them more faithful in the discharge of their sacred trust."—*N. Y. Evangelist.*

WORK AND PLAY; OR, LITERARY VARIETIES.

By Horace Bushnell, D.D. 1 vol. 12mo. Price $2 00.

"A variety of themes which are treated with that calm, philosophical and scholastic habit of thought for which the author is distinguished. No one can read him without having his mental pulse quickened, and his mind newly furnished with the results of a deep thinker's study."—*New York Observer.*

The Round Table says:—"There is much in the style of Dr. Bushnell, as well as in the mould and treatment of his conceptions, which reminds us of the stately prose of the older writers, now of Milton, now of Jeremy Taylor, and then again of quaint Sir Thomas More * * * In all his writings, we trace the vigorous workings and the splendid results of a powerful mind, equally moved by a taste for philosophy, for poetry, and for politics."

From the American Theological Review.

"This volume contains the best orations and articles of the author; and this is another way of saying that it contains some of the best literature of the kind which this country has produced. Common things and thoughts are clothed upon with light and beauty. Dr. Bushnell is a poet, in all but form; his mind moves spontaneously amongst the highest subjects of thought, and he adapts these to the general mind so the it is elevated by communion with him."

From the New Englander.

"The reader will here find not less of truth or more of genius, perhaps, than abounds in the author's other writings; but the truth is from a wider and more varied field, and the genius is more free and sportive in its creations. Those who are acquainted with Dr. Bushnell only through his theological writings, will do well to read this volume of literary varieties, and fill out their conception of the theologian and divine, with that of the philosopher, the scholar, and the man of letters."

REV. DR. P. SCHAFF'S

HISTORY OF THE CHRISTIAN CHURCH.

Comprising the First Three Centuries, from the Birth of Christ to the Reign of Constantine the Great, A. D. 1—311. 1 vol. 8vo. $3 75.

"Dr. Schaff possesses a true Teutonic erudition, which he expresses in the best Anglo-Saxon clearness, and with a Celtic vivacity and effect."—*Methodist Quarterly Review.*

"This volume seems to us to have all the merits of the author's previous publications, which are too well known to need description here, and which have placed him in the first rank of contemporary writers on Church History, not only in this country, but in Germany and England."—*Princeton Review.*

"Dr. Schaff has written a perspicuous, animated, often eloquent, and always trustworthy narrative. This is high praise when we look at the deficiencies of the best of the current works in this department."—*New Englander.*

"The *North American Review* says:—With this book we are greatly pleased. At the commencement of each section, a list of authorities for its contents is given, and from the sources thus indicated, the author furnishes a free and graceful narrative of what is properly embraced under each title. . . . . . The work is equally well adapted to the needs of the students and the edification of the general reader.

"A familiar acquaintance with the sources of historical knowledge, a mature judgment, a sound, nervous logic, and a lively imagination, pervaded by the energy and warmth of a living faith, and a glowing heart, are all brought to bear upon this work." —*Mercersburg Review.*

"This vol. furnishes proof that Church History can be presented in a way which shall not only instruct, but interest and edify. The reader is drawn along from section to section, and from chapter to chapter, by the natural and necessary succession of subjects, and charmed on every page, by the clear, concise and vigorous style. If any excellence belonging to it impresses us above another, it is its admirable adaptation as a text book in Church History;—we shall be greatly mistaken if it does not as such take its place permanently or extensively in the seminaries of our land."—*The Guardian, (Rev. H. Harbaugh.)*

"This volume, whether as a book for general reading or as a text-book for students, is one of the best—perhaps we ought to say the very best—with which we are acquainted, on the eventful periods it embraces."—*New York Examiner.*

"No one can doubt the author's qualifications, both intellectual and religious, for a historian of the Christian Church. He writes under the responsibilities of a Christian conscience, and with the enthusiasm of a Christian heart."—*Christian Mirror.*

"Ministers, theological students, and lovers of Church history will prize this book for its clear, perspicuous style, and catholic and liberal spirit."—*American Presbyterian.*

"It combines, in a happy manner, the thoroughness and accuracy of the German critic with the practical spirit of the American teacher. The style is scholarly, yet clear and animated, the descriptions are brief and bold, the generalizations philosophic, yet not obscure or needlessly abstruse."—*Central Christian Herald.*

"This history is a noble monument to the genius and learning of its distinguished author. It is genial, truthful, transparent, and animated with a soul whose sympathies throb in unison with the great and good of all ages."—*Lutheran Observer.*

HORACE BUSHNELL—HIS HOME-LIFE.

BY SARAH K. BOLTON.

Two things made for Horace Bushnell a name; an uncommon mind, and an uncommon wife. With either, life could scarcely have been a failure; with both, it could not but be a success. His wife was his better self. Born of an aristocratic Unitarian family, reduced from affluence to the need of self-support, the young daughter, with her mother, opened a boarding school. The mother was cold, elegant, self-contained; the daughter, not less dignified, but with a warmer heart and manner.

While in her teens, a religion with a divine Christ in it, was born into her soul. She knew her duty, and that duty was to erect a family altar in that home of young ladies where no one had ever heard her pray. What the struggle was before that mother and unconverted sisters and those young lady pupils, can only be known by those who have had a like experience. The result was that mother and sisters and nearly all the scholars were soon believing in the Savior.

Soon after, the young student came to their house to board. What wonder that the spiritual life of this girl, a trifle older than himself, came to be a power with him. He admired her superior intellect, and loved her noble nature. The union which followed, cemented by mutual respect and dependence, that knew nothing but a grand equality, that had individual aims but an undivided interest, developed, even with the weakness and pain of an invalid life, all that was noble and grand in Horace Bushnell.

What Carlyle says Louisa was to Frederick the Great in judgment and advice, he, often in the midst of his State conferences, excusing himself a short time to learn her opinion and counsel, what the wife of John Stuart Mill was to him as an inspiration in all that was esthetic and pure, what Lady Belaconsfield was to Disraeli, whom he so pathetically says at her death, "believed in me when men despised me," such was Mrs. Bushnell to the gifted author of "Nature and the Supernatural."

When the aristocracy as well as the thinkers sought the North Church and its preacher as one of the attractions of Hartford, of New England even, or when the churches went wild against him because of his supposed heresy, Mrs. Bushnell kept steadily on the way of saving souls, and saving her husband. For years she taught a large Sunday school class, one rule of which was, that no one could enter it unless unconverted, and could not remain after conversion. They must then be at work. For years she was leader of a "Woman's Prayer Meeting," and her prayers will never be forgotten by those who heard them. She begged for us, as she used to express it in her prayer, what she herself had learned, "*the interior intimacy of a divine friendship*." If any one was dying and needed the consolations of the gospel, she was sent for. Her dress was plain, in accordance with her profession, and vanity or display found no sympathy with her, even among her children, some of whom married wealthy, and had the means for such display.

She was fearless in her defense of right. Though very modest, at one time she rose to speak in a North Church prayer-meeting, a thing unheard-of for a woman, remarking that she "wished to say a word if there was no objection." The deacons were dumbfounded, and instead of giving the wife of their pastor a cordial opportunity, were silent as death. In a very gentle yet queenly way she said, "I see there is no objection!" and proceeded. Such a woman was not afraid to have her poet daughter, whom Charles Dudley Warner thinks very gifted, a teacher in the public schools, when teaching was considered plebeian by the aristocracy, of whom Hartford has her full share. Such a woman, loved in her handsome home and loved out of it, shaped the destiny of Horace Bushnell. No wonder he used to say that "natural scenery lost half its beauty when not seen through her eyes"; that "other women might be better looking," but to him "she was the best looking woman in the world."

Dr. Bushnell had his grand traits of character, his manly support of what he considered right, (how he ever wrote his "Reform against Nature" with such a wife, was a mystery to his friends; the strongest argument against Woman Suffrage perhaps, and yet his weakest book, and the one that will be soonest forgotten), his untiring industry, his invincible will, and above all a desire to do his whole duty to his God. Others will think and write of his books, his pulpit power, his comprehensive mind, but those who knew and loved him best will cherish, most of all, his home life, and the example to the world of a blessed marriage, that largely made him what he was.

Cleveland.

DR. BUSHNELL.

Dr. Bushnell has been rightly classed with the Broad-church clergy of the day. —*Presbyterian.*

This recognition of sin as a tremendous fact distinguished Dr. Bushnell from most writers of what are called liberal tendencies.—*George S. Merriam.*

As a theologian Dr. Bushnell is much more readily described by his aberrations from the old and long-accepted standards of orthodoxy, than by any positive and settled beliefs of his own.—*N. Y. Christian Advocate.*

He was always a thoroughly sincere seeker for truth, and in his most heretical days was perfectly sound and settled on that corner-stone of all things—the distinctly supernatural origin and authority of the Christian religion.—*Independent.*

There can, we think, be no question that the profound change in the Calvinistic theology, so recently wrought in New England, is largely due to Dr. Bushnell. —*Universalist.*

His real services consisted in bringing out some hidden or forgotten relations of old theological truths, and in impressing the conviction that the whole truth is not contained in, or bound by, any single and partial formulas.—*Evangelist.*

I am constrained to think that he has done vastly more good than harm, for he was an earnest soul seeking for truth, and his truth will be felt long after his error has spent its force.—"*Silex,*" *of Hartford, in the Examiner and Chronicle.*

It is our conviction that wherever he has departed from the belief held by the church for many generations, respecting the person and work of Christ, it will be found that he was in error; and that he has added nothing to a clearer understanding or a better statement of the doctrines of sin, atonement and forgiveness through the blood of Christ.—*Vermont Chronicle.*

Taking him all in all, Dr. Bushnell was one of those representative men whose fame is independent of mere ecclesiastical relationships. His personality was projected into everything that he wrote and said for the public. His speculative errors will be lost sight of in the blaze of those better qualities which he used with such splendid effect. And the odor of those sweet spices which he poured over his only Master's head and feet will fill every house into which his words have carried his loving testimony.—*Christian Intelligencer.*

In personal appearance Dr. Bushnell was slight. His face was powerful, and suggestive of wonderful acuteness. His features were sharply chiseled. His forehead was rounded and full; his lips straight, and impressed with an air of decision; his eyes so deep-set in his head that they puzzled the skill of the artist who molded them in clay or painted them. He was nervous and energetic in movement, exceedingly forcible in speech, and an extremely interesting talker.—*Letter to Examiner and Chronicle.*

A poet in theology, a constitutional liberal caught and held in the net of so-called Orthodoxy, a soldier in courage and a master of spiritual strategy, a man capable of bringing the loftiest and most subtle thoughts to the service of the most practical interests; a proud, yet humble, a strong, yet gentle spirit; full of womanly feeling and manly vigor of thought; shut up in a frail body, that would neither allow him to work continuously, nor to idle enough to recruit its ever-leaking strength —what a valuable life he has lived, what a fine career he has closed!—*Liberal Christian.*

1876.

Rev. William Caldwell
with the regards of
Isabel Blake

Dec. 1864 —

DR. BUSHNELL.

No man ever more completely veiled his pre-eminence with humility. All his inferiors were put at perfect ease, as if in complete equality with him. Nothing in dress, demeanor or carriage denoted superiority—only his speech betrayed him. It might be the criticism of a poem, or an excursion into the field of politics, or the opinion of a book, or such playful conversation as springs up at the fireside, or wherever friends chance to meet by the wayside; but whatever it might be, there were always to be noted some distinctive traits of the man; the positive and intense opinion launched in bolts of speech that flashed as they flew to the mark; the grotesque remark that suddenly came from ever so far away, like a bomb-shell, to explode and make short work of empty pretensions; the natural and inevitable tone of authority, which nevertheless quietly suffered the contradiction of any feeblest dissenter; the new coinage of words that put pockets-full of common-places into hard, clean, fresh original forms; the bright-gleaming scimitar strokes of wit that sometimes parted the head and shoulders of a strutting fallacy so deftly that a little joggling of the thing was requisite to discover the decapitation. There was no lack of positiveness. He thought and believed and spake and wrote vigorously, nor conceived that courtesy required suppression of convictions. It was not a breach of friendship with him to contradict what seemed to be false, and the most insignificant man in the conference might, in his turn, fly at the opinions of Dr. Bushnell, and denounce them with perfect impunity.—*Rev. E. P. Parker, D.D., in Hartford Courant.*

A witty clergyman was once asked what he thought of a certain brother in the ministry. "I don't know how to answer you; if I should say that he is the weakest man that ever undertook to preach, I might not speak the truth, though I expressed my own opinion." If I should say that Dr. Bushnell, for "putting things," has no peer, I might not speak the truth, though I expressed my own opinion. S.

A correspondent sends, followed by a few lines of comment from his own pen, the following from an unpremeditated address by Dr. Bushnell at the 200th anniversary of the Second Church in Hartford, Feb. 22, 1870:

He rose, and after recalling some salient points in the discourse of the day before, by Rev. E. P. Parker, D.D., went on to say, "Just a word now in regard to the unmentioned people of the story. Who they were, and where their dust reposes, never can be known. But if we had their names, scarcely more would be known. The body of Moses—where was it laid? And if his name, too, had been hidden, as his body was, would he not still have lived in his people by all his works? So these unmentioned ones of your church-story are living in you here to day, as truly they that were in the gaps of the records, as they whose names are preserved. These names tell you little, and it is only a very few of them, four or five in a generation, that ever come out to be so much as spoken by their syllables. And still all these unmentioned, or scarcely mentioned, ones are yet truly alive, so much even as they once were here; and for one, I love especially to give them greeting at such times; for it is their special merit, it may be—their self-forgetting and unforward modesty—that has veiled them. And what more could their names signify, when all they did and were is alive in you, now waiting to be owned and cherished by your tenderest homage?"

Here we have an illustration, put with his characteristic felicity and force of language, of the power of "unconscious influence." The present members of that venerable church trace no good enjoyed by them to these unmentioned, because unremembered, fathers and mothers. Nevertheless these early saints, dropped out of the church record, live through the wondrous power of "unconscious influence," and will live through all coming time. T. L. S.

souls of men by law which is gracious and by grace which is law.—*Sermon by Rev. T. T. Munger, San Jose, Cal.*

DR. BUSHNELL.

As a preacher, take him all in all, he probably had no peer in the land—not in his power over the masses, but in the essential richness and value of his spiritual utterance. He addressed a high grade of mind, and had no vocation to address other, and conscious of it, attempted to speak to no other. He did not start with the question, "What do the people need to hear?" but assumed that they needed to hear what he had to say—the only rational ground for any human utterance. His charm as a speaker was subtle and strong. Reading closely from notes, he yet spoke as if in vision, with thoughts far away in heaven, in deep and mellifluous tones, and with a cadence of inexpressible sweetness, never to be forgotten. The discourses of a college life at New Haven have all passed out of mind save three or four preached by him, but these, even to the tones of the voice and poisings of the head, are well remembered; for *reality* knows no end.

His published sermons are more read than those of any other man, except perhaps Robertson of Brighton, and being read by preachers they find their way to vast multitudes, and in forms more suited to their capacity than as they fell from his lips. No one phrase so well describes them as that they are pervaded by an intense *spirituality*, or what is the same, *reality*. He took the things of God and showed them to men out of his own clear and open vision. Holding that the imagination was God's door of entrance into the human mind, and himself having one wide and high and ever open, his discourses have much of this divine poetry about them, which, however, is felt to be the soberest reality.

Such a man was sorely needed; he came and did his work well. His influence is not easily measured or traced, just because it is so high and fine; but also because it is such, it is everywhere amongst us—here, in California, where he spent two busy years, and all over the land—helping parents in the Christian nurture of their children, quickening the preacher, quieting the doubts of the skeptical, assuring the conscience-stricken that their Saviour came not to condemn, but to save, and persuading all that God is yet present in his own world, still working in nature and in the

ANOTHER GREAT MAN TAKEN AWAY.

Earth has lost, and heaven has gained, another of our best known and most valued ministers. Rev. Horace Bushnell, D.D., died on Thursday, the 17th inst., at his residence in Hartford, Ct., in the seventy-fourth year of his age. He had long been in such feeble health that the event can take none of his friends by surprise. Twenty years ago they looked for an early departure, and only an extraordinary tenacity of life, coupled with an indomitable will have brought him to such ripeness of years. Dr. Bushnell was the last of the grand series of New England theologians, who have done honor to Congregationalism by their genius and their piety, and have exerted a modifying theological influence upon the opinions of their respective generations. Edwards, father and son, Bellamy, Hopkins, Emmons, Taylor, Finney, Bushnell —there they stand, a galaxy of light on questions of doctrine. No one actually swears by any one of them; indeed we all take large exception to the teachings of each; yet we recognize the service which they have respectively rendered to Christian thought, in their day and generation. No longer does any minister call himself an Edwardean, a Hopkinsian, an Emmonsite, or a Taylorite; and we presume that few would choose to be distinctively known as a Finneyite or a Bushnellite. But no minister can afford to ignore the works of these men, in his study of divine truth.

Dr. Bushnell was born in Connecticut, and in that State he lived and died, being ever proud of its history and jealous of its fame. His birth-place was among the hills of Litchfield county, in the little rural town of New Preston, but a few miles away from the spot which gave birth to Rev. C. G. Finney; and Mr. Finney, who was ten years the senior, has been heard to tell of his teaching a singing school, at one time, where Horace Bushnell was one of the pupils. What a career for those two young rustics an astonished prophet might have unfolded to them! He was educated at Yale College, but did not enter a theological seminary, after his graduation, occupying himself for two or three years with journalism and with duty as a tutor. He was settled over the North Church (now the Park Church) in Hartford, and remained the pastor some twenty-five years, till broken health compelled his resignation. But he could not be idle, and his teeming brain and autocratic will compelled his feeble hand to drive the pen, till a small library of volumes had been brought before the public. And what a monument to his genius and piety they are! "Discourses on Christian Nurture," "God in Christ," "Christ in Theology," "Nature and the Supernatural," "Work and Play," "The Vicarious Sacrifice," "Sermons for the New Life," "Christ and his Salvation," "Sermons on Living Subjects,"

www.ingramcontent.com/pod-product-compliance
Lightning Source LLC
La Vergne TN
LVHW020936110826
845150LV00004B/879
* 9 7 8 1 4 2 5 5 5 1 9 6 4 *